CW00500508

Royce Kurmelovs is a journalist and writer whose work has been published by the BBC, Al Jazeera English, *Vice*, *The Guardian*, *Crikey*, the *San Francisco Bay Guardian* and various other publications. Royce grew up in Salisbury, South Australia, and now lives in Adelaide's west. Royce's second book, *Rogue Nation*, will be published in December 2017. He is also working on a third book, for publication in 2018.

The Death of HOLDEN

The end of an Australian dream

ROYCE KURMELOVS

UPDATED EDITION

hachette AUSTRALIA

hachette
AUSTRALIA

First published in Australia and New Zealand in 2016
by Hachette Australia
(an imprint of Hachette Australia Pty Limited)
Level 17, 207 Kent Street, Sydney NSW 2000
www.hachette.com.au

This edition published in 2017

10 9 8 7 6 5 4 3 2

National Library of Australia
Cataloguing-in-Publication data:

Kurmelovs, Royce, author.

The death of Holden: the end of an Australian dream/Royce Kurmelovs.

ISBN: 978 0 7336 3882 4 (paperback)

Holden automobiles – Australia.
Holden automobiles – Australia – History.
Business failures – Australia.
Automobile industry and trade – Australia – History.

338.762922220994

Cover design by Luke Causby, Blue Cork
Cover photographs courtesy of National Library of Australia, Highway Patrol Images/Flickr, jeremyg3030/flickr, William Carram/Alamy Stock Photo
Typeset in Sabon LT by Kirby Jones
Printed and bound in Great Britain by Clays Ltd, Elcograf S.p.A.

FSC
www.fsc.org
MIX
Paper from
responsible sources
FSC® C104740

Books and cars are not built alone.
For people who work with their hands.
For those who lent me their stories.
For the friends who lent me their couches.

Again, thank you.

Contents

Preface

TURNING IT OFF

My first memory of work is the rumble of my father's V8 engine at five-thirty in the morning. I would wake to the sound of the window frame rattling in the wall and listen to him go. At night, he'd come home smelling of sweat and loam dust, go to the freezer, scoop ice cubes into a short glass and pour himself a scotch. Then he'd turn on the television and eat whatever dinner my mother made that night.

It was routine. Something dependable – like everything else growing up in that same little house just off Main North Road in the same neighbourhood with the same people for 23 years. My parents had picked the place up as newlyweds for $40,000. Over the years they rebuilt parts of it and threw on a new coat of paint to make it their own. They never made it rich, but they made enough to get by. Not everyone is so lucky.

You never really understand something like that growing up in the middle of it. That house never changed, but the world around it did. Australia got rich sending iron ore and coal to Asia. South Australia was getting by just fine for the most part, coming out of a decade when the State Bank collapsed and dragged the local economy down with it. Our family in that house might have got by just fine too, but our neighbourhood and the others around it belonged to a region where the rust had set in 30 years before.

As an adult you look back and you can see it in the little things. The hardware store that closed down. The liquor store that didn't. The high-school teachers who broke lesson plans with impromptu speeches about education and good jobs. The ones who didn't. There were the friends who went off to university to make something of themselves and those who didn't. Those who learned trades, and those who didn't. Those who got out by joining the army. Those who stayed because they had kids early. That one friend who left school to chase a dollar, who ended up working so hard as a waitress that four years later she collapsed on the bathroom floor of the restaurant and still went to work the next day.

If you were born in or around the 1950s, it's the kind of thing you would have been there to witness. If you were born after 1990, by the time you hit adulthood the good jobs would be gone or going and you would have no idea what it was like.

The last of the good jobs where I grew up were with GM Holden, that proud old lion down by the roundabout on Philip Highway. It was a ten-minute drive away, maybe less. You saw it driving past through rain, peering out from behind the window wipers as the water beat down against the glass. You saw it driving past with the heat bearing down on metal, with the windows lowered and an elbow resting on the door frame. Even if you never really thought about it much, the feeling was that it was always there and always going to be. Another part of the landscape, fixed and certain like a distant mountain.

Only, it was always closer than you knew. Autowork was never really in my blood. My father was in construction, though my grandfather worked at the Holden plant for 18 months when he first migrated here with a young family and found himself in need of work, fast. To this day, the old man says it was a good job for someone whose accent was too thick and English too thin. My mother still tells the story about the Christmas party the company put on that year, about the food they served and the presents they gave the immigrant children.

Then there was everyone else. Growing up you don't realise just how much people depend on a place like that. As a kid you could always tell whose daddy worked at the plant and whose didn't. You could tell by the car they drove and the house they lived in and because people told you he did, though you didn't need really understand what that meant because you couldn't appreciate then what a good wage was. The factory out that way paid people's mortgages and rent, let them bring kids into a world that was predictable. It paid for dinner that night, breakfast in the morning, the shoes their kids wore to school, drinks at the pub after work, and when the factory shut down over Christmas, there was money for a holiday. People were comfortable because of it. It gave them enough that they had time to be happy.

And then one day you hear they put a bullet in that old lion and told everyone it was for the best. Told everyone it meant progress. Keeping the place alive would have been bad economics, they said. It would have been too political. So too was killing it, really, but those who pulled the trigger promised that things would be better afterwards when they brought in something else. Only problem is that for a long time things hadn't been getting better for the people where I grew up and most of us knew they probably weren't going to.

I never worked a day in that factory or in its supply chain. I never really had a chance. Instead I got out, got educated and moved for a time to another neighbourhood, near where another Holden car plant used to operate. That plant closed years ago and you can still see the scars. My life, whether I knew it or not, has been shaped by the fortunes of the car factories and smelters and shipyards. Still is. So too have the lives of many Australians.

And when the factory closes and the Australian car industry dies, it will be the end of one story and the start of another. When the television cameras have gone away, the photographs have been taken and the speeches about loyalty and service have been made, everyone will go home and life will go on. The story about the mess of steel and glass and rubber that make up a four-door family sedan will be done then, but the other one, the one about flesh and bone, will continue. That story isn't about macroeconomics or global finance, and neither does it have a happy ending. It is about a people who made a life in places like Elizabeth, Geelong, Broadmeadows and Dandenong on the promise of good pay for hard work and how that promise was betrayed.

This book is a work of reportage which tells that story, written at the time the closure was taking place, before we understood what it meant.

Chapter 1

THE BITTER END

IT WAS TWO WEEKS UNTIL CHRISTMAS.

Just another Wednesday. Day shift had been running since six in the morning and now that the clock had ticked on past midday, those working the assembly line at the Elizabeth Holden factory were looking forward to going home. Another shift done.

Except there was movement behind the main administration building that looks out over Philip Highway. A shop steward had noticed figures on the grass setting up a stage, thought it was weird and called up to the Australian Manufacturing Workers' Union (AMWU) seniors' office to ask what was going on.

Darryl Waterman answered the phone and said he didn't know anything about it, but the senior promised to take a look. He hung up and went down to investigate with Leanne, the other AMWU senior.

There they found Bob Glass. Now retired, back then Bob was Holden's Director of Vehicle Assembly Operations and the factory's second in command. Glass refused to answer their questions and told them they'd both find out with the rest of the workforce.

Leanne said she needed a cigarette. Together they went outside and talked over what Bob had told them. Both had a pretty good idea about what it meant.

'The union had been telling the company that if you do get to a point where you are going to pull the pin, make sure the workforce is the first to know, because in the past, decisions have been made and people hear about it on the media before we're told in the factory,' Darryl says, remembering the day.

Rumour spreads like fire through large factories, so the pair decided to keep it quiet and went back to their office, where they called Jon Gee. These days he is a South Australian Labor Party rep for the seat of Napier, but back then Jon was an organiser for the AMWU. Darryl and Leanne told him what was going on and what Bob Glass had said before suggesting he get over to the factory, but he was already en route. In the hours before the closure, someone in the company had been calling around anonymously to the major suppliers and anyone with a stake in the factory to tell them it was over.

Darryl and Leanne met him at the gate. He arrived at the main admin building just as word was getting around that the company were shutting down the line and pulling everyone out onto the grass. Jon shook hands with both seniors and looked each in the eye. 'I think the decision we've all been trying to avoid is upon us,' he said.

It was the middle of summer, 2013, and the clock was pushing 2pm. By now, there was nothing else for the three union reps to do except join the rest of the workforce outside. Together, everyone listened to Holden CEO Mike Devereux announce that the company would close the factory in 2017; then Richard Phillips, Executive Director of Manufacturing, took over the microphone.

Richard was boss at the Elizabeth factory. Tall and square-jawed with an athletic build, Richard was a native son of the region. He'd come up humble, having grown up in Salisbury in Adelaide's north. His father had worked as a sales manager at the local Big W and Richard had started his working life as an apprentice fitter and turner on the factory line at Holden, where he was awarded Apprentice of the Year in 1991. From there he had climbed the ladder, eventually making it to Detroit where GM taught him how to run a factory before they brought him back home to Elizabeth in 2009 and made him Director of Vehicle Assembly.

By 2012, he was running the place and only a year later he found himself up on stage with the GM men telling the world it was all over. Richard praised the workers for their loyalty and service, and talked at length about the state of the business. There was no easy way to say it, but the factory would close in 2017.

Merry Christmas, Elizabeth.

On the grass, the mood among the workforce was sombre. For a while they had known this might be coming, but now it was really here and the reaction was matter of fact. This was happening and it sucked. But it wasn't up to them anyway and the more time went on, the more people just wanted to go home. Mostly they were happy they weren't coming in for the afternoon shift in an hour.

The company then put out an official notice to all Tier 1 and Tier 2 suppliers, those companies that made all the little pieces that went into each car, and from the grassy lawn in Elizabeth, or the City of Playford to use its official title, the news rippled outward. Next to hear about it were the suppliers down the road at the Edinburgh Parks Industrial Estate, just outside neighbouring Salisbury, an old colonial town built along the trade route that eventually became Main North Road.

Then the news thundered south, radiating out along the plains past Mawson Lakes and Gepps Cross, down towards Adelaide. The car industry once dominated out that way too, from Holden's Woodville factory in Adelaide's west that operated in the 40s, to Mitsubishi's Lonsdale factory right down near Reynella. Having a car factory in your neighbourhood was once a sign of progress. Then the 80s rolled around and the big factories started to close, one by one.

And as a century-old South Australian company, CARR Components had seen it all. By this time the firm was getting by making parts for Holden's Commodore and Cruze models from its factory at Netley in Adelaide's west, tucked away by Adelaide Airport.

Adam Reynolds, CARR Components' engineering coordinator who had spent more than half his life in the automotive industry, was standing in the main office when the news broke. If the reaction out the front of Holden had been one of muted despair, the reaction on the factory floor at CARR Components was that of paralysis. No one wanted to believe it. Holden was 'bigger than the Roman Empire', as one former Holden worker put it. It wasn't going anywhere.

Now it was and the news ricocheted through the rest of the building.

Out on the factory floor, a 50-year-old woman got talking to Reynolds. She had spent most of her working life at CARR Components and factory work was all she knew. She wore hopelessness like high-vis.

'Well ... what do I do now?'

'I don't know,' Adam told her.

What else do you say to someone whose entire future had just been brought into question?

'I don't know.'

Chapter 2

THE VERDICT

Michael Wetherley was on jury duty the week Holden's fate was decided. The day it happened, he was sitting on the only case he had been given during his entire tour with the South Australian judicial system. It was the third day of the trial and he'd got up early that morning to get a bus into the city.

The morning paper had a big double-page spread speculating about whether GM would quit the country, and Michael had bought himself a copy. Joe Hockey had publicly dared the company to leave in the days before and now the government was saying GM had already decided to go and just hadn't told anyone.

Some of those in the jury pool who knew Michael worked at the factory tried talking to him about the whole situation. Those conversations ran the full gamut of opinion and all seemed to follow a theme. 'It would be sad if it went,' someone would say. 'And it would be rough on Elizabeth,' they'd point out. 'Because, you know, Holden is the only thing out that way.'

Then would come the counterpoint: 'But really, it was inevitable.' 'The government wasn't going to keep handing out money forever,' they would say, and that much everyone could agree with. But then the other comments would start. 'We're just wasting the money,' the opinion was. 'Why should they get any more? They should just close.'

With that, the verdict was in and it was unanimous. It was sad but inevitable, and the day it was all decided, Michael didn't learn he would be out of a job until later that night. It's no-phones-allowed in the hermetically sealed world of a sitting jury and he spent the day listening to the trial of a man from Christie Downs.

'You know, those bogans down south,' he jokes, remembering it. 'The bums who used to work for Mitsubishi.'

The guy at the centre of the case had used a gun to win an argument with his neighbours and for three days the jury had listened to the prosecution make its case while the defence responded with the suggestion that every witness was lying. Through it all, they never heard from the accused because he never took the stand. Instead, the defence lawyer closed her case, and Michael and 11 other good men and women disappeared into the jury room to deliberate.

As this was all happening, one of the biggest moments in Australian economic history was being made. Everyone Michael worked with had been told they no longer had a job. Afterwards, State Premier Jay Weatherill made the 40-minute drive north to the Old Spot Hotel, where he bought rounds for the men and women of Holden who had listened as the company thanked them for their loyalty, thanked them for their service, but said it was no longer required.

As the party wrapped, Michael and the jury found their guy guilty. The court thanked them for their time and by six o'clock he was turned out onto the street. On the walk to the bus, he switched on his phone and the first text was from a friend talking about the end of something. It didn't register and Michael had no idea what he was on about. He sent his wife, Cheryl, a message telling her he was out and she called him while he was on the bus.

When Cheryl found out, she was at home on the computer typing a letter to Tony Abbott about how his government shouldn't let the factory close. Her husband worked there, but that wasn't why she was writing the letter. It was too important to the country, she thought. She wanted Australia to be a country that made things. All countries should make their own things to some degree. People need something they can touch. If you let go of the factories, then you're starting from scratch. It didn't make sense to close it down.

She had just hit save when the news came on to say the factory was dead, and the irony wasn't lost on her.

Over the phone, Cheryl told Michael what had happened and his initial reaction was muted. When he got home, his supervisor called. He had been trying to get in touch all day to let him know what would happen next. That was a question the bus trip home had given Michael a chance to think about. Suddenly, all the questions that those on the shop floor had been asking for the past five years had been answered, only to be replaced with new ones. What would happen now? How would it work? What would happen to all the people?

Then the other thoughts started to creep in. It sure would be something to be there right at the end, Michael thought. This was no small thing. An event everyone would talk about for years to come. Maybe Michael might even be around to help build that last car, to actually be there when it drives off the line in 2017 and closes that period of Australian history when the country used to do its own heavy lifting.

Chapter 3

SCREWED

DARRYL WATERMAN KNEW THEY WERE SCREWED AS SOON AS he saw the Chinese factories.

Back then he had been one among a group of senior factory figures, including union reps and area managers, who went on an expenses-paid company fact-finding trip in April 2013. Over a two-week factory shutdown, the group visited the Vauxhall plant in Britain and toured Chinese car plants run in partnership with General Motors (GM) in Shanghai and Shenyang.

There was nothing unusual about this trip. The company did them once every few years as new people rose to senior roles. The idea was to put the Elizabeth factory in its 'global context' and time was mostly spent plane-hopping, dealing with jetlag, or touring factories.

Waterman went in thinking they were supposed to be looking at production processes to see what could be brought back to Elizabeth. First stop was the British plant. And it was impressive. Ever since Margaret Thatcher, the country had let its manufacturing base shrivel as companies offshored to China and in doing so helped build the new Chinese middle class. When MG Rover collapsed in 2005, everyone seemed to agree the British car industry was basically dead until the global financial crisis collapsed the UK's financial services sector and made the government look twice at its manufacturing base. With rising wealth inequality and an economy beset by austerity and recession, car making had new meaning with all the money needing to be spent on new machines and research. During 2014, British Prime Minister David Cameron even went so far as to give a speech to the World Economic Forum where he told British companies to 'come home'. There was already a steady trickle of British companies 're-shoring' for better-quality production and shorter delivery times from local supply chains, and he wanted more to follow. Britain was to end the 30-year contraction in its manufacturing sector and become the 're-shore nation'. By 2015, the British car industry employed 130,000 people and was generating £10 billion a year for the national economy.

But it was the massive Chinese factories that surprised the Australian union reps. They went in expecting sweatshops and low-quality vehicles. What they found were massive factories, full of momentum, with happy workers capable of pushing out hundreds of thousands of cars a year. The year Holden announced its closure, the Chinese car industry produced a little over 18 million vehicles. Australia made a grand total of 210,538. Where the Japanese once outcompeted the Americans by learning how to build cars better through lean manufacturing, the Chinese did it by sheer scale.

'That's when we sort of thought, shit, we're in a bit of trouble,' Darryl says.

When asked what was missing from the Elizabeth operation, he said, 'Lots of things.'

Mostly, it was the high Australian dollar that did it. So long as the Australian dollar was sitting around 80 US cents, car makers were earning good money. It didn't matter much if their only export markets were obscure Middle Eastern economies or that the size of their market share had been winding back into the single digits for years. Those problems were manageable until the dollar started creeping up towards parity and stayed there, making imports cheap while Australian cars became more expensive to make and more expensive to export.

Parity to manufacturing is what drought is to agriculture. For a farmer, no rain means no crops, and a growing debt. For factory owners, a high dollar means high production costs and little return. In both cases, things will eventually change. Fresh rain will fall again and so will the dollar. The question is how long they can hold out, because the longer it takes, the more likely farmers and factory owners are to go broke. Left unchecked, this is how dustbowls and rust belts happen.

'And you know, that's why we're not going to continue after 2017, because there was just too much that we were up against,' Darryl says. 'But one of the things that we were trying to do was change the Enterprise Bargaining Agreement [EBA] to something that would allow the company to get some more money out of the business, to try and reduce their costs and get more productivity. The company was struggling running the way it was with the Australian dollar, the drop of tariffs, the cost of labour and the cost of production, full stop.'

While still in Shanghai, the delegation met with two GM reps at the company's Asia headquarters, one of whom was GM's Executive Vice President James DeLuca. Over take-away pizza and cans of Coke, the two GM company men promised to do what they could to help Elizabeth, but at the end of the day, they said, they needed $20 million in savings from a variation to their EBA, $70 million in further government support over the next ten years, and GM Board approval to keep the Elizabeth factory alive and give them the next two models.

This was the first the unions had heard about changes to the EBA. Vauxhall in the UK had just negotiated a change to keep the factory open and now the company wanted the same for Elizabeth. The company offered to help with the EBA, but this was union territory. If it was going to happen at all, it needed to come from them.

Once home, the first thing the company had to find out was whether a variation halfway through the previous EBA was legal within the strict confines of labour law. It was, so the real problem came during negotiations when the company wanted to cap the amount awarded to retrenched workers under the Voluntary Separation Package (VSP). This meant lower payouts if the company suddenly wanted to downsize the operation by 400 people.

This did not go over well with the workforce. VSP agreements have traditionally been uncapped and tied to how long a person worked for the company. The change would punish a worker for their loyalty, because anyone who had worked the shop floor for 20 years and held out to the bitter end may have taken home less than if they had bailed right back when things started getting difficult.

So, the union reps were sent back and the cap was removed. In the end, the unions made deep concessions that amounted to $20.2 million in savings. The variation would mean a three-year pay freeze and less break time, and allow the company to call people in for overtime when they needed it, despite a national standard that prohibited just that. The unions didn't like it, but they were convinced it needed to happen, so it did.

Not that it meant much. The sacrifice was a nice sentiment, but a false hope. Ever since the US government had to bail out GM in 2009, the company has been brutal about closing old operations to prove to investors that everything is under control. While Vauxhall might have been spared the knife, the Opel plant in Bochum, Germany, wasn't. In April 2014, the GM subsidiary announced that the Bochum factory would close at the end of the year after more than 3000 workers turned down a company offer to keep production running until 2016 in return for a freeze on pay rises.

The reality for Elizabeth was that the factory's fate was never to be decided by labour conditions, but by a handful of very important people in Canberra and Detroit. The fact is, the Holden badge may be draped in the Australian flag, but the company itself is a wholly owned subsidiary of General Motors and American to its core. While no one in company management will ever say so on record, or even in private and especially to a reporter, the election of Tony Abbott's government in late 2013 changed everything. Any industry support promised by the previous government was not coming and globally GM was looking for reasons to close plants. The Australian government simply handed them a good one.

About two months after Holden made its future known, Toyota followed. Its factory in the Melbourne suburb of Altona only opened in 1996 before it was rebuilt when the facility was gutted and expanded and up-scaled to build hybrid cars. The place still had the shine on it when the company told its 2500-odd manufacturing workers it would be shutting down along with the rest in 2017.

Toyota has never closed a vehicle assembly plant anywhere in the world, and Australia had been the first western country in which the company tried to build cars outside Japan, way back in 1963. Since then it has built 3.2 million of the things, 2 million since it opened the Altona plant. Even as it stared down the end, the company was on track to build 90,000 cars in 2015, twice as many as Holden and five times as many as Ford. The Toyota Camry had been the top-selling medium-sized sedan for over two decades and it had a viable export market in the Middle East. Closing was never on the agenda.

But once Holden said it was pulling out, Toyota had to follow. As much as they compete, the car companies are symbiotic. A single car is made up of over 30,000 bits and the companies that supply Holden with everything from nuts and bolts to stereo systems also supply Toyota and Ford. It's why Holden's decision sealed Toyota's fate. One without the other increased the risk of a supply-chain collapse, and while both companies could have limped on without Ford, Holden and Toyota needed each other to survive, and without the big three, a good chunk of the little operations that fed them parts could not keep going either.

Chapter 4

LOCALLY SOURCED

As of 11 December 2013, the Australian car industry had four years before Holden and Toyota would turn off their factories for good and it wasn't long before the car companies started to cut back on their orders, forcing the supply chain to consolidate.

As the first job losses trickled in during 2014, Adam Reynolds at CARR Components was among them. Then he was 41 years old, a big man with a gentle disposition. He had spent his working life in plastics and was more or less born to it. His father once ran one of the biggest plastics factories in the southern hemisphere before he sold his share and retired in his thirties, leaving the company to eventually become Trident Plastics.

'South Australia used to be a big plastics mecca at one stage,' Adam says as he talks about what life was like in the 80s when work was easy. Adam had started out at 17, leaving high school at the end of Year 10 and picking up a job as a machine operator at Blown Plastic Products. Pretty soon he was job-hopping his way through the industry until he landed at Philmac, an iconic South Australian plastics factory that first started in 1929 and specialised in making valves used in irrigation.

'There was a position where I said that I could do a job, which I completely bullshitted my way into,' he says. 'They worked that out on the first day and they were going to get rid of me. They said I needed to get my act together pretty quickly, so they gave me a week and I worked my arse off and they kept me on there. I stayed there for two, three years, I think it was.

'I've gone from being an operator and having seniors telling me that people who are operators haven't got much chock, to become Divisional Manager of Injection Moulding in charge of over 40 people. And that wasn't easy in itself. It was a steep learning curve for me.'

Much later, CARR Components brought in Adam as Engineering Coordinator to do Advanced Product Quality Planning Workbooks for clients making new orders. The biggest client on the books was Holden, so when Holden pulled out, those orders stopped coming and Reynolds's service was appreciated but no longer required.

Adam and his partner had already seen the end coming as early as 2010, and had started to make plans for their family. By the time he was made redundant, Adam was on the way to earning a qualification in Workplace Health and Safety with a view to getting himself into a management position. Even then, he wasn't out of work for long, picking up contract work with AiAutomotive, another South Australian-based supplier that runs its own press shop and the state's largest e-coating facility.

This is the way it went in the car industry. Once upon a time, anyone who found themselves out of a job could usually find work at one of 700 to 800 companies in the supply chain through word of mouth or reputation. That was the nature of the industry. Supply workers would climb the chain to the big manufacturers and the suppliers would catch workers from the car makers.

It was a support network a person could count on, until the supply chain started to consolidate and work became increasingly scarce. Not long after Adam lost his job at CARR Components, he heard they were being taken over by a younger company, Precision Components, and on 31 July 2014 the factory changed hands.

At the time, AiAutomotive wasn't in any better shape. By the time Adam came on board it had been in receivership for at least two years, well before everyone knew the Australian car industry was dead. The business had only been saved when Holden and Ford started paying its bills to keep it afloat and keep the e-coating facility running. Adam, and everyone else in the building, knew then that if AiAutomotive couldn't be stabilised by the time the car makers left, it would sink, taking its workers down with it.

Chapter 5

THE NUMBER GUYS

'AND BY THE WAY, ECONOMICS IS NOT A SCIENCE, IT'S A POINT of view,' Göran Roos says when asked about the Productivity Commission's 2014 position paper on whether the federal government should have continued to provide financial support to the car industry.

'There are many different points of view, the difference is in the assumptions they make,' he says. 'If you are a Productivity Commissioner, what you have is an economic framework based on the neoclassical economic framework. So, what you get is a predictable point of view and then you look for things that support that point of view. It wasn't prejudged, so much as a predictable outcome.

'It was expected.'

An honorary professor at Warwick Business School in the UK and founder of the think tank Intellectual Capital

Services Ltd, Roos was approached in 2010 by the South Australian government, which brought him in as a Thinker in Residence. After he handed in his report 'Manufacturing into the Future' on 19 March 2012, he was offered a position chairing the Advanced Manufacturing Council.

It turned out to be an excellent career move. In places like the UK, Switzerland and Germany, the ideas Roos had been talking about have pretty much become standard in conversations about manufacturing and industrial policy. In Australia, however, his ideas are new and his work tends to be referenced alongside that of Adelaide University economist John Spoehr in nearly every conversation about the future of Australian manufacturing.

It's not hard to understand why. Roos brings to the conversation a level of nuance that doesn't reduce the whole problem to a black-and-white argument about free-market economics versus protectionism.

'I can't understand why we don't have a smarter approach to industry policy,' Roos says. 'I mean, people hate me saying that, but the key is to create an environment where winners emerge. You don't pick winners.'

He laughs when it is pointed out to him that he is unusually blunt.

'There's no use not being blunt.'

Roos's ideas come with a long intellectual pedigree, but the main concept draws on the 'Economic Complexity' reasoning of César A Hidalgo of Massachusetts Institute of Technology's Media Lab and Ricardo Hausmann of Harvard University's John F Kennedy School of Government. The basic concept is that economic prosperity depends largely on a country's ability to access 'capabilities'.

All this means is that a complex economy with access to a range of skills is able to solve problems thrown up by new manufacturing projects. In doing so, all the people in between, all solving new problems, create growth in the wider economy. Low levels of economic complexity see countries struggle to develop the wealth needed to maintain a high living standard. As a result, they face problems in areas such as crime, health and poverty. High levels of complexity mean a deeper level of capability within an economy, more entrepreneurial activity and a wider range of skills available. This generates growth and results in the higher living standards that define developed economies.

Roos names Japan, Germany and Switzerland as examples of countries with high complexity. Each, he says, scored about a two out of three on the 'Economic Complexity Index'. By contrast, the US sits at about 1.6 and Australia at 0.7.

'So, not very high to begin with,' Roos says. 'This is why sophisticated economies try to develop and maintain industries that "drag up" economic complexity.'

Car making and defence manufacturing are two such industries. Roos gives the example of a university graduate who designs a product and wants to set up a company to produce it. They can't do so alone. What they need is someone who knows plastics, some other people who know how to bend metal and more still who know how to build an efficient production line. If there is no one who can do this locally, they will go somewhere else to find someone who can. The local economy then misses out on new growth, new tax income and new applications for old skills where new industrial processes push boundaries and solve new problems.

This is what the car industry provided. In Roos's view the industry's end, and the wider hollowing-out of Australian manufacturing, will have knock-on effects for the rest of the economy, forcing the country to become more dependent on primary industries and low-end services. Roos says this will lower the amount of overall wealth, as people earn less, lowering the amount of tax revenue generated, making it more difficult to provide key services, and threatening the overall standard of living.

With this, the decision of a government to act, or not act, in support of an industry becomes less about 'protecting' industry or 'letting the market handle it'. Instead, the issue is whether governments should invest to 'secure higher standards of living'. Roos brushes off any suggestion that he's calling for protectionism and says he is for a free market. 'Protectionism never helped anyone,' he says. His main point is that if a country chooses to let an entire industry shut down, it must manage the closure carefully. Otherwise, economic scarring occurs where a region loses its skills base, threatening its ability to recover from a recession.

From that point, skills are 'very hard indeed' to recapture. 'And if you wait for ten years or longer, it becomes basically impossible,' Roos says.

And it's not just the cars, it is ships, it is rail, it is anything that can be made, according to Tom Skladzien, economic advisor to the AMWU, who says that for a long time now Australian manufacturing has been bleeding.

'What the mining boom did was push up the dollar,' he explains. 'The dollar went up not because we're lazy or we don't produce enough, it was because the world economy is in American dollars. It's not just the car industry either.

It's other industries such as rail. We've got core industries shedding jobs.'

What Skladzien is talking about is 'Dutch Disease', so named by *The Economist* for what happened to the Dutch economy in 1959 after the discovery of a large natural gas field. Dutch Disease describes what happens where a resource boom causes foreign investors to cash in. The sudden flood of money and huge profits generated raises the value of the local currency. In turn this makes imports cheap and exports expensive, which puts more pressure on manufacturing as economic activity increasingly focuses on resource extraction. Once the boom ends, resources run out or it just becomes too hard to get them out of the dirt, manufacturing will have withered and the wider economy is left anaemic, threatening its overall stability. Skladzien says that as of 2014, this was the state of the Australian economy and to prove it he points to Australian Bureau of Statistics numbers showing investment in mining growing at the expense of manufacturing around the same time the dollar began to spike in 2006.

Skladzien refers to Roos when explaining that economies unable to turn resources into consumable goods don't do well in the long run, as the main industries they tend to depend on are the rather straightforward work of farming, mining and tourism.

'Basically, digging up shit,' he says.

Of course, the Federal Productivity Commission would disagree. In early 2014, the Commission released its position paper 'Australia's Automotive Manufacturing Industry' on whether the government should provide funding to the car industry and, predictably, advised against future government assistance. The report directly rejected the kind of arguments made by Roos and Skladzien. Essentially, the Commission didn't seem interested in any argument that couldn't immediately and precisely quantify, in exact dollars, why the government should continue to support Australian car makers.

In terms of the arguments made by Roos, the Commission answered by reducing the issue to one of 'spillover' and then making two points on page 55 of the document. First, the federal government should only support industry to secure spillover benefits where those benefits would not be otherwise achievable by private companies; and second, the car industry was nothing special.

> In the Commission's assessment, it is unlikely that the spillovers uniquely associated with Australian automotive manufacturing are of sufficient magnitude (relative to those for other industries) to provide strong support for ongoing industry-specific assistance measures. Furthermore, the Commission does not consider that the particular characteristics of the automotive industry render generally available measures (aimed at supporting spillover-generating activities such as R&D) ineffective.

The rest of the 215-page document follows a predictable pattern. Each argument made by representatives from various car-industry lobby groups, state governments, unions and industry associations were generally brushed aside as being too hard, too expensive, too protectionist or pointless because workers were overpaid anyway. Even the idea of softening the impact of the closure over five or ten years was rejected on the basis that it might undermine the competitiveness of the market.

The whole thing was coming down, the Commission said, and it was going to happen all at once, in one clean motion.

The Commission's view that the car industry was not worth saving is one also shared by economist Richard Blandy.

'We've got to adapt to the world as it revolves around us,' Blandy says. 'Economies evolve all the time as relative costs, demands and technologies change. You've got to evolve with the world economy and if you don't, you'll be taken to pieces by those who have. Assembling cars in South Australia cannot compete with assembling cars in Thailand.'

Rhetorically, Blandy's metaphors for talking about the end of the Australian car industry are all biological. Companies, he says, must 'adapt' to changing environments. Communities must 'evolve'. Closure, like death, is part of the 'natural order' of things. The aim for economic policy, then, is not to protect the old but to provide fertile ground for something new.

Blandy, an adjunct professor at the University of South Australia's School of Business, carved out a niche at Flinders University and Melbourne University when he returned to Australia after graduating from Columbia University in New York in 1969.

The starting point for his thinking is a belief in the 'virtues of competitive markets' where prosperity is driven by competition. Where competition lags, growth stalls, leading to higher unemployment and lower standards of living. Competition does this by always working to disrupt the existing status quo in the marketplace, which gives a new company the chance to emerge, establish itself and grow. In doing so it creates new jobs. Over time, this process means jobs are made or become obsolete. All advanced economies, Blandy says, have seen a decline in manufacturing and Australia is no different.

In theory at least, this is not all that different to the kind of thing Roos would say. But, then, economics is all about emphasis, and small differences make for big changes in outcome.

'Seventy per cent of our economy is services,' Blandy says with emphasis, before pointing out South Australia has 8 per cent of the country's high-tech start-ups, slightly more than the state's share of the national economy. Blandy then refers to a report released in April 2014 by StartupAUS, titled 'Crossroads', which expands on this idea. From the outside, this vision for the future seems to be one where the South Australian economy is more or less driven by its own kind of Silicon Valley.

This was a continuation of a theme Blandy had outlined back in March with an opinion piece he wrote three days before the 2014 state election. It was titled 'Our Post-Industrial Future is a Rejection of Bigness, Centralisation and Bureaucracy', and opened with a direct plug for South Australian Liberal leader Steven Marshall. If Roos has become the darling of state Labor parties, Blandy's own star would have risen had the Liberals not lost the South Australian state election three days later.

The central thesis in Blandy's piece is that big operations have to think small to survive. It describes a post-industrial future for Adelaide that 'is not socialistic in the sense of "big government"' and made up of small-to-medium enterprises or 'the creative industries'. This refers to small, 'highly networked' businesses that are 'horizontally organised' and heavily reliant on the Internet. They are united, in Blandy's thinking, by the idea that 'small is beautiful'. What Blandy is sketching is an economy driven by start-up culture, small design firms, tech start-ups of the kind that created AirBnB, and contractors working out of co-working spaces like HUB Adelaide. In a sense, this vision for South Australia is just a twist on a set of ideas that are largely American imports.

What they promote is a vision for work that prioritises the abstract over the real; where software, finance and tourism take precedence over making, shipping and building. It is exactly the kind of cultural and economic change that Edward McClelland's book *Nothin' but Blue Skies* chronicled in the American rust belt where post-industrial communities have struggled and where ideas for how to cope generally follow the same pattern.

Once the factories have been used up and social blight has been allowed to set in over years or decades, poor, post-industrial neighbourhoods are suddenly 'rediscovered' for their 'grit'. These places are then remade with buzzwords like 'revitalisation' and 'renewal' for people with disposable income who had the privilege of an education that taught them a profession or how to code. Over time, the benefits tend to flow to wealthy new arrivals rather than locals who lose their job and struggle through the hard times, only to be pushed out as rent and rates climb skyward.

When pushed on whether services could realistically fill the skills gap left by manufacturing, let alone re-employ those who might lose their jobs with the end of the car industry, Richard Blandy redirects the question by talking about protectionism.

'Why do you want to protect something?' he says. 'At the end of the day, a car industry left with significantly higher protections than anything else couldn't survive. The idea you're going to be a part of some industry forever is misleading.

'Nothing stands still.'

Chapter 6

HANDMADE, LOCALLY GROWN AUTOMOBILES

EACH DAY, THE 123-HECTARE HOLDEN FACTORY SUCKS IN 402,000 car parts. They are either made on site or received in one of 274 truck deliveries or 33 cargo containers from any of 33 direct suppliers in a supply chain made up of 700 to 800 companies. The average length of service is about 17 years for the 1600 people who work the factory across two shifts, the first starting at six in the morning and the second ending at midnight. Every person there helps in some small way to build 335 cars, daily.

Every 87 seconds a new car drives off the production line. Not too many years ago, it used to be one a minute.

This process involves a complex array of individual people with different skills all working towards one, unified goal. Each machine needs to be maintained and cleaned. Each car body needs to be made from scratch. Each piece of raw steel needs to be fed into a machine, safely, and bent to exact measurements before being spot-welded in place.

Vehicle assembly is the beating heart of the entire operation. Everything and everyone is moving and every single piece, from door frames to 5-millimetre screws, finds its way into this giant shed before someone adds it to a car body, often from muscle memory alone. The work they do is quick. Each bay has a 72-second window per component. It takes 198 minutes for a car shell to make it through assembly from start to finish.

This was the glory of lean manufacturing circa 2014, before the company started to lay people off and production dropped to 240 cars a day. Economic commentators around the time of the closures liked to talk about how Australia was never good at making cars. Where they meant to say that Australia was never a true industrial heavyweight like Japan, they were right. But Australia could make cars and could make them well. The Elizabeth plant was one of the best in the world at what it did. The days when the company would stockpile parts out the back in huge bins died with the 80s. In the new millennium, the entire process had been separated out, studied and broken down. Eliminate waste; maximise productivity. Everything was put together with perfect timing and in perfect order. Everyone knew exactly what they were supposed to do, and where the next part was coming from, and where it was going. There was no room for error. Even 99 per cent accuracy was not enough, because this meant at least two cars a day wouldn't start. The aim was 100 per cent, every time, all the time, no exceptions. Stopping wasn't so much a problem then, so long as it didn't last too long. There were ways to compensate for downtime; error was the true threat.

What this kind of operation meant was steady money. Steady money for suppliers who needed stable income to make business models sustainable and plan for the future. Steady money for those who worked at the factory so they could buy TVs and cars, take out mortgages and raise families. Steady money for councils and governments who could rely on tax revenue and income from council rates to fund new projects. Steady money for drivers and shipping companies, banks, bakeries and retail outlets. Take that away and what you're left with is a gap.

No developed industrial economy ever got to be that way without a car industry. The factories could take a person barely able to read or write and give them a future. It taught them how to work and to be good at the work they did; it gave them expertise, a small slice of the essential skills base that drives a modern economy.

Expertise is not something that can exist in a vacuum. It has to come from somewhere and, once obtained, it needs to be used to create value. If there aren't opportunities to use that expertise, people either take menial jobs or they move away, and over time that expertise fades. People looking to develop new products move to where the people with skills are. With no skills base, a region's economy misses opportunities to grow, which means fewer jobs to go around. People with lower pay or insecure work find it harder to support families or buy houses, and so less money circulates in the economy. Lower incomes and higher welfare participation means fewer consumer goods bought, greater personal debt, and higher deficits for government treasuries. Those with the money to move on don't think twice about leaving their worse-off neighbours behind. As the population falls, tax revenue falls with it. Governments and local councils already struggling with issues of disadvantage in some areas have less money to do more with and so become unwilling to throw good money on bad neighbourhoods, especially if it has always been that way. If a region is not able to hang onto its skills base, its economy gets hollowed out and the standard of living drops.

Or at least that's the case according to former federal Industry Minister Greg Combet, who cites Göran Roos to make his argument.

And he should know. Before politics, Combet was a union man in Newcastle back when the steel industry was dying and a local recession was tightening its grip around the community's throat. During his time in politics, he served as the federal minister for Industry and Innovation from 2011 to 2013 before he resigned from politics altogether upon the return of Kevin Rudd. In the space of about two years, he went from trying to keep the Australian car industry running to serving as its undertaker with the South Australian government as Chairman of the Automotive Transformation Taskforce.

'What has happened is a terrible, terrible development,' Combet says. 'We could see all this coming, but we wanted to adjust over a decade or so.'

Now, an entire industry is gone, with any suppliers unable to diversify likely to fold with Holden in 2017. According to Combet, most of the 33 direct suppliers in the state fall into this category. Given the time frame of the closure, there is little chance they will diversify. Those that might will be companies further out in the chain and the smaller, family-run factories that tend to be lighter on their feet.

What's needed, then, is to manage the closure well, retrain the workforce and grow new industry. Talking about what could replace it, Combet points to defence manufacturing, food and wine, mining and gas exploration as potential opportunities.

But things change quickly. That was Combet's position in May 2014. Two months later, the Department of Defence published a discussion paper questioning whether it would be cheaper to send South Australian defence manufacturing offshore. The suggestion was there would be better value for money on an upcoming submarine contract if they were bought 'off the shelf'. At first, the Abbott government didn't say much of anything, which only confirmed they were seriously considering it.

The implications were huge. After car making, defence manufacturing is South Australia's other big manufacturing industry, employing thousands of people. So far the South Australian government has invested over $300 million in Techport, an industrial maritime hub at Osborne on the peninsula's southern edge. From there, the state was supposed to build Australia's warships and submarines, bringing in millions of dollars and securing the future for thousands employed there.

One report ripped that future away, sending shockwaves through South Australian manufacturing. The official reasons given for the urge to offshore were delays and cost overruns in the construction on the first of three destroyers – but few in the industry believed this. Cost overruns and construction delays to the tune of millions happen on the first build of any run because it has never been done before. This is why short production runs are always a bad idea. And even if the destroyers had blown the budget, the Collins Class submarines had been built on time and to spec, so why offshore the subs?

In the shipyard, the rumours started immediately. One theory ran that it was all part of Abbott's war on unions. A better theory was that a complex geopolitical calculus meant the decision had already been made and the subs were going to Japan. This would stimulate the stagnant Japanese economy and shore up the American–Japanese–Australian alliance against an increasingly big, bad China.

The takeaway is no one knew what was really going on. In mid-August 2014, Prime Minister Tony Abbott seemed to put an end to any uncertainty when he gave a speech that declared, with confidence, that building the next generation of submarines in South Australia would create a 'massive amount of work' for the local economy. Days later, Abbott gave a second speech, this time at the South Australian Liberal Party's annual general meeting. There he repeated what his Defence Minister had been saying for the past few weeks: all defence decisions would be made 'on the basis of defence logic, not industry policy'.

No matter what anyone, anywhere had to say about the matter, Canberra wanted to build submarines and warships at bargain-basement prices and it was about to show it could offshore with the best multinationals.

Chapter 7

BLUEPRINTS

Until the Chrysler factory out at Tonsley in Adelaide's southern suburbs opened in the mid-1960s, the Valiant was just a rebadged, locally made American Plymouth that lacked a certain authenticity.

That all changed once Tonsley got up and running and on 31 March 1964, the first Australian-made and -designed Valiant drove off the line. Models came and went, and two decades later in 1980, Mitsubishi took over Chrysler's Australian arm. For the next 28 years the factory continued to run from its 61-hectare site along Main South Road, about a 20-minute drive south of Adelaide, and when it finally stilled in 2008, it provided the country with a blueprint for what happens when a car factory closes.

Tom Phillips was 54 when he took over as CEO of Mitsubishi Australia in 2000. He had moved over from

Toyota, where he was the General Manager of Sales and the company was at the top of its game. Looking back, he says that were it not for his ambition, he could have ridden out the next decade as a director with Toyota and retired happy.

But Tom Phillips was a hell of a salesman who had spent his working life moving his way up from car dealerships and sales departments to the boardroom. A niggling part of him wanted the top job and he wasn't going to pass up this opportunity, whatever the risk.

From the moment he moved to Mitsubishi, he felt the weight of the company's expectations. As CEO he sat at the intersection between powerful global forces and the local colour. There were the global corporate figures overseeing the tidal push and pull of billions of dollars, in capital. There were the expectations of his sales division who dreamed of glory and riches from the man who had been with Toyota when they moved into the top position in the market. There was the media that regularly ran stories speculating about whether the Mitsubishi factory was doomed. And then there was the distrust of the rank and file who took one look at Tom Phillips and saw a man with no manufacturing background taking over a troubled business. The consensus seemed to be he was there to shut them down, an idea he denies to this day.

'The thing about it is when you're a director of a company like Toyota, you're exposed to a lot of things that go on in the factory,' he says. 'The Toyota way. The Toyota production system. You may not do it but you have an understanding of how it works and how it should flow.'

What Tom Phillips couldn't have known was that the next few years of his career would be spent making a do-or-die last stand for Mitsubishi's Australian operation. The local manufacturing arm was in a bad way for some time when he came on board. The company's global operations had felt the effect of a recall scandal in Japan, and it didn't matter that none of the cars involved were actually sold in Australia. Sales dropped and then dropped again as rising petrol prices collapsed the market for thirsty V6s. People were buying smaller, more economic cars of the kind being built everywhere but Australia, and Mitsubishi Australia was late to the game.

Then the American arm, led by Pierre Gagnon, took a $304 million hit. The year before it had introduced the '0-0-0' loan scheme on new cars, which targeted young people with ultra-generous zero per cent loans, zero deposit and zero repayments for the first year. At first the company set a sales record when 345,111 vehicles sold across North America to people who had zero per cent chance of paying them back. The next year sales crashed 49 per cent and those cars came right back as the repos (repurchase agreements) started to roll in, sending the company's finances into chaos.

And when the company underwent a global restructure in 2004 to cut its 44,000-person workforce by 10 per cent, the job of telling 670 people working at the Lonsdale engine factory in Adelaide's south they were done fell to Tom Phillips.

It was a 15-minute speech to an emotional crowd, but none of those listening were surprised. Everyone in the place had seen the line getting slower. They'd heard the rumours on the factory floor. They'd read the news stories. The morning of the closure, the local paper ran a screaming front-page story about how the Lonsdale factory was dead. It might have been good journalism but for Tom Phillips it makes for a bad memory. It was news that should have come from him.

'For people who work hard and do everything that's asked of them and then they're still out of a job, that's where I found it tough,' he says. 'You'd ask people to do their job, do it better than they have ever done it before, and then, you know, you believe that if we achieve this, we're all going to be saved. And still, you achieve it in most cases, but jobs are still lost.

'There were a lot of people who came up and shook my hand afterwards and said thanks for trying, which probably made it more difficult for me. They were producing as good a quality engine as could be produced anywhere, certainly as good as they could within the Mitsubishi world, and they still lost their jobs. They didn't deserve it, but that's the reality of the market.'

The reality of the market: that's the sound dead factories make.

* * *

It wasn't supposed to end that way. The car they were building, the 380 sedan, was supposed to have saved the Tonsley factory. It was big and spacious and handled well, but when it came out it was a flop, and hope died with its sales numbers.

The tendency among the rank-and-file in the industry is to blame the car. 'Have you ever driven the 380?' one car industry worker deadpanned when asked what went wrong. 'It was a good-looking car, it just wasn't finished,' said another.

Tom Phillips rejects this outright. 'It's a good car,' he insists, just probably not the one he wanted to build. He says this in language moulded by years of practised diplomacy. He puts the end of Mitsubishi Australia down to a combination of market forces and boardroom decisions in Tokyo and Detroit. Fuel was $1.30. The market for six-cylinder cars was 'falling apart'. He had to deal with six company presidents in Tokyo over five years. The opportunity to export to the Middle East was lost. So too was the American market, because the American arm didn't want the competition and blocked the sale. In the end, the car they built was the one head office wanted, because what head office wants, it gets.

The Australian arm of the company was sick when Tom Phillips got there and dying when he left in 2005. The man to replace him was Robert McEnery and three years later, on 5 February 2008, Robert announced the closure of the Tonsley factory and told the world all local manufacturing would end as of 31 March. The workers were angry. They knew they were struggling but they didn't know they were going to be sacked. Rumour has it between 30 or 40 cars came off the line that day with key marks from tail to tip.

When the last 380 rolled off the line at Tonsley on 27 March, about 500 workers lost their jobs. Around 430 stayed on for the next year to help mothball the plant and stockpile enough spare parts to last a decade. At one point, cheap Chinese labour from a state-owned enterprise was brought in to help gut the factory. They paid those workers as little as $1.90 an hour, though when the courts got involved, the Chinese company said it had paid them a stipend for what amounted to Australian wages after those workers had returned to China. The court believed them, but still fined them $14,850 for taking their time to make the payments.

Combined with the closure of the Lonsdale plant further south, and the downsizing at Tonsley in 2004, direct job losses from Mitsubishi totalled 1700. In one survey, more than half of Mitsubishi workers who responded had worked at the plant for 21 years. On the other side of town, the average length of service at Holden is 17 years.

It took nearly a year to haul away the machinery, but by the end of 2009, the 61-hectare site was reduced to a giant, empty shed that dominated the landscape at the shoulder of Main South Road. The closure was said to have sucked $370 million out of the local economy, with a flow-on effect of $230 million. Real estate values in the surrounding suburbs started to stagnate and fall as people moved away looking for work, or struggled under the weight of a mortgage. Of all the employees who found themselves out of work after the closure, a third found stable new employment, a third found unstable employment and a third haven't worked since.

And these were supposed to be the good times. An era of easy work and decent money. Two-car garages and widescreen TVs, three, maybe four bedrooms and a joke doormat that reads: 'Welcome to the nuthouse'. This was a time when South Australia, and the rest of the country, were supposed to be doing well. When there was a skills shortage. When the mining boom was making it rain for anyone who signed up to Fly-In-Fly-Out. A time when both sides of state and federal politics were keen to support the displaced car workers.

For all that, the Tonsley factory site sat idle for about five years, because the South Australian Government and Mitsubishi first had to negotiate a handover and decontaminate the site. Then someone had to work out what, exactly, they were going to do with the 61-hectare piece of real estate. At the time, there was a lot of talk about bringing in 'advanced manufacturing' and opening a hub for TAFE and the local universities. Supporters pointed to how the site was close to the city, Flinders University, arterial roads and a public train line.

It was a good idea and eventually the site would become home to the Australian Industry Transformation Institute, led by Professor John Spoehr, and aimed at building up businesses making medical devices and researching nanotech. The problem was, getting it back up and running took time. Work on turning the site into the state government's vision of an education and retail hub only began in 2014 under the very forward-looking, if somewhat ironic, slogan: 'Tonsley: where industry and people thrive.'

The five or so years it took to start construction is seen as a victory by Tom Phillips. As he says, anyone who deals with government or business knows how new projects tend to move at a glacial pace.

But five years is a long time to everyday people, especially car workers whose work moves in regular 72-second intervals. It might have been a win for those who called the shots, but for workers with 20 years of industry experience and a mortgage to pay, it was just too long.

When Mitsubishi announced it would downsize in 2004, the federal government set aside $10 million for a Labour Adjustment Package and a $45 million Structural

Adjustment Fund. The idea was to attract new investment so growth would soak up the excess labour, but this was a failure. Many firms that moved in did not meet their employment targets and those that did tended to set up out by Elizabeth to be closer to what was left of the state's manufacturing base.

Another $380,000 had also been set aside by the South Australian government specifically for financial counselling, career counselling and résumé preparation, but despite lots of talk about a skills shortage, no funds were available for actual skills retraining. Jobnetwork providers didn't seem to help either, because they tried to apply a model designed for long-term unemployed people to the recently displaced.

In spite of this, people did their best and their stories, be they of struggle or success or just getting by working as security guards or taxi drivers, have been studied and reported and made into digestible statistics. By industry, 36 per cent found other work in manufacturing, 11 per cent in retail, 7 per cent in construction, 6 per cent in health services and 2 per cent each in mining and defence. Anecdotally, at least, the security check-in at Adelaide Airport is still largely staffed by ex-Mitsubishi workers.

Only 15 per cent of former Mitsubishi workers surveyed by Flinders University academics said they earned more than they once did, with 11 per cent saying it was about the same. The rest averaged three jobs a year, went into early retirement, or didn't work again.

And that's just the people. The widespread withdrawal of heavy industry brings with it local environmental problems. The residents around Tonsley and Clovelly Park learned this when the area just south of the former Mitsubishi plant was found to be contaminated with trichloroethylene (TCE), a chemical used by nearby parts maker Monroe to remove grease. TCE usually finds its way into soil, air and drinking water after escaping factories through waste water or run-off. It is odourless and doesn't show up in medical testing, but long-term exposure can cause liver problems and raise a person's cancer risk. All of which is exactly why the Environmental Protection Agency sealed off part of the area in late July and tried to relocate residents while they did more tests. The locals were not happy: testing had cleared the area three years earlier.

At the time of writing, no one knows what will happen to the Holden site on Philip Highway. Speculation has it that it will be sold off to a real estate developer to turn into more urban sprawl. Others still bank on an eleventh-hour rescue by a company willing to take it over and keep Australian car making alive. Right now, word is the land beneath that factory is so heavily contaminated, it will take years to scrub clean and no one will ever make a home on top of it.

Chapter 8

GOLDEN HOLDEN

DONALD ELLIS IS A TALL MAN IN THIN, WIRE-FRAME GLASSES. His hearing is bad and his blue eyes are on their way out too. Mrs Ellis, or Marj as she is introduced, is out the back in the kitchen.

'So, you're the one who's come to talk about the glory days,' she says.

There are two single-seater reclining chairs facing a television in the homely living room and the carpet is soft underfoot. On the walls are paintings of Australian native birds, and the bric-a-brac on the shelves makes it easy to miss the solid-looking gold clock that's been given its own space.

'Holden gave this to me for 25 years of service,' Don says, picking it up in both hands. 'They gave you a choice: either a mantle clock or a watch. I chose the clock.'

The company was good to Don Ellis. It wasn't a charmed life, but it was a comfortable one, with a comfortable retirement. Holden even gave one of Don's sons an apprenticeship, even if he never really used it. Holden was only one of two companies Don ever worked for after he started adult life at age 14-and-three-months as a purser on a cruise ship with the Adelaide Steamship Company.

Don goes to fetch a black-and-white photo. It's a portrait of him from way back when. In it, he looks solid and broad shouldered with a slight smirk. He's staring down the barrel, back straight and leaning slightly forward with his arms crossed in his lap. Then, he wore a crisp uniform and tie.

Today he is wearing a burgundy sweater vest with a red-and-blue check shirt and he's talking about his time on the ships. That was when the Adelaide Steamship Company was still around and running cruises along the east coast in summer and southwest in winter. Out of that gig he travelled the country, learned a skill and even found a wife when Marj stepped on board while the ship was docking in Brisbane in 1954. She had won a competition for a free cruise and a year later they were married. They have been together ever since.

After that the company started talking about selling off its fleet, so in 1956 Don walked out and walked into a salary at Holden's old Woodville factory along Port Road, because he knew how to pay people on time and in the correct amounts before anyone dreamed payroll software would make a good part of the job redundant.

As a kid growing up in Adelaide's west, Don had known the plant. Like everyone who lived out that way at the time, he still remembers watching the workers ride their bicycles to the factory. There was a bike rack down the centre of old

Port Road, and there the workers would leave their bicycles by the hundreds. Like any young boy growing up with a car plant in the neighbourhood, odds were he would end up there some day. It just took Don a little longer to get around to it.

'I wasn't overawed,' he says of the first time he walked into the place. 'Not in the least. It was as I expected it to be. But it's a marvellous thing, overall, how they make a motor car. Just to see from pieces of metal, what they can do with them, paint them and put them together on the assembly line. How they're built. The way they are built.'

Four years at Woodville saw him transferred to the infant factory at Elizabeth in 1960, the same year the body hardware shop went into operation. Two years earlier construction had started with a ceremonial pouring of concrete. Don was around almost from the very beginning. He was there the first year Elizabeth went into operation, at a time when the whole complex was nothing more than an administration block and a small press shop.

'Over the next few years I saw that entire plant built, day by day,' he says. He watched as the factory doubled in size, then tripled and kept going. The body shop and vehicle assembly line went into operation in 1962. In 1963 the Queen visited the plant.

From the moment he moved to Elizabeth, if someone came in looking for work, Don Ellis was probably the man they would see. There would be an interview and they would be given a form that asked for a list of their last five employers. These were then checked thoroughly by Don and his office to make sure the applicant was telling the truth, and after that they were sent for a medical exam to prove they could cope with working on the line.

In those days, it was men who did the heavy work. Women only made up a fraction of the company's workforce and while those numbers increased 40 years on, it was still the case in some parts of the factory, such as the assembly line, right up until its close. When Don did hire women, they usually found work on the industrial sewing machines making things such as car seats. Men of the era had no patience or skill for such detailed work. Theirs was the heavy lifting of the assembly line or the dark, deafening work feeding steel into the machines that made the panels in the press shop.

At its best, Holden employed 30,000 people Australia-wide. That's 60,000 hands before automation, and Elizabeth employed more people than all other Holden operations. Thousands of people came to work every day at the plant and Don was responsible for making sure they were paid on time, every time, even when their wives came in to collect their pay packets on their behalf.

When the factory was big enough that the company wanted to start showing it off, Don was also the first to give tours. Once the labour force hit its peak and there was trouble with the unions, Don was made the first Industrial Officer and his job was to go around to union meetings to give management a detailed report on what they were after.

'We had problems in those days with Communist Party people infiltrating the work area,' he says. 'The Secretary of the Communist Party out at Elizabeth, he also worked there as well and he was very good to get on with, wouldn't you know it.'

Don Ellis got a solid 27 years out of the company before he retired at 55. It was 1983 and around that time he says a downturn was hitting. Anyone over 55 was being asked to leave with a generous compensation package.

'I got a special offer, a golden handshake in other words,' he says. 'I was given the choice of leaving at the end of Christmas, when the factory shut down, or coming back next year and leaving at the end of January.'

Don chose Christmas and retired at 55.

Much has changed since then. The bloodletting of the 80s saw all those with institutional knowledge and experience walk out the door and into well-funded retirement. A few years after Don left, automation began in earnest when the first robots started to appear and the company stopped hiring people off the street altogether. Then they started cutting back the workforce and the numbers dropped little by little. By then the Woodville factory was gone entirely. A Bunnings hardware store now stands in its place as a mausoleum to the factories. The surrounding neighbourhoods still shows the scars.

As does Don. His hearing is gone and there's a chance it has something to do with the clang of the press shop whenever he had to go onto the factory floor. His eyes are going too, but that's just old age. Eventually he'll fail a test and they'll take away his licence, he says. He's had it since he was 16. He's never had an accident and he's owned four motorbikes over his lifetime and driven nearly every Holden model produced at the factory during his time with the company.

And it's funny, because as he talks about the motorbikes he rode and the cars he drove, there is something different about the man sitting in his lounge chair in this living room in a quiet suburban unit.

His back seems straighter and his jaw looks a little more square.

Chapter 9

GOING HOME

EVERY DAY, CANTERBURY CLOSE NURSING HOME MOVES TO the same basic rhythm. Once the nightshift hands over to the morning shift, its residents are woken up, cleaned up, dressed and taken out to breakfast. There are six residents per carer, some more ornery than others. Those with more mobility need to get up first – if not, they'll sure as hell do it themselves and if they're a fall risk, that makes trouble for people like Nick Pettina.

Once Nick Pettina took care of the machines that built people's cars, now he takes care of people's grandmothers, and in a lot of ways, he says, the work he does at the nursing home is no different to what he used to do at Holden during his 36 years and eight months of service. Each day begins with the same basic rhythm, but what happens after is pure improvisation. Some days, something will happen that throws it all out of balance, and some days, it's just a matter of going through the motions.

Nick started in the plant on Monday, 17 January 1977. He never wanted to work in a factory, he says; what he really wanted was to be an artist. He loved to paint and draw, and he played guitar in a band he stuck with up until he was 23. They made a bit of money out of it, he says, had a few late nights and he even got his name on a record. If he had his way, he would have kept going, but his father sat him down as a 16-year-old and said, son, get a grip. Get a real job.

So he did.

Holden was the obvious choice. When his father came over from Italy after World War II, he had worked for a time at the plant with Nick's uncles. It's what made the factory an intergenerational monument. A guy would turn up to work knowing his uncles had helped keep the machines running, or his mother had worked the industrial sewing machines and his brothers were over in one of the other plants.

Inside, the press shop was run mostly by Italian men, though their numbers among the rest of the factory were nothing like out east where the car factories were built so migrants would stream off the boat and onto the production lines. At Elizabeth, the Brits dominated. These were hardened union men who came out as Ten Pound Poms and weren't afraid to stand up to company management, a trait GM's Detroit management did not expect when they built the Elizabeth factory.

When Gideon Haigh tracked down historian Mark Peel for his 2013 book *End of the Road?*, on the origins and state of the car industry, Peel told him GM had been expecting a workforce of 'Australian Mexicans'. At one time, Peel had gone back through the company's records from the 70s when industrial action and wildcat strikes raged, and found it was possible to trace the dawning realisation among Detroit executives that their migrant workforce actually had backbone.

It was in this environment that Nick applied to work at the Holden factory. He liked fixing things and working with his hands, so signing on as an apprentice fitter and turner made sense. He did his first year of basic training at the Woodville plant, which had then been set up as a trade school for the new apprentices. There he learned how to operate a lathe and a milling machine. He learned how to use a pedestal grinder without taking his fingers off and how to use a file grinder without grating the top of his knuckles. After that he was sent over to Elizabeth, where he rotated through the plants to learn how each worked. He ended up spending most of his time in the metal stamping plant where they made the bonnets and the boots and the floorpans. It was big stuff and big engineering.

It was also big noise. The first thing Nick Pettina remembers is the monstrous clamour of the press shop. 'It sounded like the roar of the ocean on a stormy day,' he says. It was a new world for a newly minted man who had never set foot in a factory before. Then he was marched out onto the floor and shown the equipment he would be maintaining. These were huge, 20-metre-high presses. Big and mean and hungry, worth millions of dollars with complex control systems and gantry cranes running along the top that carried big coils of steel almost as tall as he was. The steel then fed into the machine and into a blanking press that punched out the basic shape of the metal.

That was before the robots were brought in towards the close of the 80s, when everything was still done by hand. From the presses, the basic shapes would be moved to other machines that formed them over four or five stages and a finished panel would slowly take shape. Two men would feed the panels of unformed steel into a machine and two men would take it out.

'It was noisy. It was dirty. It was dark. It was dingy. It was horrible and I kinda thought to myself, I didn't really want to end up down this neck of the woods,' Nick says. 'I would rather have been in the vehicle assembly plant where it was nice and clean. Everything was clean there, because it had to be because that's where the car was being assembled.'

Over time, the stamping plant went from being a low-tech shop to being high tech and Nick Pettina had a front-row seat from 1977 right up to 30 August 2013. As the tariffs started to come down, the factory was cleaned up and noise reduction was introduced, which helped a little. Lean manufacturing would later be introduced and the factory stopped stockpiling parts in huge bins they kept out the back where they would rust until they were needed, cleaned off and put on a car. Robots were brought in, though before hydraulics the early robots worked with a system of belts and chains that would wear down quickly and had to be replaced. They also took away jobs. The first robot in Elizabeth was installed in a welding booth in Plant 1 and took the job of a welder.

The robots might have been unpopular because they took away jobs, but that machine in the welding bay and the others to follow made the place safer. They also needed a different kind of knowledge to keep running. Guys like

Nick Pettina had that task but first had to pick up a whole new skill set to program the things and tweak them to make sure they stayed precise.

Nick was also around to watch Richard Phillips rise from an apprentice fitter and turner who worked under his supervision, to boss of the Elizabeth plant. To this day, he is proud of Richard.

In fact, Nick had been there so long and seen so much, he never planned to leave. He and a friend had done their apprenticeship together and by 2013 were the last two left standing from the year they joined. They were the class of 77 and they were going to be there until the end, one way or another. 'We always said, they're gonna have to drag us out kicking and screaming, because we're going to be the last to go.'

If Nick's father set him on the path to the factory, it was his mother who got him out when she was diagnosed with early-stage dementia. She was 82 years old then and lived alone, so Nick and his wife started visiting every night to make sure she was eating and taking her medication. They paid her bills and took her to the doctor and out to socialise.

Both knew that in time she would begin to slide backwards. So in 2013, Nick took a package. He wasn't completely comfortable with it, he says. He had spent his entire working life at Holden. It's where he learned his trade and spent his adult years. It's where he helped train countless apprentices and sat on boards and actively helped shape the company as it is today. He had invested in the place and it had invested in him. The idea of leaving such a substantial part of his life behind made him feel uncomfortable.

But he did it for his mother. He even went to study a Certificate III in Aged Care so he could better understand what was happening to her and how he might best take care of her. He didn't have a plan for what he would do after that. He thought he'd work part-time, maybe as a gardener, or perhaps he'd go back to being a muso. He didn't know. Then he started to learn about the aged-care industry and how 6.1 million of 23 million Australians are aged over 55, though just 6 per cent live in retirement villages or aged-care facilities. As they grow older, many aren't going to be able to look after themselves and many of their kids aren't going to have the time, money or knowledge to do it for them. Instead, they're going to live in a home. Some of them won't want to be there and will tell their kids so, but many will have no choice and neither will their kids. Those kids will visit once a week, or a fortnight, maybe, and in their own way they'll be helping to drive the $18 billion aged-care industry to grow another 4.7 per cent in 2016.

That's when Nick woke up to the idea that maybe he wasn't supposed to be caring just for his mother, but for other people's mothers too. Maybe he could do some good in the job, so he spoke to a few people and found an organisation whose values worked for him. He arranged a four-week placement at the Canterbury Close retirement home as part of his course and something clicked.

Just like his trade at Holden, it was non-standard work. Just like the plant, there were safe ways of doing things and unsafe ways of doing things. Each day was different, and whatever happened, just like at the plant, Nick and his team would have to manage it. If the devil was rising and someone was out for a cigarette, it just wouldn't work: in the factory, that meant down time and thousands of dollars in red ink; in a home, it meant someone might die. Each person has to work in sync, he says, they need to function together as a unit.

And just like Holden, that's not something a person can appreciate from the other side of the wall. Not that most people even think about that. They just expect their car to start when they turn on their ignition and they expect their grandmother to be waiting for them with a smile and a shawl over her lap when they finally turn up to see her.

'To someone who hasn't seen it, who hasn't walked through it, who hasn't seen what is behind the wall, you can't really appreciate it,' he says. 'We used to have tours of people that would come through and you would show them around the plant. And by the time they would walk out, they would go, wow, I didn't realise there was so much involved in building a car. I didn't realise it was so high tech.

'But I don't think the normal Joe Blow off the street sees it like that. Ah yeah, you're just someone putting bolts on a car or whatever, you don't need skills.'

But that's a conversation Nick doesn't have time for. He's been off the floor for about an hour and he's left his team a man down. So he says goodbye and good luck, and disappears into the white halls of the Canterbury Close aged-care facility.

Chapter 10

A GOOD JOB

JEFF JURGENS WAS BORN IN THE WRONG ERA. TEN YEARS earlier, he'd have spent his working life at the Holden plant and he'd have retired happy. Even so, he has nothing to say but good things about the company and his time with it. Sure, there were always problems, just like any other workplace, and waiting out the clock at a factory sucked some days, but that's life. Work sucks. You've still got to do it.

Working in the paint shop at Holden was a good job, Jeff says, one with good people, which paid good money. It gave him everything he has, he explains, and then he lights a cigarette.

Jeff left school at 14 after the first two weeks of Year 9. He had been so sure he was leaving school, he never even bought books. All he was waiting on was approval from the school to follow his older brother up to Alice Springs so he could work with horses. Horses were the family trade, he says. His father had been a jockey, as had his uncle and his brother. Horses even brought his parents together – they met at the races where his grandfather had been a horse trainer. So when the permission came through, he left to be a jockey just like the other men of his family.

Jeff got a good few years out of it, but before long he had grown too heavy and was at a disadvantage, so he went to work on a cattle station up the Strzelecki Track where he learned how to rough it under a starry sky.

He was about 20 then and getting homesick, so after three months working on the cattle station, he moved back to Adelaide. His sister-in-law tipped him off to the fact Holden was taking people on. It was 1988 and it was a job Jeff had promised himself he'd never do.

'It was factory work,' he says. 'Procedural work. Inside. I said I would never, ever do it.'

But he did it anyway. He landed the job and the money started coming in. Like everyone else starting out, he was surprised at the size of the place. At that time the factory had 'something like 5000 people' running around, and the unions and so many moving parts and personalities and nationalities. Greeks. Italians. Vietnamese. Cambodians. More.

'You take it for granted when you jump in a car and go to the shop,' he says. 'It's a lot of little pieces. We built a world-class car and people took it for granted. When we see it out on the road, we take pride in what we built. When people drive our cars, we had a part in that. We built it.'

It took him a little while to get used to the rhythm. At first he resisted, but he soon picked up the line speed. Next thing he knew it was 2009 and 21 years had gone by.

He had risen to leading hand, looking after a team in the paint shop, and he was taking a package. He had a family. He had kids. He had a house.

It was a tough decision to take the package and even then he waited to the very last minute to decide. Everything had been pretty uncertain around that time. Rumour had been around that the factory was done. The company had started cost cutting because of the GFC and because it wanted to get the next model, so the pressure was on to deliver. In the years before, GM had started operating factories in China and they had been bringing over guys to be trained at Elizabeth. Those training them knew in their gut they were probably training the people who would eventually take their jobs. Still, Jeff had turned down the previous two offers and this time around he struggled with the choice: stay, or go.

'I thought I was going to work there forever,' he says. 'We had bought a house close to my employment when we had a young family. Nicole was two and Luke wasn't born yet. Everything we have is basically because of Holden.'

Even when pushed, he doesn't offer one clear reason why he took the package that fateful day in 2009. All he says is that there were many reasons and there was a feeling it was as good a time as any to take the money and step down.

There is a tendency among some to talk about the end of the car industry as a 'liberating' experience. The thrust seems to be that money paid to prop up the factories was being 'liberated' for use elsewhere, like the $4 billion the federal government shifted from subsidising automotive manufacturing to subsidising the agricultural sector in July 2015. The people who work the line would also be 'liberated' to do something else with their life, the thought seemed to run. When this kind of talk starts, the whole shutdown gets painted as a favour to the couple of thousand men and women who would be out of a job in 2017.

Only, people like Jeff never asked to be liberated from the factory. Never asked to be turned out to scrape together a living in the service industry. It may seem like a quaint, old-world notion to those who talk of car factories as the dark, dingy places of the past and joke about how they were living off taxpayers' money, but those like Jeff who worked in the factory took pride in what they did. They were men and women of substance. They woke up each morning, slid into their car and went into work where they did their jobs. Every day, without question. They earned their living, took care of their families as best they could and contributed to something bigger than themselves. At the end of the day, they had something to show for their labour. The plant was their place and there they mattered.

'It becomes a way of life,' Jeff says. 'Every morning, you get up and go to work. That's the way it was.'

Even after he was liberated from factory life, Jeff would still follow the same familiar rhythm. He'd wake up at five every morning, because that's what he'd always done. In those early months he had nowhere to go. At that time, the company helped him get into a three-month course doing a certificate in Transport, Warehousing and Logistics. Out of that, he got an MR truck licence, which can cost a couple of thousand dollars. Even then, it didn't make life easier for Jeff, who went out into a job market very different from the one he knew over two decades ago.

'I was off for a year and I had three months doing that course and the rest looking for a job,' he says. 'Even with that certificate, it was very hard because I had no experience. I applied for at least four or five jobs every day and, 98 per cent of the time, you don't hear back from them. Hundreds and hundreds of jobs and I only got two interviews.'

That was five years ago and since then the job market has only got harder, Jeff says. Though the global financial crisis had just hit when he left, Australia managed to survive the worst of it. The mining boom hadn't hit its peak yet and there were jobs to be found. Eventually Jeff did find work driving trucks, but it took longer than expected and by then the money from the package was running out.

Five years on, he has managed to get himself into another manufacturing job on contract, painting and blasting the warships with the Australian Submarine Corporation (ASC) down at Osborne. It's well paid, earned after a period of struggle, but still the 'valley of death' – where a gap between projects meant a drop-off in work – started to hit the shipbuilding industries and people were being laid off. Jeff was made redundant for four months, but was called back on contract as a cleaner on the ships. He was more than fine with it, he says. He's getting older now and it was easier than what he had been doing before. It also meant a regular pay cheque.

Even today, Jeff is still in the factory. When he talks about his time with Holden, he uses the present tense. It's as if he never left. Like he's still one of the guys, even though he doesn't see anyone from the plant much anymore. Sometimes they cross paths while they're out and when they do, they'll sit down somewhere, get a beer or a coffee and shoot the shit for a while. Remember what it was like. But mostly, the people he saw every day for 21 years have dissolved from his life, except for his cousin who still works at the plant. His cousin's getting on now and Jeff worries what he's going to do when the place closes, just like he worries about all the others. He knows what it meant to work for Holden and he knows what the end of it will mean for his people, good people who built the cars everyone else took for granted.

It was those people he thought about when he heard over the radio the place was closing. He had been driving a truck that day and for him the news was huge. There had been rumours for a while, sure, but he never thought there would actually come a time when Australia didn't make cars. Jeff didn't need 50 pages of economic modelling to know what it meant. All he needed were those few wayward years on the open job market.

'It's the small businesses,' he says. 'The local shop. The local pub. The footy clubs. You have to pay fees for your kids to play sport. Can they afford it? I don't know.'

He lights another cigarette.

'You know, in ten years' time, when things get hard for those families and their children, people are going to say, "I told you so."'

Chapter 11

OVER IT

JUNK MUSIC PLAYS IN THE OLD SPOT HOTEL SPORTS BAR. IT'S mostly pop classics. 'The Final Countdown' by Europe. The Stones. Over in the back corner by the bathrooms are a couple of pool tables no one is using. At the other end are the flat screens where the horse races are playing next to the cricket. All high def. Almost no one is in the place at one in the afternoon this day and if the two distant-looking bartenders mid-shift were honest, they'd say they really don't want to be there. The only thing keeping them from floating out the back are the couple of regulars nursing beers and staring up at the TV screens waiting for their horse to come in.

It's also the closest thing to an unofficial Holden workers' bar outside the Central Districts Football club. When the line breaks for the year near Christmas time, they head in through the doors at the Old Spot for drinks before they head into the city and get up to no good. The bar itself looks out along Main North Road. Around the other side of the building is a small, dimly lit restaurant known locally for its famously average food. Through the restaurant is a dark room lined with pokie machines that fill it with a certain glow. Every now and then one of those perched on a stool feeding dollars into the neon abyss stops for a moment to go outside for a cigarette. Nothing has changed in the place over the past two decades and nothing probably will over the next two. But the beer pours cold and the sandstone-brick pub built along the Little Para River over a century ago, back when the traders used to follow the track south to Adelaide and when the area used to be filled with citrus trees, is about as close as you get to a local this far out in the 'burbs.

It's also where Michael Wetherley agrees to sit down. He orders a Coke. He doesn't drink much anymore, he says, ever since that fateful Holden break-up day a few years ago when one drink became two, two became more and he woke up the next day promising never again. And for the most part, it stuck. These days he doesn't touch the stuff much and when the guys in the factory go out to play at the end of the year, he's the volunteer designated driver.

Michael is a tall, thin guy with an athletic build and a laidback attitude. He's a cyclist, and a mate has just got him into running. If he could swim, that same mate would be getting him into triathlons too, but cycling is his first love and every morning he rides the 5 kilometres into work from his home in Elizabeth.

Michael may live in Elizabeth these days, but he grew up five minutes further south in the streets and parks around the Old Spot. Michael's mother was raised on a farm in England and his father is originally from Grimsby, a struggling port town in northeast Britain. After emigrating to Australia, Michael's father, who was university educated, worked in the lab at a fertiliser plant out at Port Adelaide. Those years were good ones, no better or worse than any others and as far as Michael is concerned, kids then had more freedom than they do now. When he was young, he says, they used to get on their bikes and ride up to Para Wirra, a national bushland reserve where the grey kangaroos come out at dusk or in the early morning. Now kids are barely allowed down the street.

In school, he spent more time messing around than hitting the books. Studying just wasn't his thing. His younger brother was the studious one, and he ended up earning a PhD in geology and moving to Western Australia.

Michael's own path through adulthood seemed tied to the Phillips clan. Michael went to Salisbury High School, where he played cricket with Richard Phillips's older brother. When he got his first job, it was working with Richard Phillips's father, the sales manager at the local Big W. Years later, Michael ended up working for Richard Phillips at the Holden plant.

These days he's married with three kids. He and his wife, Cheryl, have watched their two girls grow up strong and smart, and their young son is not far behind them. Ask Michael what he wants for their future and he just wants them to be happy and get a good job doing something they love, he says, so they don't have to end up working at a place like Holden.

Not that Michael hates the place. He likes it well enough – it's the best job he's had, he says – it's just not high on his list of things he'd rather be doing. Still, the money from the factory is enough that Cheryl chooses not to work and instead stay home to be with the kids. It pays the bills on their house, and carrying the Holden name meant they had no problems getting a mortgage on the place.

'You could just walk into a loan,' Michael says. 'I mean, a guy walks in and says I work at Holden and they know he's getting paid, he's getting pay rises. It's just the security you have.'

The ice in his drink rattles up against the glass as he speaks.

'Without Holden, everything would have taken longer.'

* * *

Factory work doesn't get busy. It doesn't get slow either, but that's usually the first thing people who don't know the inside of a factory ask someone who does.

'Been busy?'

Factory work doesn't change. Each day is the same. It is never busy and it is never slow. The line moves at the same, steady pace day in, day out. It starts at the same time as yesterday and it will start at the same time again tomorrow. The job you do is the same job you've done a thousand times before and it doesn't matter if no Holden dealership in the country sold a car yesterday, the factory is still going to push out 200, maybe 300 more. As it will today. And tomorrow. And the next day.

Once the day starts, it's just a matter of running down the clock until you can leave. It is work that means having the same conversations with the same people, and weighing up whether you are getting paid enough to be there as the next job comes down the line.

And Holden paid well. So well, Michael stayed. Before he got the job working general assembly, at the point in the line where the chassis is married to the body, he was making broomsticks at a plastics factory for a living. The pay was crap but the job was easy and Michael hated every minute of it. When he heard Holden was going to be putting on a third shift and had contracted labour-recruitment agency Manpower to handle the application process, he was one of 'about 7000' applicants. The agency weeded out the no-hopers and after the initial round was over, they started prepping those like Michael who made it through on how to cope when the Holden people called them up for an interview.

It was a long process, stuffed fat with interviews and dexterity tests. There was one at the recruitment agency that involved inserting screws to time and doing 'little things' with his hands to prove he had the dexterity. There was another one at Holden that involved putting a cut-out of a tyre onto a sensor board and hand-starting the nuts in the right order. Then there were the others at the medical centre to get a baseline level of strength.

Michael wanted the job. His working life had been spent in retail and drifting between labour-hire companies before he went to work at the plastics factory. Holden was a shot at something more. It was close to home and it was more of a career than a job in a place where maybe he could work towards something, maybe even move up. Most of all the pay was good.

So he made sure to push hard against the sensors on every test. He'd pull and he'd push and in the end, he pushed so hard he threw his back out and had to take the next few days off from making broomsticks. When the people in charge at the plastics plant asked how it happened, he had no hesitation about telling them a story.

* * *

By May 2015 Holden started retrenching workers. Production had fallen from over 300 to 290 cars and then to 240 a day. A shutdown had been planned for 22 May, and about a month before, the company had given each person an envelope detailing how much they'd get in a package if they were suddenly asked to leave.

But not enough people wanted out and when too few put their hand up, the company got busy firing people. It was the first time it had to do so in half a century and of the 270 who lost their jobs on 21 May, at least 80 were pushed out the door.

That morning, everyone in Michael's section felt odds were good they'd survive the cull. The company needed them there in general assembly and if a guy made it through to smoko, he knew he was safe. Still, the company had told everyone to clean out their lockers in an effort to try to eliminate the walk of shame. It was a nice gesture by management, but people still knew what it meant when the company men came around to tap someone on the shoulder and say, grab your things.

Michael survived, and so did the guys on his line, but another man he used to work with was let go. It was the first sign the closure was real and it was happening. It also had a flow-on effect for the parts suppliers. Those factories ran on low margins with a high volume and as the number of cars per day dropped, the number of parts Holden needed fell and the suppliers had to start letting people go.

To smooth the pillow, Holden had set up Transition Centres at its Elizabeth factory and at three other sites in Victoria. They had paid $15 million into the federal government 'Growth Fund' and set aside money to help retrain and reskill workers staring down the barrel of the industry's closure. The centre was open to those employed at the suppliers and anyone who wanted to do a course or get a new qualification could access up to $2000 to help cover the cost, though as 2017 bore down, the company upped that figure to $3000. Career counsellors and fact sheets were made available and there were people to help write new résumés and run computer-skills courses, all after hours.

Problem was, no one was turning up. A lot of people had kids and a lot of people who work at Holden don't live in Elizabeth. If their kids needed to be picked up from school, there was no time to stick around after their shift to talk résumés and interview techniques. Then there were those who just couldn't wait to get out of the place at the end of a shift and those who just didn't want to think about it at all. The end was still a year or two away and they'd deal with it then, they guessed. So by about November 2014, the company was telling its people they'd give them half an hour during work hours to head down and take a look. Those who did were in for an education.

'It was interesting, at the beginning,' Michael says. 'They had this graph up in the Transition Centre and it said, these are the things that people at the factory said they would like to do and then this is the percentage of actually decent jobs that are going to need people. And it went up the other way.

'When it got to aged care, like 50 people said they'd go into that and there's going to be thousands of jobs in that industry. But everyone was saying they wanted to go into manufacturing or transport.'

But manufacturing is dead. The company had been saying it over and over. So too were the career counsellors at the Transition Centre. It didn't change the fact people still wanted to make stuff. Even those who wanted to get into truck driving or the transport industry were in for a shock. Nobody wanted drivers who had never driven, and where they did, it probably made more sense to hire an 18-year-old.

* * *

Cheryl's invitation to High Tea came by post. It had been addressed to Michael and invited any women connected with Holden to RSVP for the event. It didn't say what the event was for, only that Holden was 'exploring its feminine side'. Cheryl didn't know what that meant, but she was curious to find out, so she put her name down.

When the day came, Cheryl turned up in a black dress with little blue flowers she had made herself. That's because Cheryl is a 'serial crafter' and artistic by nature. Before the kids, she got educated, travelled and worked at labour recruiting agencies, including Manpower, the very same organisation Michael had applied to when he was trying to land the job with Holden. That was before the pair had met. Afterwards, after he got the job, after they got together and after the kids, she chose to stay home to be with them.

Theirs was a house of makers. Michael helped make cars and Cheryl made dresses as a soldier in the modern sewing movement which had been driving a revival of the art ever since it stopped being taught as a core skill in schools. Making things gives a feeling of self-reliance, she says. Knowing how to make a thing from nothing helps give it value. Few can design, stitch and sew a dress from nothing, but Cheryl can and she had already designed the black dress with the little blue flowers when the invitation to High Tea gave her a reason to finish it off.

The event itself was held in the Transition Centre. It was a nice set-up and there were about 100 other people present, seated along three long trestle tables. Some women worked for the company, but most of those present were partners and wives.

Once settled, what Cheryl really wanted was a cup of tea. Bushfires had been tearing through the hills that day and the air over Adelaide was dry, of the kind that sneaks up on a person and makes for a powerful thirst.

Only, there wasn't any tea. It's a detail that makes Cheryl laugh to this day. There were tea cups laid out, but no tea at an event that called itself a High Tea. So there was nothing to drink after a hot day in a room full of people who had gathered together for a purpose not entirely clear. It was only when radio personality Amanda Blair opened the night that Cheryl understood it was a session for the women of Holden about what the end of the factory would mean for them. Which was lovely and all, but Cheryl could really have used some tea.

Instead there were a series of motivational talks. The message, in a nutshell, was to make sure that when their husbands came home with their money when it was all over, not to let them just sit on the couch and watch TV. Amanda

Blair told a heavy story about a friend who once had a drug addiction but overcame it to become an emergency room doctor, while a psychologist spoke on how to cope with change and the need to 'stay positive'. There were others who spoke about volunteering and those who made sure everyone in the audience knew if they ever needed help or support, they could always find it at the Transition Centre.

Which was nice and supportive and everything, but frankly Cheryl was already there. She had dealt with the news months ago and found the announcement a relief after the wall of noise that had been knocking about the TV channels for months on end, speculating about whether her husband would be out of a job.

Even afterwards, people didn't seem to understand that the announcement that the factory would close did not mean work would stop tomorrow. People kept asking Cheryl whether Michael was still working. He was. People also wanted to know if they were devastated. They weren't. They had a family to care for and lives to live and the shutdown was probably a bad bigger picture, sure, but they weren't living every day in 11 December 2013.

Meanwhile, the company was doing its best to be supportive. It had opened the Transition Centre. It was reaching out to the wives and partners of the workforce. It was even giving families the chance to tour the factory, which again was nice but bittersweet.

Cheryl's daughter hadn't been interested in going to see it, but her son was. In previous years the company had been too worried about security to allow such a thing. It was why they didn't even allow their workforce to have camera phones for a time. Only now it was all coming to an end, they had softened and took the kids around on a little cart to show them how it all worked. They even let them choose where they wanted to visit in the plant.

Cheryl and her son chose the paint shop. In the past, few visitors would have been invited into the area, but this time they had the whole experience. They were put in the 'space suits' and had to stand under an industrial fan to blow off any dust before they were let loose inside. Out in the rest of the factory, the tour guide was even good enough to drive everyone around to the point in the line where Michael worked so the kid could see Daddy.

For a child it was a grand adventure, but for the adults who understood the subtext, there was something else to it. This thing they were seeing was amazing, but they also understood they were only seeing it because it was about to be given away.

That's when Cheryl turned to the woman sitting behind her.

'It's kind of sad, isn't it?'

* * *

A year out from 2017, Cheryl is tired of the sadness. It has been there ever since the company dropped the third shift a few years back and it's been a slow, sad unwinding ever since. When the announcement was made, Cheryl was relieved, not glad. In the years and months leading up to it, she had grown tired of all the talk and the speculation and the assumptions that they had been living with for the last ten years. She had grown tired of the pressure to buy Holden. She was tired of the people who thought they knew what they are talking about. She was tired of the constant wondering about what things are going to be like.

Michael has been talking with Cheryl about going into aged care when it's all over. Or perhaps disability care, though he doesn't know much about that. That graph at the Transition Centre stuck with him and the couple have been talking about it for a while.

At first it surprised Cheryl, but Michael kept coming back to the idea. It helps that the company is offering money to cover the costs of doing the course. His plan is to get qualified by about October 2016, when the next round of redundancies will take place because the company will want to get rid of people before the next pay rise falls due. If he can, Michael wants to stay, but if the company men come around to tap him on the shoulder, he wants to be ready.

He says it's strange, though. Most of the people he talks to don't seem to be thinking about the end just yet. He'll come across them at an event or during some down time, and he'll ask them what they plan to do when they leave. Mostly, he says, they just shrug.

'They're like, oh, I don't know, just not thinking about it,' Michael says. 'And then they ask you, are you going to stay for the end? And I say, well, I'll see what I can do, but we can't all stay to the end.'

Chapter 12

LIBERATED

WORKING ON CONTRACT FOR A COMPANY IN RECEIVERSHIP IN an industry that is slowly coming apart means no future. No future means struggling to pay bills and not being able to get finance, which means no new car and no mortgage. It means selling the house and putting everything in your wife's name because she is the only one with a stable job and odds are that pretty soon she'll be the one paying the bills.

This is what things are looking like for Adam Reynolds going into the start of 2016, and it is a truth that weighs on him. Over a beer he tells how AiAutomotive has so far picked up extra work making chassis for Jayco Caravans and the company extended his contract. He loves the job, he says, loves the people he works with. Across the shop, quality has improved because everyone is making the extra effort. Even so, the factory isn't back to full health. It may be able to pick up extra work making spares for the car industry, but sooner or later it will have to restructure because the volumes they're getting just aren't enough to carry on as they are. When they do, they'll have to cut back staff, and there's every chance that means cutting back on Adam.

Which is the problem. Adam is a man who has always worked. He has always been able to find a job and he has always been able to bring that money home to his wife and kids. He is also a man who likes kicking goals. He works hard and he gets results. It was an attitude that meant he used to never have a problem finding work.

Not now. It's a year out from 2017 and Adam has been looking. He has also never been a man to sit around waiting for the worst to come and for the past six months he has been doing what he is supposed to do. He got in early, got qualified and got the paperwork. He finished a Certificate IV in Work, Health and Safety. He finished a Diploma in Management. He is working on a Certificate IV in Training and Assessing. He even followed his aunt's advice from years ago when she told him the way to get a job is to pick out the companies he wants to work for and then farm out his résumé to them all. It worked back then, why shouldn't it work now?

Except he rarely hears back and some days it's the silence that gets to him.

'No one wants to touch you because you don't have runs on the board,' he says. Out of all the applications he put in, he only had one response, from the shipyards at ASC. They called him in for an interview, put him through a psych evaluation and a medical, and when it was over he thought he'd nailed it. The job was his. Finally some good news.

And then nothing. He never heard back. It may have had something to do with the crunch hitting defence shipbuilding industry towards the end of 2015. Or it might not have. Adam Reynolds can only guess, because they never answered his follow-up emails.

It's the same story with his qualifications. Now that he has the paperwork, Adam has been applying for jobs in HR doing Training and Assessing, but no one seems to want him because he has neither trained nor assessed.

'I'm back to where I was when I was 17 years old,' he says. 'I feel frustrated. I feel angry. I just don't know what I'm going to do anymore. I really don't. It's hard to feel as though you have purpose in life when you don't know what you're going to do.

'Before this happened, I had all these dreams and aspirations. I'd been able to afford, basically, everything. We were going so well with paying our mortgage off, our cars were paid off. We were starting to build a bank balance. Then ... all of a sudden, the automotive industry decided they were going to pull the pin.

'Going from, like, I think a reasonably good-paying job now, I'm going to have to take at least a 25 to 30K cut in annual pay. I'm 43 years old and that's a massive kick in the teeth.'

A week ago, he had a hit off another job. It was one he was probably qualified for, one he could have picked up and run with. The company had even got back saying they wanted him to come in for an interview, but somehow Adam just couldn't do it.

The sequence played through his mind and he imagined going up against a panel again, shaking hands, laying on the charm, getting to know them and then, after all that, still having to face the prospect that it would be for nothing and they'd say no, sorry. Or they'd say nothing at all.

It was just too much, so he didn't go. Instead he told his wife he was unsuccessful, but that was a lie. It was a lie from an honest man who hates liars, to the woman who has stood with him for 16 years.

'This whole situation is making me do things that are not me,' he says, pausing a moment. 'At this stage, right now, I'm destined to sit on the unemployment queue and that's the cold, hard fact about it.

'I don't want to, I want to work. I want to make a difference. I want to show my son this is how you get things in life. You work hard for it. You play hard, have fun. My future at the moment, everything I've known has been manufacturing. I've done the right thing ...'

He doesn't finish the sentence. He doesn't have to.

Chapter 13

CANOES

Glen Dalimore goes to sleep late and rises early. It means he can be sure he'll always get to sleep at night, he explains as he makes coffee at the kitchen counter. 'As soon as my head hits the pillow,' he says, stirring the cup. 'Though one of these days, I'm probably going to drop dead from a heart attack.'

Glen is a 43-year-old fitter and turner who has been practising his trade for a quarter of a century. In that time he has moved back and forth between the car industry and defence manufacturing, but right now he's working on the shipyards out at Osborne as a pipe fitter on the Air Warfare Destroyer project.

There are four unions on the shipyard, and Glen is a union rep with the Australian Manufacturing Workers' Union, which has been helping fight the Australian government's plans to offshore shipbuilding. Glen is across every aspect of the issue and since October 2014 his name has been put forward as a public spokesperson for the union's campaign to keep the $50 billion submarine contract local.

Since then, Glen and the other guys on the yards have been watching as the industry slowly shuts down for lack of work. In June 2015, Forgacs started laying off guys from its yards in Queensland, and in August BAE did the same when it sacked 150 from its Victorian operations at Williamstown and then 200 more in November. As 2016 picks up, it's South Australia's turn.

'We've managed to shift around and rearrange the chairs on the *Titanic*,' Glen says. 'Beginning next year, we'll be losing workers every quarter. November 2015, we had 1150 workers, nearly 1200. By the end [of] 2018, ASC will be down to 250 workers, full stop.'

For the past five years, guys like Glen have been talking with both the right and left sides of politics about submarines. It used to be talking submarines with those on the right meant the bottom line and unions. Talking submarines with the left focussed on anti-war politics and jobs. The point was, Glen says, to get people talking about how Australia is going to be buying these machines anyway, so the issue becomes whether spending billions for someone else to build them makes any sense.

That is what Glen is talking about at his family home in the Adelaide Hills, where he and his family live on the flip side of a postcard. It's a part of the world filled with sprawling paddocks and livestock, and the soft orange glow of a setting sun behind the distant hills. Shadows are starting to reach across the paddock and up the walls of the old Federation-era cottage he and his wife have been slowly restoring. It's very much a life worth fighting for.

And Glen has been on the front lines of that fight as AMWU's union delegate for the past two years. All told, shipbuilding is worth about $250 billion to Australian manufacturers, and South Australia alone has sunk over $300 million to build Techport at Osborne, an unremarkable peninsula out in Adelaide's west. This tied the state to the defence industry and gave it something other than car manufacturing to help keep the lights on.

Thousands – mostly men – went to work in the shipyards building warships for the federal government. It was hard, heavy work on the giant steel structures. They built the Collins Class submarines, which started out badly but came good; they built the Air Warfare Destroyers and a couple of offshore patrol vessels, and then they were supposed to build the new submarines.

Even about a decade ago, those on the shipyards had been talking about a situation where the end point on major projects lined up and everyone would get laid off until the next project came online. It was a problem that would see thousands of skilled tradesmen put out of work around the country. The solution was a rolling build: orders come in large enough numbers that by the end of the production run, those built first would need to come back in for an upgrade or service. What this does is provide certainty to the workforce and allows the companies who build them to train up their employees. Over time, it eliminates errors from the process and speeds up production. In contrast, having to stop and start means skilled workers go off and get new jobs, and to get them all back again ten years later costs serious money.

'Once they go, that's it,' Glen says. 'Building a ship is like no other skill. It takes years for a non-shipbuilder to become adapted to a trade in shipbuilding.'

Mismanagement of the country's shipyards started under the previous Labor government. As 2013 drew near, the unions and shipbuilding reps started warning about a drop-off in work. The valley of death, they called it, and to avoid it Labor had promised a rolling build with a new fleet of 12 submarines. Thing is, they never got around to actually putting in the paperwork.

Which shouldn't have been a problem, because in a show of bipartisanship the Coalition backed the idea of a local build before and all the way up until the 2013 election. They would build the subs in Adelaide, they said, and if they were elected, it would take about 18 months to choose a new design. No one wanted to screw around with national security.

Once in government, that attitude changed. Australia had been buddying up to Japan in the face of a more aggressive China and then, on 29 July 2014, a defence discussion paper took issue with cost overruns and delays on the destroyers. It suggested future contracts could be offshored to get better 'value for money' for the taxpayer.

At first, PM Tony Abbott refused to say much of anything, but when he did finally start talking, it was about how they were going to go offshore to Japan, or Germany, or maybe France. No one was quite sure which. What they *were* sure about was that the local Australian shipyards wouldn't be involved. Things were only made worse when a conspiracy theory started circulating in the shipyards about a secret defence deal with Japan that meant the contract on the subs was already decided, making everything else just theatre.

There were so many objections to all this, those on the shipyard didn't know where to begin. For a start, they said, there was a difference between submarines and destroyers. Yes, the fleet of Collins Class submarines had problems at the start, but they worked out in the end. The destroyers, on the other hand, were never built in large enough numbers or for long enough to iron out the wrinkles, so of course there were cost overruns and delays in the schedule. They'd never done it before and first times always mean mistakes are made.

By the time October 2014 came around, there was enough of a backlash that a group of South Australian federal Liberals were in revolt. Among them were former ADF test pilot Senator David Fawcett and Senator Sean Edwards. Things worsened a month later when the government started talking about privatising ASC and Defence Minister David Johnston stood up in the senate and told the country the government shipbuilder couldn't be trusted to build a canoe.

'It was a gut-punch,' Glen says of the reaction in the shipyards. 'Morale in the yards fell.'

So the unions upped the stakes. They sent a canoe to Johnston's office, and by December he had been sacked, but that didn't slick the anger. The feeling was that Canberra had taken away the car industry and now it was taking away shipbuilding.

'Name another manufacturing industry in South Australia,' Glen says. 'The car industry is going. We have some industries around, but they're on the edge. It will be a skills drain. Completely.'

Glen runs through the basic arguments about keeping shipbuilding alive.

'It's not about union jobs for the boys,' Glen says in a moment of frustration, but an industry that is about to be torn down because of a political failure and, when it goes, it will take down the livelihoods of thousands of people who depend on it. All the money, all the time and training that has so far been invested to give Australia an industrial base since World War II will have been flushed.

And it was during World War II when Australia was supposed to have had the realisation that a nation of farmers and miners was not enough. The country's manufacturing base had been expanding slowly up until 1940. Once Imperial Japan began stomping around the South Pacific and all the British promises of naval support fell through, Australia came dangerously close to being cut off from its allies. So Australia jerry-rigged a war economy in places like Salisbury and Geelong. It built ammunitions factories, and companies including Ford and International Harvester gave over their plants to support the war effort. Thousands of Australians, men and women, went to work in the factories and learned new skills, but then the country had nothing on the scale of Detroit, what Franklin D Roosevelt called 'the great arsenal of democracy', whose factories built the guns and tanks democracy needed to drive fascism out of central Europe and the Pacific.

After the war, that industrial base expanded rapidly as thousands came home to find work in the factories with a new understanding of the world around them. It was hoped the Australia of the new millennium, with its kilometres of coastline, had learned the need to do its own heavy lifting. It was supposed to have understood the importance of maintaining a minimum level of independence and self-sufficiency. The thought a modern Australia would suddenly contract out everything to the Japanese and then have to drive their 'off-the-shelf' submarines back to Kure, Hiroshima, every time the things needed an oil change was a joke to those who used to build them.

Only, the punchline was made up of guys like David Coulthard. Dave is a boilermaker at ASC who has spent the past four years working on the Air Warfare Destroyer project. It's January 2016 and Dave explains that ASC are expected to cut staff next week, and he may very well no longer have a job in a few months.

Dave speaks with a voice as deep as a bass drum and doesn't waste time getting to the heart of things. He is a man who has spent his life building Australia's ships, since he signed onto the navy at 16. He's 45 now and a lifetime in the trade has worn his body down to a nub. His work means spending eight hours a day putting things together inside a space no bigger than a pool table, and for every hour put in, it strips a little more cartilage from his joints, leaves a little more dust in his lungs. His shoulders, back and knees, he says, are 'wrecked'. His eyes are 'gone'. His lungs are 'stuffed'. But even so, he loves the job. It is work he knows and work he has been doing in one form or another most of his life.

These days, however, it has become more a means to an end. Dave's been divorced twice and is currently a single father of a 16-year-old son and a 14-year-old daughter. He's proud of them both, he says, and for a while his son was thinking about starting an apprenticeship as an electrician alongside his father at ASC. Or he was until he came to understand the work involved and decided it wasn't for him. Now the boy wants to be a doctor. Which Dave wholeheartedly supports, though the professional world is one he doesn't understand.

'It's an easier life for them,' he says. 'Easier existence, but you don't have as much of a fallback without a trade. If you're a doctor you're pretty safe, I guess. But then, I don't know a great deal about it. My old man was a motor mechanic and my grandfather was a bricklayer.'

And before he mended cars, Dave's father built them. He loved the work and loved the cars he helped make, just as Dave loves his trade now. Dave says the day Australia learned car manufacturing was dead, his father was disgusted. He knew what it meant. Knew it would mean thousands out of work when there wasn't much else out there. It's a view Dave shares.

'You can probably throw a blanket over Elizabeth and Salisbury and say that's it,' he says. 'And if we lose shipbuilding, South Australia is screwed.

'What's left? Tumbleweeds.'

That's the bigger picture, but right now there are more pressing matters. Work on the destroyers is winding down and when it does, the company will start laying people off. Dave could go in the next round, or it might be the guys he works alongside. The last time the company laid off 50 to 100 guys was hard enough. Most of them still haven't found work again.

If he's out of a job tomorrow, Dave thinks his best shot would be to go overseas and work on an oil platform or a gas field, though he says that would be hard on his kids and he has to think of them. They sometimes ask if they could buy a house and settle down. It ain't going to happen, but that's not something Dave can say to them. They have a pretty good idea about what's going on as is. They even get into arguments at school about it when the other kids repeat what they hear from their parents or the TV about how industry shouldn't be government funded, or that it just shouldn't exist.

That's when the teachers step in to back his kids up.

'They say, if there are no jobs here, what is everyone going to do? What are you going to do when you leave school?' Dave says.

They know better than most how not everyone gets to be a doctor or an architect.

Most people can appreciate the sweat that goes into building a ship from nothing. The average household car is made up of about 30,000 components. The average naval-grade warship is a complex floating city made up from tiny bolts to huge, prefabricated steel hull blocks. Making it all fit together is hard and often shitty work. If it doesn't line up, the weight transfer will kill it. But it's something that has to be done and if so, Glen asks, why not do it here?

That's the 50-billion-dollar question and while Canberra takes its time to answer it, one way or another, those in the industry are about to be laid off for lack of work. They've done all they can. They've protested and rallied and lobbied and made noise. They've sat down with politicians and reporters, and they've nutted out the issue so many times.

Now what they want is for someone to hand them their future so they can feel its weight, turn it over in their hands and breathe it in. Unless that happens, everything else is just words in the air.

Chapter 14

MEANWHILE, HEADING NORTH

IT TAKES JUST MOMENTS FOR THE METAL SHELL OF THE FOUR-wheel drive to roast. It's October in Leigh Creek and grand final weekend in the biggest country town of the region. Summer has come on heavy like it always does in this part of the world, so it's a small mercy when the automatic doors of the pub slide open and out flows cold air. Ever since James Harrison first experimented with an ice machine in 1851 on the banks of the Barwon River in Geelong, modern, industrial air conditioning has done more to unlock Australian productivity than any interest-rate adjustment ever could.

Inside the pub, men with tanned skin and broad shoulders have brought their families to watch the football. They drink with their wives or with their mates and shout at the TV screen. Their young sons loiter around the pool table awkwardly holding the cues, while their older daughters gather near their mothers. It's a pleasant vibe, for the most part, except it is a very quiet afternoon. For a town of 549 people, there are 20 present, at most.

This is because, at this moment, Alinta is getting ready to close the whole thing down. In the same way that Holden meant everything to Elizabeth, Alinta was everything out this way and that made them king. Officially, they leased the town from the state government but the company may as well have owned the land, owned the houses and even owned the air above if it had the will.

The energy company also owned the massive open-cut coalmine just outside town. The Telford coalmine stretches across the horizon from the edge of town and when the wind picks up the coal dust inside the mouth it makes a black whirlwind, the top of which can be seen over the massive dirt hills piled high around the rim.

The company has made billions over the past three decades ripping brown coal out of the ground at that mine and sending it south to burn in the heart of South Australia's last two coal-fired power stations in Port Augusta. Earlier in the year, the company CEO had been talking about how they wanted to keep at least one of the Port Augusta plants open until 2030. Everyone thought they were safe, they had nothing to worry about, then a month ago the company turned around and said it was closing it all down.

Coal-fuelled power was just too costly, the company said. The plants were too old and there was just too much pressure from wind power to justify keeping them open. The aging power plants had clocked a loss of $100 million over the past four years, with $200 million already spent on extending their shelf life, and they just couldn't compete. It was money down a black hole in a state like South Australia, which leads the country in drawing 40 per cent of its energy from wind and solar. Even as the federal government undermined billions of dollars in investment in the renewable energy sector, South Australia's Labor government quietly cornered almost half the renewable energy projects in the country to at least bring some work into the state. Rooftop solar and wind generation was at the stage where it was undermining mass-market electricity producers such as Alinta. So the demand wasn't there, the power plants weren't needed anymore and neither was the mine that fed them.

The Telford mine didn't export its coal and it didn't make sense to. The price of thermal coal had fallen to an eight-year low in October 2015, at a little over US$46 a tonne. There was no export market that would justify the effort to get it out of the ground and put it on the back of a ship, even if the company wanted to. For as long as the mine had been running, the only people burning that coal were those operating the power plants. No more power plants meant no more mine. No more mine meant the company had no more use for Leigh Creek.

Not too long ago, the idea of Leigh Creek without a coalmine was unthinkable. The mine literally built everything out here. Before 1982, Old Leigh Creek sat on an area where the open-cut pit is today. Then the company came along and asked the whole town to move to where it now stands before the coal pit swallowed Old Leigh Creek whole.

Moving was the best thing to happen to the township. The mine brought easy work and good pay. It brought a school and a hospital and a swimming pool and sports facilities and air conditioning. The town started to service anyone for kilometres around who needed food or fuel or the postal service. With the mine and the company, Leigh Creek suddenly found itself significant.

Now Leigh Creek is just another used-up mining town across post-mining-boom Australia, or the United States, or Europe. Swap out the name and Leigh Creek's story is no different to any of them.

Leigh Creek could be Marree further north, back when the rail line closed in the 80s, moved further west and the state government never finished sealing the road to the town. Leigh Creek could be Roxby Downs, the modern city in the middle of the desert that serviced BHP's Olympic Dam uranium and copper mine. For years the company had promised a massive expansion of its operation that would turn it into one of the biggest of its kind in the southern hemisphere. Everyone was just waiting for the go-ahead, which would have made South Australia – and the local people – rich. It never happened and from August 2012 BHP started cutting back.

When 2015 closed, so did the mine. The state government guaranteed the town would be supported at least until 2018. What happens next is anyone's guess.

And all people can do is guess. Ever since the announcement, conversation always turns to the mine. In the well air-conditioned pub, a man in shorts and a T-shirt is ordering a beer. He leans over the counter to ask the woman pouring it how long she's been out here.

'Six years,' she says, though she's only been working for three. She came out with her husband who works in the mine – and then all talk stops.

Both know what comes next.

It's the same for Steven Hoddel, a pit boss over at the mine. He's a company man to his core and his loyalty to Alinta is complete. He won't talk about Alinta, he says from under his ten-gallon hat and dark glasses. It's not hard to understand why. He has given the mine the best years of his life and Alinta has been good to him. All he'll say is that it's a crappy situation, but 'there's no more money in it'. As far as he's concerned, it's done. What's there to complain about?

Reading between the lines, Steven Hoddel is worried. Work at the mine will dry up soon, but his wife still has a 12-month contract teaching in the school at Leigh Creek. For now, the family has to stay put and he is about to find out what a sudden surplus of free time does to a working man.

Those with the freedom to leave are already packing up, and those who haven't are looking to. Anthony Brady lives out at Copley, about five kilometres up the road. He grew up in Old Leigh Creek and then New Leigh Creek, before moving away to Port Augusta and coming back with his kids to the Aboriginal community at Copley.

The Bradys, Anthony says, have coal in the veins and at least two generations have worked on the mine. When he first walked into the pub and heard people saying the mine was closing, he thought it was a joke. The mine would never close. Then a few weeks ago news came that the whole thing was done. He doesn't work on the mine, but now he's planning to shift his family back to Port Augusta.

'I've got to follow the hospital,' Anthony says. 'When Leigh Creek goes, the hospital's going to be gone and there's not going to be much school for the kids now.'

He has four children, three girls and an 11-year-old boy with epilepsy for whom he cares full time.

'I brought my kids back up this way to get away from city life,' he says. 'City life is too fast, you know? Out here, it's slow, you know? It's good, they can take their time growing up. In the city you've got to grow up quick or you miss out.

'Myself, I got it easy. Back when the mines were running full strength, when I was a kid, we had everything. Swimming pool, football, sports, it was all there. But this younger generation, these new ones coming up, there's nothing for them.'

Then there are the hopefuls, those like Nigel Carney, another Copley local who thinks it is possible to avoid being swallowed up by that nothing. He believes the town can have a post-coal future. As proof, he points to the state government's promise to fund the town for at least three years and how one company has been talking about setting up to make gas and fertilisers from the remaining coal in the mine. There's even talk among some locals about boosting tourism to the Flinders Ranges or growing frankincense, only no one knows what exactly is going to happen next, making it difficult to take the first steps towards making those ideas a reality. Just try securing finance for a new business venture when there's every chance the place will be a ghost town in 12 months.

'It's the question mark that we want removed,' Nigel says. 'There's some pretty smart people up here and the ideas floating around are realistic. If we get some statements from the government that these ideas are going to be funded, then that question mark goes and we have more a positive flux of energy.'

Until that happens, though, all the ideas are little more than talk, and Leigh Creek's life after coal depends on whether anyone out there cares enough to make it happen. On that point Carney is both hopeful and pessimistic. Most people think coal evil these days. It's the devil's mineral and Leigh Creek is just another small outback town in South Australia, the fly-over state.

'Coal's got a bad name, right?' Nigel says. 'No one wants to talk about coal, but then how do you help mining communities transition away from coal? Maybe coal's got such a bad name that no one cares about the people who depend on it.'

It may have happened in a different place, under different circumstances, but that's how the autoworkers' agony came to be shared by the coal workers and why even from way out here beyond the Flinders Ranges, not far from the desert, past where RM Williams made his trademark boots, it is still possible to hear the call of a Holden engine.

Chapter 15

PORTION CONTROL

STEELE NUGENT IS A LITTLE GUY WITH A BIG BEARD AND A sense of humour to match. These days he is a bike mechanic in the family business along Main North Road, but for a time he worked in the lunchroom at Holden's Elizabeth plant.

He had finished high school in 2007, but didn't graduate and was in need of a job. He was studying at TAFE in the meantime and trying to figure out what he was going to do with his life now that adulthood had found him. His mother knew someone who knew someone at the Holden Canteen Society, the independent third party that ran the factory cafeterias. She put in a good word for her son and not long after, they called him in for an interview.

That's how Steele became 'The Canteen Guy' at the Holden plant. The global financial crisis was about to hit and when it did, the company started tightening the belt on just about everything. The years leading up to it were good years, fat and happy. Not long before, the company had gone to three shifts and about 5000 people worked at the plant. There was decent money to be made catering to the car workers, selling them TVs and doing their taxes. Factories needed lawyers to write contracts, accountants to do the taxes and all the little bits and pieces necessary to run the factory had to be shipped and trucked and sold. Homes needed financing, insurance needed paying and there were mouths to be fed. All that was required was an incorporated body, a friendly smile and a just-sign-here-please.

It was a time of plenty. Though he can't put a dollar figure to it, Steele's feeling around then was that he was being paid entirely too well for what he was doing. Partly, this was because the Canteen Society had a huge historical significance to the workforce. The Society was independent and ran off what it made in the lunchrooms, but then GM Holden contracted to run certain services, such as the tea service, which had been included in an EBA long past and fought for by the workforce ever since. The tea service would come up and down the lines for anyone who wanted it. It was a marginal expense, but one the company had been trying to cut for years at every negotiation.

The other reason Steele felt the pay was too high was because the whole place just ran so smoothly. 'Like clockwork,' Steele says. A typical day would mean going in for an afternoon shift and helping to clean up the dining area. Then at three o'clock the line would break and the people would file in from the plant. Things would stay busy for about an hour, then they would filter away again, leaving the cafeteria staff to clean up. That was it. There was nothing much else to do. The next few hours meant standing around trying to look busy while they ran down the clock.

Wednesdays were the only exception. On Wednesdays Steele would be turned loose in the factory with a map and an electric-powered delivery cart. He'd drive that cart out to the satellite canteens to drop off pre-made sandwiches and cakes. It was a four-hour task and the map marked out the fast routes through the factory, but that missed the point. Life was supposed to be about the journey and there was nothing else to do on most days, so Steele would take the long way around to look at the factory.

Not that it lasted. Pretty soon Steele felt guilty that he was getting paid so much to do so little. He worked to live, that much he had figured out, and if he was standing around doing nothing, there were at least ten other things he'd rather be doing with his life. So when an offer came through to work full time as a landscaper, he decided study wasn't for him and he took the job. It paid less, but the work was outside and was more mentally stimulating than wiping surfaces and slinging schnitties in the evenings.

It was good timing too. About two weeks later, the first tremors of the global financial crisis were felt. Holden started looking to cut the fat, and the contractors were the first to go.

* * *

Not all of Elizabeth is hurting. The average annual income for the region was pegged at $41,089 at the 2011 Census, compared to $51,923 nationally. Still, there are some families in the area who have not worked in three generations and the worst off among them tend to find their way into Selina Franke's dining room on a Monday afternoon.

Every Monday, Selina drives in from Riverton, a small country town about an hour further north, to volunteer at AnglicareSA's Mission on Elizabeth Way. The Mission provides counselling and financial support services, but it's the free lunch for which they are best known. Between them, Selina and her team serve anywhere from 90 to 140 people during the day, and the thought that the plant will close in 2017 is terrifying, she says. They can barely keep up as is.

Today's special is soup. All the chicken that went into the soup was Selina's. Whatever food AnglicareSA gives her, she matches with food she brings from home. If she didn't double what she had to start with, she says, it just wouldn't stretch.

Outside, there is a slight chill on the wind and the sky is overcast, but inside the Mission is alive and full of movement. Everyone is friendly and people are talking. No one swears. They're asked not to by one of the volunteers, a deeply religious woman who is moved by such things. So she asks them not to curse and she always asks nicely, and those present always keep their promise out of respect.

Selina tells how a fortnight ago two pregnant women and a young boy came in looking for a meal just on the edge of cut-off time. By then, everything was gone and they were packing down the kitchen. They had no choice but to turn them away.

'It really hurts us to say there's nothing left,' says Selina. 'But then you get a tin of baked beans or offer them something – but that's not what we want to offer them. We want to offer them a good, hot meal, you know?'

Selina is no stranger to hard times. For over 40 years she ran a string of hotels with her blind husband, starting with the Queenscliff on Kangaroo Island and ending with the Blake Motor Inn. Soon after the pair retired, their son Richard passed away.

He was 36 when he ended his life and the subject is understandably hard for Selina to talk about. Around her neck she wears a lock of her son's hair that she touches when she thinks about him.

'It's not right for parents to bury their kids,' Selina says as she tells how at first she had trouble coping, so she got in touch with BeyondBlue. Through them she learned how suicide is at a ten-year peak, with an average of seven deaths by suicide a day, and how men account for three of every five such deaths. For Indigenous people, this rate is 2.5 times higher for men and 3.4 times higher for women.

This is how Selina came to the Mission. She wanted to help in some way to keep people from making the same decision as her son, and the people at BeyondBlue thought she might be able to do some good and suggested she get in touch with AnglicareSA.

Turns out, they were right. On one of the first Mondays volunteering, Selina found herself face to face with a young man who was talking of ending his life. He's safe now, she says, and he still comes in to see her.

This is what Elizabeth looks like now as it runs down the clock to 2017. Making cars in Australia was never something that could be done alone and it was never going to be easily turned off or cut cleanly away. It was always going to be messy.

And some of the places the car factories called home are already messy like Elizabeth. Some parts of that city on Adelaide's northern edge have been in recession since it first started to shed its manufacturing base in the 1980s. The people who make their lives in these kinds of places have been doing their best to get by ever since.

Chapter 16

JOB HUNTING WITH JESUS AND CHARLES DARWIN

IT'S 10AM ON A FRIDAY, THE SMELL OF GRASS IS IN THE AIR AND a crystal blue sky stretches above. Mark Waters is mowing his lawn when a pair of boots step onto his driveway. He lets the engine of the lawn mower idle a little as he looks up and says to take a seat on the second-hand couch beneath the front porch of the Californian bungalow. He'll be done in a minute.

Mark is average height, average build with tanned skin and an honest face. He's 32 years old and grew up in Jamestown, South Australia. He's easy going and clever and, when he has come into some money, he'll shout a beer without a prompt.

Until he shattered his wrist in 2010, he had also always been someone who worked. 'They put in a metal plate,'

Mark says, pointing to the scar on his arm. That's when he lost his job as a contract labourer and first went on welfare. A year later, things started to get back on track until June 2012, when he 'snapped' his leg playing soccer in his backyard and he was right back where he started. It wasn't until June 2014 that he picked up a casual position as a delivery-truck driver working for below-minimum wage at a discount furniture store.

'I tell everyone they only paid me $13.50 an hour,' Mark says. The company didn't care that it was below the minimum wage. It was a buyers' market and they burned through three, four guys in the time it would have taken to notify the authorities. They were so bold they even printed it onto an official payslip Mark still keeps in a plastic sleeve. He passes it over to prove it.

After that, Mark left and was back on the government money at a sum of about $500 a fortnight, plus whatever extra in rent assistance. The poverty line for the June 2015 quarter had been calculated at $517.77 per week.

'I had to scale back my whole life,' Mark says. Once he would have liked to have had a family, he says. Settle down. Maybe even buy a house. But a year in, that was a dead dream. By then he was living in a sharehouse with other, older factory workers who had lost their jobs. Bills had to be watched and a hot summer or cold winter took its share. The Internet cost too much and using a computer meant a trip to the library. He had no savings but the debts still had to be paid and for a while even registering the car was a gamble of cost versus return.

Just doing the grocery shopping takes work, he says. Time has to be spent figuring out which store has what specials and then the guys in the house pool their money to buy in bulk. Bacon, Mark says, is the poor man's best friend. It comes cheap and in quantity. So do eggs and together they go halfway to a decent meal. Failing that there's always the $6 help-yourself Chinese food in the city where something is always happening.

Mark loves the city. Between keeping his jobnetwork provider and Centrelink sweet, Mark still needs to live. He reads more these days and he has got to know his neighbours. Every now and then he picks up small cash-in-hand jobs or fixes broken lawn mowers or appliances. Sometimes he goes for walks or heads into the city, where there is live music and buskers and the Art Gallery, which is always free.

Mark even has a favourite painting there. It's of colonial Sydney soon after it was first founded, with only a handful of buildings and a few horse-drawn carts. Sometimes he goes there to stare at it. There's also a golden chalice, he says, heavy and encrusted with jewels.

'It's like something an ancient king would have drunk from,' he says.

His eyes widen when he talks about it.

* * *

It's an unusually cool morning in an unusually warm November when Mark drives out to the industrial estate beneath the new expressway in Wingfield, South Australia. He's there to door-knock local businesses, go factory to factory and look for work.

When he was younger he'd turn up at reception in high-vis clothing and work boots, tell them he was ready to go.

Sometimes the manager would come out and have a chat to him. Right now he can't be bothered, and walking around an industrial lot he flags down a forklift driver and asks for reception.

Opening the door, the air conditioning pours out and a receptionist appears from a side room. She is neatly casual and her posture visibly grows tense as soon as she sees him. With a smile and a confident voice, he gives her the pitch.

His name is Mark Waters, he says, and he is a casual at a plastics factory right now, but the position is going to wind down over Christmas and he's looking for some extra work after the holiday period to get him through. He has a forklift licence and is an experienced truck driver, and he hands her his résumé.

The receptionist tells him there's nothing going right now, but she'll keep the paperwork on file just in case. When she takes his résumé in both hands, she looks at it for a moment and doesn't seem to know quite what to do with it. Mark knows it's not going anywhere but thanks her anyway with genuine gratitude.

Mark's never had a call-back from a résumé drop and doesn't expect to. Most companies want you to go online these days, he says. Some even have 'No jobseekers' signs in their reception area. If the rejection rate in the real world is high, online isn't much better. Companies have computer programs that screen a résumé for the necessary experience and instantly send a rejection letter if it falls short.

'When I was younger, there was work for everyone,' Mark says outside. 'Now it's an employers' market and they all want you to go online. Even the job agencies want you to look online. They say cold canvassing isn't really looking for work because it isn't advertised. I say it is. You never know if you go into a place and their driver has just got another job somewhere or turned up late for the 50th time that very day. They may remember you and say, "Hey, let's give that young bloke a try."'

As of August 2015, 77,000 South Australians were officially unemployed. As of May 2015, there were 8800 job vacancies in the state, which meant at least nine candidates for every position, putting aside variables such as level of qualification, experience, age, location, or competition from those looking to escape bad casual or part-time jobs. By October the unemployment rate had eased to 7.7 per cent, down from 8.1, but South Australia remained the worst-performing economy on unemployment in the country, even worse than Tasmania, an island state with half the population.

* * *

Richard Nixon made 'workfare' famous, but as an idea it started out as the product of the left. The idea that a government might put its unemployed to work in return for a welfare payment originated with 1960s American civil rights leader James Charles as a means to end welfare dependence. In Britain, it was the Labour Party who caught onto the idea well before the Tories ever uttered the phrase.

The idea then filtered out to Australia during the 90s under conservative John Howard, who made it a core part of his welfare policy. Even if the program was scaled back by its successors, Australia has always had affection for the idea and it continued to exist in some form under the next two Labor leaders before former Prime Minister Tony Abbott expanded it under his stewardship.

It's no surprise why. As Minister for Employment under the Howard government, Abbott was the one who gave bloody, screaming birth to Work for the Dole in Australia the first time around. It was his signature policy and Abbott was responsible for moulding it to accommodate ideas of 'mutual obligation' and 'individual responsibility', a direct reflection of Abbott's own personal ideology. Better yet, as a policy it tapped into the evolving Australian mentality towards the poor and unemployed. Society had an obligation to feed people who could not feed themselves out of circumstance, it was once thought, and then people started talking about morals. If Australia was going to feed a man or a woman, it was only going to feed those who deserved it. Those on welfare had to 'do the right thing'.

When Tony Abbott took down Kevin Rudd at the 2013 federal election and installed himself in Canberra, Work for the Dole came back in a big way, only this time around it would go further. Abbott scaled up the program to include thousands more people than ever before and allocated about $1 billion to get it rolling over the next three years. His government was going to break welfare dependence, Abbott promised, and they were going to teach the unemployed a little self-confidence in the process.

So they set up 18 trials around the country for people aged 18 to 29, including one out at Elizabeth in South Australia – and it didn't work. One study on the trial program from ANU later found only 2 per cent of participants had work after taking part, but that didn't matter at the time. The Abbott government insisted it had been a success and as of

1 July 2015 the entire program was going nationwide. They were going to get the young and unemployed back into the labour force and build new skills. Young people, Abbott said, needed to 'work or learn'. It was a message echoed among his ministers. There were the 'lifters' and there were the 'leaners', they said.

Not everyone was so sure. The Australian Chamber of Commerce and Industry and the Australian Council of Social Service didn't like it and suggested the program needed work. Others, like economist Jeff Borland from the University of Melbourne, rejected it outright.

'What they've done is taken a bad program and made it a more important part of the activities that unemployed people are required to do,' he says months after the program rolled out. 'What the best of these programs do is build up people who are unemployed, build their skills and give them an opportunity to start out in the workforce through an employment placement. And Work for the Dole doesn't do those things.'

Borland rattles through the criticisms like a machine gun. Community organisations that take on Work for the Dole projects are not contracting out that work. At its best, a workfare program should reskill people, but under the present program there is no formal training and there is no support offered to help people with the specific problems keeping them from finding work. Borland's own research shows taking part in Work for the Dole means the unemployed are no longer focussed on actually looking for work and are less likely to find a job in the six months following their stint. The government says his research is outdated.

None of it mattered, though, and the program scaled up. Nothing changed again when Tony Abbott was dropped on 15 September and Malcolm Turnbull cleaned house, removing Eric Abetz as federal Minister for Employment and replacing him with Western Australian Michaelia Cash. The new Employment Minister doubled down on Work for the Dole, saying it was here to stay, it was good, it worked, and any problems just had to be ironed out.

Work for the Dole ended up getting Mark Waters a job, just not the way it was supposed to.

In early 2015, Mark's case worker offered him a chance to work on a project helping to restore a church and Mark jumped at it. He had been on the books for a while and saw it as something to get him out of the house. On site, he joined a group of 15 people who were going to repaint the inside of the church, do some gyprocking and other odd jobs. They'd learn a few new tricks and at the end have something to show for it.

Everything started out fine, but quickly the mood on site began to change as relations between the participants and on-site supervisors broke down over a growing list of complaints. Mark says that among other things, the site lacked proper safety gear and basic tools, and offered no real training. None of the participants were trusted with real-world tools and even when they were, often there weren't enough to go around. It also quickly became clear they were a burden; idle hands meant to stay busy.

'The work was meaningless,' Mark says. 'We were basically painting the same walls over and over.'

Mark talks about being made to dig a drainage ditch with a screwdriver and nearly being knocked from a ladder that had been set up in a busy stairwell, supported by a block. There were serious concerns from the participants about the high ceilings of the church and the lack of scaffolding, he says, but if anyone complained they were seen as a troublemaker and the site supervisor just asked someone else to do it. Then someone fell from a plank of wood suspended between two trestles and the organisers finally shelled out for proper scaffolding.

On the morning of a ministerial visit to the site, Mark and a supervisor clashed over a cup of coffee. Mark had just made himself a cup when the supervisor told him to throw it out. Mark refused and the man erupted into what Mark describes as verbal abuse.

Coupled with the safety risks, it was enough to push him to lodge a formal complaint with the jobnetwork provider that managed his case. He says his case manager listened to everything he had to stay, solemnly took down his details and told him they would find something else for him to do, like working to restore vintage cars at the Birdwood Museum.

This sounded pretty good to Mark and he walked out of that meeting feeling like things were looking up. Almost immediately after, he had a phone call from an upper-level manager telling him he had been found a job at a plastics factory. It was casual, they said, but the pay was good and if he didn't like it, they'd find him something else.

'It was a bribe,' he says. 'I was quite surprised because I have no experience working in the plastics industry. Never in my life. It was a very surreal experience.'

The basics of Mark's story are supported by Byron Stone, who was working at the same site. How he ended up there was different to Mark. Now 28, Stone first left home when relations with his parents turned bad. It's a period in his life he doesn't like to talk about and all he'll say is that he was homeless for some time, couch surfing between friends.

Since then he has been on his own, working mostly for labour-hire companies doing contract work. He has washed bricks by hand for a company that recycles them by the tonne and worked as 'scab labour' at Westinghouse's whitegoods factory near Elizabeth to help keep the place running while the company laid off its union employees and shut it all down. He remembers watching people being called into the manager's office one by one to be told they were no longer needed.

The last job he held was working for a turf farm in the Adelaide Hills, growing the lawn for the Adelaide oval redevelopment. When that wound up, he was back on welfare right around the time the government made it mandatory for anyone under 30 to do at least 25 hours Work for the Dole a week. The two met on the site and Byron repeats the same complaints as Mark. There was no safety gear, he says, no training, no proper equipment and, above all, the work was pointless.

The site, he says, had three months' work for a six-month project and the supervisors saw it as their duty to keep people working, even when there was nothing to be done. Be difficult or backchat a supervisor and they would use an app on their smart phone to dock the backchatter's pay $50. Start an argument and they wouldn't hesitate to cut them off entirely.

Then one of the other participants made a complaint about the lack of tools and activities on site. From that point on, the organisation doubled down in trying to keep participants busy and Byron was told to pick clovers from the church lawn. They called it weeding, he says. On another day, they were made to weed the garden of the church-owned property next door and had to edge the lawn by hand. They weren't even given a pair of scissors.

In that time, Byron had been talking to everyone he could about the Anti-Poverty Network and pretty soon word got around he was agitating on site. It was enough to draw the pastor out from his office to talk to Byron about why he didn't like Work for the Dole. Byron took his inspiration from Jesus when he explained there was a jobs crisis outside the church front door and that Work for the Dole punished the poor for something beyond their control. The pastor took his cue from Charles Darwin when he ended the discussion by telling Byron some people in society had to lose before he walked away chuckling to himself.

* * *

South Australia's general attitude to protest is casually indifferent at best and hostile at worst. It's especially so out in the suburbs of Middle Australia where politics is something that happens somewhere else and is beamed in through the television in the evening. In the areas around the old car factories, the feeling is that politics and politicians gave up on ordinary people a long time ago, making the notion that a local MP would actually come around knocking on doors something of an event.

It's why political movements tend not to get much play out in the suburbs. Political organisers don't usually make the effort to speak, and the people who live there don't make the effort to listen. The biggest current political movement to get any real reach into the suburbs is Reclaim Australia, which has so far tapped into the deep distrust of professional politicians and the genuine fear Australians more broadly have felt every time they come home from work, crack a beer and tune into the evening news where their leaders would talk of 'death cults' in front of seven Australian flags.

Both Reclaim Australia and groups like the Anti-Poverty Network trade on organising de-industrialisation's refugees and both spring from a rejection or suspicion of the political system, only where Reclaim Australia finds unity in fear of an enemy that threatens the Australia that was, the Anti-Poverty Network looks forward to the kind of world it wants to create.

Unlike Reclaim Australia, the Anti-Poverty Network is a local South Australian development. It is a loose collection of other groups fighting single-issue causes out in the suburbs, in the places where the dole queues grow and all the good jobs dried up years ago. Together, they support each other and have been waging campaigns against programs like Work for the Dole and compulsory income management ever since the group was formed around 2013.

Pas Forgione is mostly responsible for keeping it going and these days he gets paid an hourly wage to raise hell. For the past two years he has been a full-time activist and organiser for the group, which started out as a single-issue fight against Julia Gillard's plans to manage the income of welfare recipients when her government was lurching to the right to shore up her leadership.

It was an odd decision. Everyone else who calls themselves an activist in these parts usually fights their cause on the steps of Parliament House along North Terrace. Traditionally, these have been university students with upward social momentum and newspaper-slinging socialists trying to bring on the revolution, one paper at a time. It's a mix reflected in the battles they choose. Issues such as good pay, stable jobs and decent support networks lack the pathos of barbed-wire-ringed refugee hell holes and Pacific Islands sinking into the ocean because of climate change. As a rule people don't like to think about work more than they have to and those people who are hurt when a company offshores a warehouse operation or a government tries to earn votes by tightening conditions on welfare payments are not always nice, don't always dress like young professionals and don't always speak the Queen's English.

'If you've never had to deal with the welfare system, you wouldn't have too much of a reason to think about these things,' Pas says. 'The most interesting conversation to have is with people who are middle aged and they've been working all their lives and right out of the blue they're out of work and no one told them Newstart is this hard.'

Family got Pas thinking about these issues. His was a migrant family with a colourful history. His father first came out from Apulia, Italy, in 1972 and his mother was born here, but her family had emigrated from Naples. Pas's grandfather and namesake had fought for Mussolini in World War II and reportedly kept a photo of Il Duce – an irony not lost on his socialist, atheist and gay grandson. It is a story Pas tells along with the one about his great-uncle, Pio of Pietrelcina, a man who claimed both the stigmata and the power to be in two places at once and who was the 39th most popular saint in all of Italy as of 2014. He died in 1968 and was canonised by Pope John Paul II in 2002 as the patron saint of civil defence volunteers, teenagers and 'stress relief'.

The Australian branch of the Forgiones ended up a little more humble. Pas's father worked as a labourer, his mother a kitchenhand. Pas was the oldest of three kids and while the family may be doing all right now, he says, he remembers a time when his mother had to borrow from the neighbours to buy bread.

Just as for Mark Waters, Centrelink helped Pas land his job, just not in a way it ever intended. When Pas finished university and couldn't find work, his experience of the welfare system was the same sobering grind faced by every other recent graduate. Eventually he was on Newstart long enough that his job provider put him into the sunnily named 'JobClub program'. The program was designed to be an intensive, supervised work-search activity, but in essence it involved spending eight hours a day sitting in a room on ten-year-old computers, scrolling the Internet. By then, Pas was knee deep into organising and instead he used the time to write editorials and print the leaflets, handouts and fact sheets needed to run a campaign.

That also meant meeting with public officials, unions and church groups, but the only way to get out of JobClub was to have a job interview. So that's what he told his supervisors, who took one look at the sneakers he was wearing and wouldn't let him leave. He couldn't go to job interviews wearing those, they said. He should buy new shoes. Pas said he didn't have the money and the supervisor said he should buy himself a new pair and jobnetwork would reimburse him.

Which was alright by Pas. He was using the system's resources to take down the system and he was getting a new pair of shoes for his trouble.

He never did get those shoes, but by 2014 Pas was getting paid to organise full time after the Adelaide Centre for Homeless Persons interviewed him for their magazine and brought him on board. Since then, the organisation has been growing every time they hold an event or head over to hand out flyers to those lining up at another Centrelink office.

'What I find incredible is the amount of people on a welfare payment out there who still accept all the government's rhetoric about lifters and leaners,' he says. 'People feel so humiliated to rely on a welfare payment and people don't want to get involved with us because they don't want to see themselves as that "class" of person. They say, "I'm one of the good people."

'But I've seen people have that moment where something has been fucked and they realise they've done nothing wrong and just because they're unemployed doesn't mean they're a bad person.'

* * *

Mark used to look down on the unemployed. He confesses this between the sound of roaring semitrailers as he sips a grande latte from a service station coffee shop along what used to be South Road. That was before his injury and, really, he is ashamed to say it, but that's the truth.

'You work all day and then learn about the world from the seven o'clock news,' he says. 'What you forget is it can happen to anyone. Anyone could hurt themselves just like I did and be out of work for a long time. They don't realise how easy it is for it to happen and when it does you have to get rid of things like the Internet. It becomes impossible to service a mortgage. People take what they have for granted.

'But then, that's the social contract, isn't it? You work, if you can, and you pay your taxes and in return you get education, healthcare and welfare. I really do believe in that.'

At the time of writing, Mark doesn't have to worry. Right now, his job at the plastics factory is paying $1000 a week and he's been using the money to save and pay off his debts. Eventually it will wind down and chances are he'll end up back on welfare. If he doesn't pick up something permanent, he may end up back on Work for the Dole.

'You get used to being poor,' he says. 'All the depressed thoughts come in the first year. After that you just accept it.'

As far as life goes, he says he doesn't have any real plans. He did a business management course about a year back and thinks he'd like to put it to use. Maybe start his own business as a courier, but for that you need to buy a van and that takes money. Money he doesn't have and money he can't get through a loan in his present circumstances. Besides, the last time he tried setting up a business mowing lawns and doing odd jobs, Centrelink shut him down because he hadn't done the proper paperwork.

'Still,' he says, 'life is pretty good. Adelaide is a beautiful city. I've got it pretty easy. I just feel sorry for those under 30.'

Chapter 17

WORK VERSUS THE HUSTLE

THE MAN WE'LL CALL BLAKE SITS DOWN AT A TABLE IN A coffee shop behind the District Court building in the centre of town. It's a cheap place, but an honest one. Inside the strobe lights hum and the coffee machine hisses and people heading to work early are coming in for their flat whites and lattes and cappuccinos to go.

Blake's not here for the coffee. The man in his mid-20s who works two jobs has come in earlier this morning to talk about his kid brother. As the woman working behind the counter brings over his coffee he says he knows crime is going to go up when Holden closes.

His little brother, he says, 'steals shit'. The kid is 17 and part of a group of about seven other 15- to 18-year-olds earning $800 a day shoplifting from higher-end retail stories. They target stores that sell name-brand consumer goods and electronics retailing for over $300. They then knock $200 off the sticker price and use Facebook like an auction house to move the items quickly. If the police are ever able to track them down, the items are usually gone and there isn't enough evidence to get a conviction.

Their customers usually walk away happy. One guy who bought a pair of designer sunglasses later asked Blake if his brother could get him a new phone. It's a business operation and if these kids had the benefit of support, capital and an education, they could maybe make a few honest dollars, but then who's going to take that risk on them? It's safer to stick to what you know.

Blake runs through the nuts and bolts of it. They work in teams. One will distract the sales staff while the other cracks a display case in the time it takes to say, 'Hi, can you help me out?' Each gets a share and as a group they regulate each other's behaviour. Sometimes, Blake says, someone gets cocky and hits the same store too many times. This leads to more attention from security and their image being circulated around the chain, keeping them from going back and costing them income. This sometimes creates friction within the group, because the idea of getting caught terrifies them to their core.

'They're naturally paranoid,' he says and this fear gradually eats away at those ties that connect them to everyone else in society. Anyone who might have the will or capacity to stop them becomes an object of distrust. Over time, they become ever more isolated. 'They know that when they're caught, they're screwed, so they do anything they can to separate themselves from their family.'

Their parents, says Blake, run the range from those living off welfare to ordinary working people. There's no type or profile. Even if they find out about what's going on and make their kids' lives miserable for it, it doesn't matter. By that point, each of those involved is dependent on his 'brothers' and operates on the idea that it's 'us against the world'.

Blake has been trying to talk his kid brother down for some time now. To anyone on the outside looking in, this world his younger brother has made for himself is a fairytale, but to him it's a reality. Blake has been working to overcome the alienation and distrust his brother has built up. It's why he doesn't want his name used. He says he's been trying to 'close that gap' and 'bring him closer' to push him in a new direction, but the other kids are a problem. Asked why they do it, he says most have drug dependencies or mental-health issues such as depression and anxiety, but what it all comes down to is the money.

'These kids won't work,' he says. 'This generation will have no problem risking something. If you ask them, "Why would you not want to work?" one or two of them might have a career goal, but most of them are, like, "Why the fuck would we work when we can get this shit for free and just sell it, make instant money? Why work like a slave in McDonald's for minimum wage when I can make what those guys make in a week in two days and have everything I need?"'

The youth unemployment rate out where Blake lives is 16.3 per cent. It's a figure that hovers between 15 and 20 per cent depending on the season. Nationally, youth unemployment in Australia as of November 2015 was

12.5 per cent. For a point of comparison, Greece, a country experiencing a full-blown, bloody-knuckled economic crisis, had national youth unemployment sitting at 47.9 per cent as of August 2015.

And it's hard work finding a job in the region. Just ask Cameron Rowe, whose high school senior year wasn't a good one when he failed two subjects and missed out on 20 SACE points.

'I graduated but then I didn't,' Cameron explains. 'They gave out envelopes to everyone including people who didn't pass and they have certificates in there. Mine didn't have a certificate.'

What went wrong?

'I probably wasn't as committed to school as I should have been.'

Cameron's mother is a payroll officer with SANTOS, his father a truck driver and together they responded to news of their son's results like any other tax-office-fearing, law-abiding, working-class citizens: they waited for an appropriate amount of time to pass and then they told their son to get a job.

But Cameron Rowe had no real skills. He'd worked at Rivers during high school, but nothing that could be developed into what might be called a career. Once he could have walked into an apprenticeship in the car industry, but those positions dried up a decade back. Instead, he started to hang out at Twelve25, a youth centre in Salisbury where the people in charge had him doing admin work to give him some marketable skills. At the same time he was applying for apprenticeships and traineeships in a process he describes as 'painful'.

'My parents had the impression that it was easy to find a job,' he says. 'Which is ridiculous, because you apply for so many jobs and you get one interview and hope for the best.'

In May 2014, he found work with a big chain convenience store, working nightshift permanent part-time. He moved out of his parents' house and into a sharehouse in Adelaide's south with his partner and a friend. The idea was it would give him a chance to get it together and for a time things were looking good, he thought. His job was stable and he was independent. Yes, he was a trainee and the pay sucked, but a retail job didn't need a qualification and was the start of something.

He doesn't talk much more about the company or the conditions he was working under. Anyone who has worked a low-rent job with little bargaining power learns quickly to always speak positively about their time with the company and to never badmouth a former employer. It is not a good look, the accepted wisdom goes, and no one wants to be marked as a troublemaker.

And Cameron Rowe sure isn't a troublemaker. He's one of the good kids from a working-class neighbourhood with a quirky sense of humour just trying to do his best with a bad hand, but his silence on certain details doesn't stop the picture coming into focus. When he signed up to work with the company, they brought him on as a trainee, on trainee pay, and he would have had to stay a trainee with them for a year before anything changed. To earn those extra dollars, the company had him working towards a Certificate in Retail. On their website, College Australia describes the qualification as one for those 'wishing to begin a career in the retail industry'. It goes on to describe it as a prerequisite for entry-level retail jobs earned by working in 'various retail store settings, such as specialty stores, supermarkets, department stores, fast-food outlets and retail outlets'. There are 14 units all up, at $150 for each level-two unit, which puts the course fee at somewhere around $2100. Not everyone can pay up-front, of course, but interested applicants can ask about the flexible payment plan.

On the job, Cameron worked nightshift. He started at 10pm and worked right through to sunrise. As it turns out, nightshift in an all-night chain convenience store wasn't nearly as romantic as he imagined. There were no weird characters or strange happenings. Hungry customers turned up at the same rate as the lunch rush, except there were fewer staff to deal with them and people were tired, so they had no patience.

Cameron made it about eight months before he quit. Without an income, he had to move back in with his parents. He still needed a job, so he started following his passions. He began a Certificate III in Laboratory Skills at the local TAFE and took on more volunteer work, all the while putting out 70 job applications a week until he had a call-back from a supermarket that needed someone to stack shelves from 8pm until 2am. He took it and was genuinely excited to be making money again while he was studying. He's still looking for work, he says, but there isn't much around. It's the same story that gets told all around the region: Cameron is eager, he's a nice kid, but there's just not much out there. He's started out inexperienced and unqualified in an economy that places an ever-higher premium on entry-level jobs. When he looks for work, he's putting out those 70 or more applications a week in a place where everyone else who is serious about looking for a job is doing the same.

It's why one of the first things Anglicare's CEO Reverend Peter Sandeman says is that some families in the region surrounding the Holden factory have not worked in three generations. The textbooks call it 'compound disadvantage' and it happens when one generation falls on hard times and passes on its bad luck, just like the interest in a savings account. Maybe they lost their job in a downturn, or they were injured and could no longer work. Whatever the circumstance, as parents they handed down that bad luck to their kids, who grew up with even less work around, and chances are they passed it on to their own kids. In no time at all it starts to add up to something significant.

'This is an area that is already hurting,' the reverend says. His organisation has been trying to fight the effects of compound disadvantage for decades. 'There are all sorts of stereotypes,' he goes on. 'Some were that these people didn't want employment. That they were all on drugs. That they were all unreliable. So we had to break through that myth.'

Low self-worth is the other issue. Being born in a region that has been in recession for 30 years means being born a problem. From birth, these people are another liability for a case worker to manage, first by teachers and then by welfare officers or employers. Signs of resilience may be interpreted as signs of hardship or a problem attitude. School is boring. University is too hard, too long and costs too much money. Better to find a job and start earning. Except there aren't many jobs out there. Why? They don't know. They just know they're not there and all the good jobs are going to someone else anyway. Why bother? Break a person's heart enough times, they stop trying.

Which is the danger the reverend sees in the end of the car industry and whatever happens after. The question isn't so much what it means for the current workforce, but for their children.

'If you happen to be at a certain age or location, it's going to be very hard to get out of the way,' he says. 'My kids, if they are unemployed, they have us to fall back on. If you come from a family where Mum and Dad and your grandparents have never worked, you have no support network.

'Unless we're very careful, we may have the potential for a lost generation.'

Chapter 18

DUMB MISTAKES ARE FOR LIFE

LATE ON A FRIDAY AFTERNOON IN A SMALL HALL BEHIND THE old Methodist church in Port Adelaide, a small group of women with Seeds of Affinity, a support group for women transitioning out of prison, are helping to pack up. The group meets every Tuesday and Friday, and among them is Annette Bates.

Annette was 23 the first time she went to jail. Now 43, she knows about prisons and she knows about dumb mistakes. That's how Annette ended up in this situation in the first place, so when she says the end of the car industry is bad news for the people who live around it, it's worth listening.

The women Annette met in prison had no chance. Maybe they made a mistake. Maybe they were shoplifting or playing with matches, or someone talked them into a robbery.

Maybe they killed their husband. Maybe that husband was abusive. Maybe it all happened because they had young kids and no support, or maybe it happened because they went from one bad relationship to the next. Whatever the story, they all ended up doing time in Adelaide Women's Prison (AWP), about half an hour north of the city, next door to the Yatala Labour Prison, which houses the men.

During their stay, Annette says, the women had nothing to do except talk about their kids and how much they missed them. That's how she knows that Holden closing down is going to be bad. 'Those people that are struggling, those people who are doing their best to make ends meet, they are screwed,' Annette says.

'They might as well dig a big hole and bury Elizabeth. There's not a lot of stuff out that way, so that most people either work at Holden or travel into the city and those that don't are living off those that travel into the city or work at Holden.

'What are they supposed to do? How does anyone think they have half a chance?'

It doesn't help that Australian prisons, on average, are not exactly set up to build life skills. There were 2876 female prisoners Australia-wide at the end of 2015, 163 in South Australia spread between AWP and another facility further north. AWP itself is 50 years old with a 148-woman capacity. It does not have separate wings to segregate prisoners by offence. Instead everyone living inside is left to mix, so those serving time for a minor drugs offence rub shoulders with stone-cold killers.

Prison taught Annette to keep her screen door locked at all times. It also taught her how to inject drugs. She says things might have been better if they were able to undertake training courses, but only those serving very long sentences get access to them. Any other resource set aside for rehabilitation had a way of going to the men next door because men will burn the place to the ground to get what they want. Women tend to just endure.

Once they get out, few are equipped to deal with life outside, she says. Inside, they are treated like teenagers until the day they are turned back onto the street where, as a certified crim, they have to find a job, raise the kids they'd been missing and make sure the bills get paid on time, every time. Sometimes they're alone, or sometimes they end up back in that bad relationship with a man who talks with his fists. Sometimes they make another stupid mistake or sometimes it's just all too hard. Annette says she knows too many women who have chosen to go back inside. However it happens, in the end odds are most will end up at AWP, talking about their kids and thinking about what they're missing.

* * *

On the numbers, South Australia is pretty good on crime. For as long as anyone can remember, crime across nearly every category has been falling, even in poorer neighbourhoods with a reputation for violence. It is a trend seen across the developed world for the past 15 years and no one is exactly sure why. The more out-there theories put it down to the de-leading of petrol, aging populations and better access to abortion for young women in bad situations. Another idea is that it has something to do with better, data-driven policing that has become less reliant on outright intimidation. Others look to all those video games soaking up hours for bored young men.

Victoria is a different story. On the face of it, crime across the board has been rising for the past five years. Again, it is not entirely clear why, but Victoria has 5.791 million people, high housing prices and more police, and in 2013 introduced strict new bail laws that have seen a record number of people breach their conditions. More people means a better chance of something going wrong. More police means a better chance it will be discovered. Everything else is just a contributing factor, making for a debate about what effect the end of an industry that operates across some of the most disadvantaged areas of the country will do to the people living around it.

At least in South Australia, the end of the car factory at Elizabeth won't do anything to crime, according to Ferdi Pit, now retired after a long, distinguished career as a police officer, finishing up as the Elizabeth station police chief.

'Most people who work in the factories don't live in Elizabeth,' he says. If you ask him, any social impact from the end of the factories will be dispersed, spread out across the places where its workers live and won't turn up in the numbers. It's a good theory, but on another night, another officer leans up against a bar. The officer was off duty and what followed was not an interview, just a conversation where the end of the car industry came up.

'A lot of people are going to hurt,' they say, and the first thing they expect to see is more domestic violence. It's the same feeling a friendly criminal defence lawyer gets. They get enough people coming into their office for dumb mistakes, they say.

'If Legal Aid aren't coping now, just give it a couple of years.'

* * *

Once a person is in the system, they are in for life. Just ask Annette. She got two and a half years for a $100 drug deal the first time around. It was 1996 when she was convicted after being picked up in a police sting. The police at the time had been looking for information on a local drug dealer and had picked up a friend. That friend then suggested Annette as someone who might get investigators further up the chain. So they did a deal with police and that fateful night that friend called Annette as she was heading out to dinner and asked her to pick up something. Annette was going out anyway, so she said sure, why not? A little while later, she was met by police cars while leaving the Hungry Jack's car park. Once they had her, they thought she would cooperate, but she didn't and that was the end of Annette Bates.

Annette left prison with a different world view and a positive test for Hep C. After that her first and only priority was getting a job, because Annette was always a woman who worked. Having her own money meant everything, but she bulged a disc in her spine while lifting a client and she couldn't go back to being a care worker, which was all she had ever known. Instead she found herself a job as a courier, sometimes driving up to 250 kilometres a day and loving every metre.

Distance never mattered. What was important was the freedom of the open road, the ability to roam wherever she wanted, when she wanted. As a courier, she was her own boss, getting paid to drive, being able to work when she wanted, how long she wanted, so long as she delivered. That's all anyone cared about. That's all she cared about.

Then, in 2013, she was busted again for driving under the influence and a judge sent her back to prison. It was another stupid mistake, she says, one she deeply regrets. She lost her licence and spent 18 more months back inside AWP, where many of the women were familiar faces. She left again with her bad back getting worse, no licence and no job in a world where everything had gone online. Annette has never owned a computer and even if she had one, she wouldn't know what to do with it. She still owns an atlas and if she wants to know something, she'll look it up, or go to the library and find a book.

Which is a problem, she is finding. Just putting in a job application now means getting a bus across town to the nearest unemployment office and using their machines. She's not the only one, either. She knows one woman from AWP with a work release who has been in so long she doesn't know what a mobile phone is or even how to buy and use a bus ticket. When she went in, mobile phones were still bricks.

What Annette needs right now is work. With work she'd have half a chance, she says, and she's getting there slowly. Soon enough she'll get her licence back and then she can start applying for jobs again. Until then, she spends her days sitting in her living room, talking to her cat and staring at the walls.

'Sitting in here is no different to sitting in a prison cell, except I've got to pay for it, but I'd rather pay for it than be in there,' she says.

'Not everyone feels the same way.'

Chapter 19

THERE'S ALWAYS THE FAMILY BUSINESS

Pulling up to the house where Dr Nathan Rout-Pitt lives with his girlfriend, Amy Boffie, and his mother, Beverley Rout, the street is deserted. It is Christmas time 2015 and a heatwave has settled in across the Adelaide plains. The lawns on every house lining the street in Brahma Lodge died off weeks ago and it's possible to feel the heat rise from the concrete footpath.

Nathan has seen the car and is already standing in the driveway, against the backdrop of the yellow brick house, with its little bay window in front and an enclosed garden out back. A tall, thin man with wire-frame glasses, Dr Rout-Pitt reaches forward to shake hands. Earlier this year, he finished his PhD in genetics research, but up to a few weeks ago, he had been stacking shelves at a local supermarket.

Inside, where the green curtains of the living room block out the sun and the old wall air conditioner hums on high to keep back the heat, Beverley Rout sits silhouetted against the bay window in her armchair while she watches television. Tubes from the oxygen tank at her side snake their way across the carpet and up to her nose. The cancer is slowly killing her. It has spread throughout her body and it is easier to list those body parts that are cancer free: bladder, pancreas and kidneys.

It has spread so far that the 58-year-old has trouble breathing and she knows she isn't going to be around much longer; she just doesn't know when it's going to happen and she's never asked. Otherwise, she'd just sit there thinking about it.

Next to the television is a Christmas tree. Underneath are carefully wrapped presents, crisp white paper with nice, neat red bows.

'I went a bit overboard this year,' Amy Boffie says as she watches her young cousin Violet play with a toy phone on the living-room floor. Amy is 25 and very much in charge. The house is in her name and she rents from a family friend. Her uncle, Violet's father, lives across the road and she helps him out occasionally by looking after the little one. Violet is already strong and loud, just like all the women in her family, Amy says, usually because they have to be.

Amy hasn't seen her father since she was 12. He left when she turned five, and then he came back again after a few years only to leave again a few months later. The last time

Amy heard from him was five years ago when she read in a newspaper that he was going to jail for something stupid.

So Amy was raised by her mother, who worked in a wrecker's yard. The guys who owned it treated Amy like she was their very own and let her have the run of the place. No one told Amy off, for anything. At home, her male cousins would never play Barbies, so she played trucks in the mud and the dirt. Before she grew up and 'got realistic', she wanted to be a palaeontologist; she wanted to dig stuff up and discover things. She never wore a dress or the colour pink until she was 18, when she started going clubbing in Adelaide with her friends.

Around that time she moved out of home. She put in an application for welfare while she finished up the schooling she missed when she stopped turning up because she was bullied. After that she got herself a job at Hungry Jack's because she didn't want to depend on government money. Then she began working towards getting herself qualified as a personal carer. 'I just wanted to do something where I could help people,' she says.

It was around that time she and Nathan met at a bar. The way she remembers it, she had been standing by herself when a tall man came over and told her she looked bored. She was and together they danced and had fun, and when it was all over she actually gave him her real number. Up on the living-room wall is a shelf with three wine bottles and one sake bottle, one for each year they've been together.

At that time Nathan was doing research for his PhD in genetics and medical science. 'I investigated how the accumulated glycosaminoglycans in various mucopolysaccharidoses, or MPS for short, affected the production of bone-forming cells and their ability to produce a mineralised matrix,' Nathan says. 'Some MPS disorders result in bone deformities such as short bones and decreased bone mass, so I was trying to work out mechanisms behind this problem.'

More than that, he was working towards something. He loved science and he believed in it. The work he would do could help people, he thought. He was going to make a career out of science and he and Amy would make a life together.

Amy had even studied aged care full time for three months to get out of Hungry Jack's. She studied from nine in the morning until four in the afternoon, when she went to work, where she could end up staying until one in the morning. She did her placement at a facility with 135 residents and a 150 staff. Her grandfather, also a careworker, showed her around the place before she started. Nathan didn't get to see her very much in those three months, she admits, but all that study paid off when she landed a $20-an-hour job with the facility where she did her placement. Then in July 2014, Nathan finished his research and his funding ran out. With the money left over, the couple went on a holiday to Japan. Both say they probably shouldn't have, but neither regrets it. Life is more than dollars and cents.

When they came back, Nathan started looking for work, but the federal government wiped millions from research funding in 2014 and took more in 2015. Some labs shut down overnight, others put a freeze on hiring until they could work out what was going on, while those that were looking to take on new staff had their own PhD students to worry about.

Nathan put out application after application but wasn't getting anywhere, so he started applying for lower lab-tech positions, only no one wanted to hire a PhD for the role because they'd have to pay him too much. That's when he started looking overseas. He had some interest from Canada, but the idea of uprooting their life and moving away from family scared Amy. In the end, it proved something of a moot point when Beverley was diagnosed with cancer and moved in with the young couple.

But Nathan still had no work, and Amy was paying the bills. Sometimes he would tutor, sometimes he would umpire football. It didn't pay much, but at least he was paying his half of the rent. Over time, the pressure built and the couple started to fight. The littlest of things would set them off.

'Stupid things,' he says. 'Just because the pressure was there.'

'Our favourite saying during that time was "Go back to your mummy",' Amy adds.

At first Nathan had been too proud to try Centrelink. He had a PhD. Why should he? But when he got desperate enough, he went in only to be told Amy earned too much and that he would only be entitled to $20 a fortnight. Eventually it got so bad he decided to take any job, and Dr Nathan Rout-Pitt went to work pushing trolleys and stacking shelves at Coles.

'It is degrading,' his mother says.

Beverley Rout is a woman cut from steel. She grew up in a family of eight children in Athol Park at the bottom of Hanson Road, five minutes north from where General Motors ran its Woodville plant. Her mother worked as a cleaner. Her father worked a bar stool and drank the money away. She remembers that the family were always having their lights turned off and when she was eight years old she started cooking and cleaning the house for her mother. When she was 15, she left school and went through a string of jobs working in factories or hospitality before she fell pregnant to a man she didn't love. Because it was the right thing to do, she moved in with him. Then one morning she woke up, told him she had no feelings for him and left. 'I was 18 and stupid,' she says.

Later she met another man, got married and had Nathan. A few years later she fell pregnant again, and right about the time her baby girl was due, Beverley's mother had to go in for a triple bypass, her father had to have surgery on his bowels, and her husband left. It didn't matter. She carried on and from that point she was raising her family on her own, until ten years ago when they were old enough that she could work as a cleaner, just like her mother, cleaning apartments and hotel rooms in the city until she had to stop because her body couldn't take it.

Beverley never had any expectations for her kids. All she wanted for them was to be happy. In primary school, Nathan said he wanted to be a teacher like his father, who is also his best friend. He was determined. Wait until high school, his mother thought, but when he got there he discovered his love for science and grew determined to do something more.

In September 2015, Nathan was awarded his PhD. He was the first in the family to ever finish university, let alone a PhD, and Beverley was fiercely proud, but the cancer meant she couldn't be there to watch.

So the day of the ceremony, Nathan told the officials he had to leave. They weren't happy, but he said it was a medical emergency and promised he'd bring the gown right back. He charged home back along Main North Road and when he got there, he took a photo with his mother. Amy holds up the photo on her phone as proof. It's a happy memory.

It also happens all the time in this part of the world. Families don't push their kids into higher education. Instead they let the kid choose and once they decide, the family does what it can to get them through. They may not know what's involved, they may not know what life will be like afterwards, but what they have is a firm notion that a degree means a good job, good money and an easy life somewhere else that will make all the risk, stress and sacrifice worthwhile.

So they marshal what resources they have and they stand by their kid. Even if they don't say so, in their private moments they'll think to themselves how happy they are that their child isn't going to be like Mum and Dad. They'll be a professional, that line of thought runs. They'll work with their head, not their hands, until their back or knees give out, and when their kid graduates they'll quietly tell their friends how proud they are of all their son or daughter has accomplished.

Out where Nathan lives the highest level of qualification for most people is a TAFE certificate. About 7 per cent of people in the area around Nathan's home hold a Bachelor's Degree and 1.4 per cent hold a postgraduate qualification. These are numbers simultaneously high and low. They're high because there's a university campus down the road at Mawson Lakes, but they're low in the broader scheme of things because children like Nathan Rout-Pitt are raised to leave. Anyone from the region with a little bit of talent and a whole lot of grit who manages to complete a degree must leave in order to earn a living doing what they have spent so long learning how to do. Except once they're out, they end up competing with everyone else without the same personal networks, without knowing how to dress like everyone else, write a professional email to the same standard, or talk nicely so they don't accidentally offend a supervisor.

As career counsellors have a habit of saying, it's tough out there. On the numbers, a little over one in four 18- to 34-year-olds around the country hold a Bachelor's Degree or higher. As a whole Australia is certified smart, but only two-thirds of those graduates were working full time four months after graduating. Now people are talking about how people actually need two degrees to get in the door.

'You know, they tell kids that you need to go to university if you want a good job and they do and they get nothing out of it,' Beverley says. 'You do all that work, he did all those years at uni. Did his PhD. How could someone do so much work and then be pushing trolleys?

'You work that hard and you should get what you want. I was listening to the TV a while ago and they're saying that a lot of students who are studying now are studying for jobs that won't exist.

'It is pretty cruel, I think.'

If it made his mother angry, it made Nathan depressed. Working at the supermarket was exhausting, meaningless work and it didn't take long for him to guess from the cold demeanour of the other employees and the excessive amount of labour he was doing that the company had kneaded four jobs into one. To make matters worse, he knew he was disposable. By contract, he was on probation for the first six months. Make too much noise about the conditions or cut corners to get it done on time and he'd be pointed to the door.

For all the years at university, for all the stress and the sweat, Nathan had graduated into the family business. Morning shift meant getting in early to clean the floors and sanitise the surfaces. Working during the day mostly meant pushing trolleys around and at the end having to clean the chicken ovens thoroughly for tomorrow. Then there were the customers.

'I really had to block people out,' Nathan says. 'You could see the way people looked down on you like you were a piece of crap. And in the back of my mind, I'm thinking, *I have a PhD. I have a PhD.*'

Nathan worked hard, didn't cut corners and people respected him for it. Even the boss recognised it and when he finally quit, she was devastated. Nathan didn't have the heart to tell her he hated the job and a friend had called from another lab to say they had three months' contract work going. Instead, he told her about his mother, and the boss promised to keep his job open if he needed it.

A new job meant renewed hope. These days, Nathan is back in the lab making viruses that can be injected into mice. It's grunt work and not quite where Nathan wants to be, but it's a start. He's hoping that the lab gets some more funding to bring him on full time while he looks for the next opportunity. He and Amy have been talking about having kids, and a little stability might make that happen.

Which is something Beverley supports wholeheartedly. After Christmas, the couple will be taking her on a holiday. Beverley's never been on holiday before. She's never even left the state. It's something she's looking forward to, because there's not much she can look forward to these days. All she wants of the future is to be in it, she jokes.

'I just want my kids to be happy,' she continues. 'I'd like to think they're going to be happy. Have no major problems. Have lots of kids.' She pauses as she hears something outside.

'Is that rain?' She asks, peering through the curtain. 'I think it is.'

Chapter 20

WHITE KNIGHTS IN THE SAUDI ARABIA OF THE SOUTH

THE TEXT MESSAGE SAID TO GO ONLINE. LOOK UP 'PROJECT Erich'.

'Hope this guy comes through,' it read.

In it was a link to an exclusive interview 56-year-old Flemish entrepreneur Guido Dumarey had given to an online motoring magazine, in which he outlined his vision for 'Project Erich'. It had been named for Erich Bitter, the German founder of Bitter Cars, a successful low-volume producer of sports-luxury vehicles that were high-end remakes of existing models. Dumarey's vision was to do the same by taking over production at the Elizabeth factory in 2017, retool the place and put together premium sports-luxury cars based on the rear wheel drive design of the

Commodore. He would produce 30,000 cars a year and had been making a lot of noise about potentially saving thousands of jobs.

He claimed the entire plan had already been thought through. Over the first six months of 2016, his people would lobby state and federal governments to make it happen. Then they would negotiate with GM to let them take over the factory and give them a free licence to use the Commodore architecture. In November 2015, Dumarey had been in Canberra to lobby Malcolm Turnbull's new government and had sought the backing of independent South Australian Senator Nick Xenophon. In early 2016, Christopher Pyne, the new federal Minister for Industry, wrote a letter outlining his support.

It wouldn't be the first time Dumarey had ridden in at the last moment to save a dying factory from the rust pile. The man had come to the rescue of an ailing GM transmission plant in Strasbourg, Germany, which had been due to close in 2014. It would have taken 1000 jobs down with it, but five years of negotiations ended up saving the plant. Dumarey sank €220 million into the factory and GM gave a purchase guarantee for the first two years of the plant's operation, along with a free licence on two of its transmission systems. Two years later, BMW was its biggest client and the plant had taken on another 350 people.

Dumarey wasn't the only one who sensed opportunity in abandoned infrastructure and a falling Australian dollar. Ethan Automotive and Red Automotive Technologies were two other companies scheming about stepping in when Holden left. Even more tantalisingly, GM had told reporters it was 'very open' to offers to take over its factory and keep domestic car manufacturing alive in Australia.

None of this changed the fact that all these plans were total long shots. Even as Dumarey was telling the world about his ambitious vision, he had not yet sat down with GM or Holden management to nut out the backbone of a deal. Even if he had, there was also the sobering fact that his plan meant moving state and federal governments to action in the space of six months – and during an election period. It meant securing hundreds of millions in finance and then rapidly fleshing out a deal with GM in one-fifth the time it took to negotiate the takeover of the Strasbourg plant. It meant sourcing and redesigning parts to build a premium vehicle and it meant securing a workforce even as the industry had been laying people off. It also meant acknowledging the fact that, even if successful, a production run of 30,000 cars a year in Elizabeth meant nothing for the national supply chain and those factories closing shop in Victoria. It meant only about 200 jobs would be saved in the Elizabeth plant, which still translated to potentially thousands of people out of work. And if enough companies in the supply chain had fallen, an Australian-built car made from 100 per cent imported parts was still, essentially, an import.

As one official put it: 'What does he think he can do that GM can't?'

Not that the men and women in the trenches seemed to care. What they wanted most of all was a white knight. As the 2017 deadline drew closer, most had been trying not to think about what it all meant. Most just wanted to pretend it wasn't happening and go to work. They'd sort it all out later. Those with family or connections in other businesses or industries made discreet inquiries about whether there was any work going, but for the most part, talk was kept to a minimum because when they spoke, it just made them feel obsolete. It was going to be bad, that's all they needed to know.

But many were also angry. Because everyone involved knew instinctively just how bad things might get, they couldn't understand why no one was fighting to save their industry. Those who were paying attention to Britain knew that by the start of 2016 the British car industry was desperate for skilled labour and had been struggling to fill vacancies. They could not understand why Australia didn't appreciate what they did and why everyone was standing by while the whole thing packed up. Holden's decision to leave had come on so suddenly and so completely that it meant there had been no time to organise a response.

Guido Dumarey was actually doing something. He raised hope of a last-minute rescue and the more he talked, the more people listened and the more they wished him to succeed.

Only the plan never made it past the end of February 2016, when Guido Dumarey and General Motors Holden put out a joint statement saying they had run the numbers and it wasn't feasible.

The factory was doomed and there was nothing anyone could do about it.

* * *

Whispers of white knights had been circulating for over a year. In a small arts bar, deep in the heart of Adelaide, a former arts advisor to South Australian Premier Jay Weatherill spoke of a plan by venture capitalists to invest in a company to take over the site.

'Don't worry about it,' he said, leaning against the counter, beer in hand. 'It's not a problem. It's all been taken care of.'

Mid-2015, another government advisor talked about how he had helped Dumarey make introductions, but refused to talk in detail about the plan. All he would say at the time was that the 'critical question' was whether the federal government was against subsidisation or car making as an industry.

If car workers were hanging out for a hero, so too were the state's political elite. The day Holden announced its closure, South Australia's leadership sat down to assess the situation and quickly understood it was pretty grim. The state's budget was headed for the red and its manufacturing industry had been shutting down for decades. The wine industry had been in recession since 2000 and agriculture needed water, which in a drying climate was more expensive to come by. To make matters worse, the mining boom was over and the $25 billion Olympic Dam expansion at Roxby Downs hadn't gone ahead. Then Canberra started talking about pulling the pin on defence shipbuilding and all the other closures started to trickle in. Things were getting serious.

But all that uranium buried beneath Roxby Downs, about 500 kilometres north of Adelaide, looked good on paper. The people who ran the state were desperate and they knew it was time to go big or go broke, and the biggest idea of them all was the nuclear option. South Australia had the world's biggest mining company sitting on top of the world's biggest source of uranium, even if BHP hadn't decided to go ahead with its expansion. The state was being called the Saudi Arabia of the global south as far back as 2007 and the idea of getting rich off cheap energy has been around even longer.

It's a vision state Senator Sean Edwards holds to. A winemaker from the Clare Valley region of South Australia, he is a Liberal man to the very bottom. His voting record shows he has moved with the party on every issue it holds dear and like any good federal Liberal politician of the era, he qualifies and caveats, never forgets to blame Labor, bags out the unions and makes sure to plug the Liberal Party's solid economic management. When asked a question that has the feeling of either being too technical or too far beyond his grasp, he shrugs it off.

'I'm just the wine guy,' he says.

One to one, Sean Edwards is likeable and his approach to industry is, within limits, refreshingly bipartisan. He is also a salesman, and what he has been selling lately is his plan to build South Australia a nuclear industry.

'The Saudi Arabia of the south? Well, yeah,' he says, answering his own question as he passes over his modelling for going nuclear in South Australia. It is a document put together with the help of Ben Heard, a pro-nuclear environmental consultant with the University of Adelaide and submitted to the South Australian Royal Commission looking into what it would take for the state to set up in the nuclear business.

It is a 48-page booklet printed on high-gloss, A4 stock, and in it the Senator outlines his vision to get involved in all stages of the nuclear cycle. He wants to dig the stuff out of the dirt and send it offshore. He wants to build the generators here and he wants to ship in the spent fuel rods, truck them out to the middle of the desert and lock them away. Combined, it would mean $21.8 billion according to the senator's figures. The kicker, he says, is the cheap power it would provide. It would produce so much energy, Edwards says, the state could give it away for free. This would create what he calls a de facto 'special economic zone' by offering dirt-cheap energy at bargain-basement prices to anyone who wanted to set up shop. It's safe, he says, and it's carbon free – though the latter is not entirely accurate, because nuclear power does emit carbon, though nothing near as much as fossil fuels. While the reactors themselves may be zero-emission, the trucks, steel and cement needed in the process aren't. It's the same for wind and solar.

The promise of energy 'too cheap to meter' is a hell of a pitch and one that has been promised ever since physicist Lewis Strauss uttered the words in a speech given in 1954 to the National Association of Science Writers in the United States. Only people back then mistook his words to be about the future of nuclear fission, when really he had been talking about the march of technology and the role of electricity in general.

It's also part of the pitch being made by South Australian company Nuclear Energy Systems Pty Ltd, founded by a group of high-profile South Australian businessmen and academics lobbying for a nuclear power industry in the state. Their efforts finally bore fruit on 8 February 2015 when the South Australian Premier announced a Royal Commission to investigate the idea of a nuclear industry for South Australia. It was a move that surprised many, given the Labor party's traditional opposition to nuclear power, and those clued in read the announcement as a way for the Labor leader to give himself the political cover needed to establish a nuclear waste dump in the state's far north.

Those observations seemed accurate when the Commission released its earliest findings a year later: it killed the dream of a South Australian nuclear power industry in saying that all that cheap power was still too expensive to get off the ground. It was a different story, however, if the state wanted to build a world-class nuclear waste 'bunker' in the middle of the desert with which South Australia could charge a premium to store 13 per cent of the world's radioactive material. It would be 'highly profitable', said Kevin Scarce, a former South Australian governor and the man in charge of the Commission inquiry. It was an investigation and a report he had worked hard on for a year. This 'sophisticated engineering facility' promised a projected income for the state of $257 billion, at a rate of about $5 billion a year, he said. If work started soon, it could be operational by 2020. All the other details would come out in the Commission's full report, scheduled for May, he told the press conference and, Scarce added, he really wished people would stop calling it a 'dump'.

With that, South Australia seemed to pin its latest hopes on setting itself up as a 'sophisticated' dump for the world's radioactive waste.

The only thing standing in the way for those who wanted to give the future a green glow was the same thing that always made for problems when conversation turns to nuclear power. Physicists and academics and business leaders can talk about how safe and environmentally friendly nuclear technology is, how advanced storage practices are, but the parts they skip over are all the people in between. People have to write the laws and regulations and sign off on the finance to build the reactors and the waste dumps. People have to run the depots and truck out the fuel rods somewhere in the middle of the desert. People do the safety checks and the quality control and the medical exams. With enough time, people forget. Give it 10,000 years, not even half the half-life of radioactive waste, and chances are people would forget what they buried out there in the middle of the desert. Instead they would tell stories of cursed hidden treasures in the same way stories were told of Tutankhamun's tomb. Long before that time comes, they will get tired or drunk or have problems with their marriages. Sometimes they may just get plain bored, or plain mean, or they may turn out to be plain old liars. When those people make mistakes in any other industry, anywhere along the chain, it might be harmful only to themselves. Not so when the job is to handle significant quantities of radioactive material, or an active nuclear facility. Even those the US Airforce trusts to babysit its nuclear arsenal have made mistakes that nearly ended in American cities being nuked.

Aside from the basic human ability to screw up, people also take convincing. Especially in South Australia, whose people still remember how the British army irradiated stretches of desert and the local Aboriginal people at Maralinga during the 1950s. They still remember Chernobyl and Fukushima with the Australian-origin uranium lying in the heart of its disaster-proof reactor. The temptation is to write off these objections as unreasonable. These events were long in the past, it is said. Some involved weaponised uranium, and Fukushima was exceptional. The world has come a long way since. Which all may be true, but the weight of that history has so far been enough to make ordinary South Australians feel uncomfortable about turning their patch of desert into the world's radioactive waste dump. Money be damned.

Give most people a choice between nuclear power and renewable energy, they will take the second. At the moment, a very different kind of green boom is on. Across the world in 2014, investment in renewable energy rose 17 per cent to $270 billion. Specifically among developing countries, that figure grew by 36 per cent to $131 billion. At the time of writing, South Australia has one of the highest penetrations of wind and solar in the world, owing in part to the way the state quietly cornered most major renewable-energy projects on the market during the Tony Abbott years when coal was the new black and the Renewable Energy Target was something to be cut down.

Prime Minister Abbott didn't have the power to scrap the RET entirely, so instead he announced a review. This review brought uncertainty into the future of the $20 billion Australian industry and, overnight, investment stalled as multinational companies had to put their projects on hold. It was enough to make Richard Inwood, the managing director of South Australian-based Tindo Solar, mad enough to give forceful radio interviews in mid-2014, during which he told anyone who would listen how the federal government had 'kneecapped' the industry.

He was angry, and rightly so. He saw himself at the bleeding edge of a green revolution, positioned as the only 100 per cent genuine Australian-made manufacturer of solar panels from his vastly underwhelming plant in Mawson Lakes. It sits about ten minutes south of Holden and 30 minutes north of Adelaide, depending on traffic. Here was a company that was innovative, growing and thought it could compete with China, he said. The hard work had been done, the concept had been proven with the help of government money from ARENA (Australian Renewable Energy Agency), and just when things were looking up, like things were getting off the ground, a new government changed everything.

Inside, the place was nothing like the expansive, moving puzzle that was the Holden factory floor. Inwood's factory was spatially neat and compact. The entire production line had been designed to fit into a room no bigger than a suburban three-bedroom home. It was also incredibly high tech and the machines it relied upon to solder and form and test each cell were, Inwood insisted, world leading. It took about 40 minutes for a brand-new panel to slide off the end of his production line at this stage of development, and up on the roof he showed off his panels in action. Every panel there was made on the factory floor below and each helped power the production line, meaning Tindo's energy costs were virtually zero. Back inside, Inwood was keen to promote his company's Australian-made credentials. 'This is quality stuff,' he said while gesturing to a panel being made. 'Not like that Chinese crap.'

Inwood then introduced Gavin Warwick, a former Holden employee, standing beneath an Australian flag that hung from the roof. Of the 18 jobs Warwick had applied for back in 2012, Tindo Solar had been the only company to take him on and, as he has a young child, the company offered stability. Three weeks after he had joined, former Prime Minister Julia Gillard visited to cut the ribbon and Gavin was volunteered to demonstrate.

'Some of the guys thought it would be funny to throw me in the deep end to see how I went,' he said.

Inwood at the time said he wanted to hire more people just like Gavin and put them to work. He had enough orders to justify a second and a third shift and eventually open a whole new factory. This was growth, he said, right down the road from Holden, where more than a thousand people were about to lose their jobs. What he couldn't understand was why the federal government wasn't interested. He was already there, he was operating and he wanted to build.

Only, no one in the wider renewable energy industry knew what was going on and no one was going to risk committing any more money until they did. Some, like Rhys Jacobs, had already committed everything. Then a 23-year-old PhD student at the University of South Australia's Sustainable Energy Centre, he had just started research on 'encapsulated phase-change materials for use in thermal-energy storage'. In a nutshell, he was working on building better batteries, big ones, for use in the Concentrated Solar Power (CSP) industry, which works in a similar way to traditional coal-fired power stations. But instead of burning coal, concentrated sunlight is used to heat a fluid, make steam and produce electricity.

The trick, however, is working out how to store that energy, and Rhys's initial design promised to halve the cost of storage, though back then it hadn't undergone a feasibility study. Like Inwood, he was angry at what he read in newspapers and saw on TV. He had started a career building something innovative that would ultimately be good for Australia and ended up watching as the federal government tore up his future. He couldn't understand how something that showed such promise was being ignored.

That feeling changed a year on when Malcolm Turnbull stepped up to take over from Tony Abbott. In doing so, it seemed he was giving the renewable energy sector a second glance by removing the ban his predecessor had placed on wind investment by the Clean Energy Finance Corporation. These days Rhys Jacobs thinks things are going to get better. A CSP company has announced it is setting up in Australia, his research is going well and he is no longer planning to leave the country at the first opportunity.

'There's a little bit of hope in our future,' he says. 'I'm not depressed as I used to be. Different governments, different policies, they change and you've just got to try and change with it, which is never good for long-term research, but that's how it is.'

Chapter 21

IMAGINEERS

On 8 September 2013, Australia woke to a new order. Labor and the progressive left had been smashed at every point of the compass. Sensing blood, Tony Abbott mustered his generals and warriors, and together they washed into Canberra, swarming down on the nation's capital from their strongholds across the country. They had lost the Senate, sure, but they had won the election. Triumph was the word of the day and over the coming weeks and months no quarter would be given, and none asked.

It was a deeply divisive time in Australia. All the progressive-liberal side of politics could do was wonder aloud to themselves how it all happened and lick their wounds as the new prime minister immediately got down to the business of protecting himself against any political threat. Every government board, council, committee or advisory body was reviewed for anyone who might pose a political threat, particularly anyone with a union acronym on their CV. The fight against WorkChoices had brought down John Howard, and Tony Abbott wasn't about to give the unions a chance to organise against him.

The first item on the policy agenda was federal assistance to the car industry. For as long as anyone could remember, the car industry had been an ideological punching bag for every Coalition government since the 1985 Button Plan to rationalise the industry. Before the election, the Institute of Public Affairs – the conservative, free-market think tank that provides the ideological ammo for the Liberal Party – published a wish list outlining a radical free-market reform agenda for the Abbott government's first term. Ending the subsidisation of the car industry was listed as item number 30. It was the first serious policy item Tony Abbott's government would deliver.

As of 2013, the car makers were more vulnerable than ever, and Holden's managing director Mike Devereux handed the government its opening. When Devereux went before the Productivity Commission on a Tuesday morning in December, the Commission aimed to draw from the Holden boss whether there was anything the Australian car industry might do to restructure. It wanted to know whether there was any way Holden could mimic what its US parent had done when it applied for Chapter 11 bankruptcy.

The first questions asked of Mike Devereux that day were whether GM Holden had decided if it would stay in Australia, and how much the company would need in government support to stay. Devereux responded by staying vague on the dates and numbers to avoid an unnecessary public showdown. He told them no decision had been made and he wouldn't publicly give a number for how much the company was asking. The government had that information, he said, and it was this vagueness that the government seized on as both an implicit threat and a weakness. The Holden boss went on to tell the Commission that for the $1.8 billion in federal assistance they had been given to date, the company had generated $33 billion in economic activity, and the Holden Cruze, the company's small car, was the fifth-best-selling passenger car in its market. What they wanted was a public–private partnership to keep going, but by then the government had already heard enough.

Tony Abbott wasn't around for what happened next. Instead it was Warren Truss, leader of the Nationals and Acting Prime Minister, working with federal Treasurer Joe Hockey, who moved with demands for a clear decision from GM. Truss opened by writing a tough-talking letter to Devereux calling for answers and giving copies of that letter to the press, and the Treasurer followed up with his performance on the floor of Parliament when he stood to answer a question from Labor's Tanya Plibersek.

There Joe Hockey beat his chest about corporate welfare and told all of Australia he could not believe the nerve of GM to ask for $500 million more than what the government had already given them. Judging from the outrage, it was as if GM Holden had asked for the $34 billion GM had asked the US Government to give to save the American car industry in 2008. It was a blistering show and images of Hockey in full flight, wearing a blue suit and blue tie, went right around the country.

'Come clean,' he told General Motors. Come right out and tell the country whether you are going to stay or go, he demanded. 'Make a commitment' to stay in Australia, he said.

'We want them to be honest with us, we want them to be fair dinkum.

'Either you're here or not.'

To this day, the Coalition line is that GM had already decided it was going, it just hadn't told anyone yet, based on a story published in the *Wall Street Journal* citing unnamed sources.

To everyone watching at home, it sure sounded like Joe Hockey was giving GM an ultimatum and it didn't take supernatural foresight to predict what would happen next. The Commonwealth of Australia was officially proclaimed to the world in 1901 and General Motors was founded seven years later in 1908. Today it operates in 37 countries across 396 facilities on six continents, staffed by 216,000 employees who produced 9,924,880 vehicles in 2014 and generated an income larger than the GDP of small developing world economies. That an Australian treasurer only three months into the job would try to work over a multinational almost as old as the geopolitical entity that gave him his office, in full view of the public, made people doubt that those in charge really understood the weight of their words.

Canberra may be 1159 kilometres away, but the long reach of the nation's capital was being felt all the way in Adelaide that day. From the moment South Australia watched the images of Hockey breathing fire about the car industry, the anger of its people stirred. They felt betrayed and as events continued to unfold, information about what the closure of the factories actually meant started trickling in.

Then the Defence Department released a white paper suggesting the country's warship manufacturing industry should be offshored and the country's shipyards started to wonder whether they had a future. Later, Canberra confirmed it would send the contract for the navy's new submarines offshore and initially blocked ASC from competing. To add insult to injury, former Industry Minister David Johnston chewed out the locals when he said they 'couldn't build a canoe'. The blows kept coming.

What these events marked was the start of a new rust-belt politics. Central to it was a fight to keep major industries alive, and where that couldn't be done, the question became what would all those people do when they lost their jobs? And where would the money come from to make it happen?

Overnight, Tony Abbott became bad news in South Australia and, with time, he managed to alienate pretty much every major Coalition voting base across the rest of the country as well as the key figures within his own party. As a leader, he was an ideological firebrand who carried the cross of the free market. He knew how to fight and when he didn't get what he wanted, he knew how to wield uncertainty like a scalpel to get what he wanted anyway. He was going to remake Australia just like Margaret Thatcher remade Britain and Ronald Reagan remade America.

Australia didn't want to be remade, however. Tony Abbott won the election mostly because he wasn't Kevin Rudd or Julia Gillard and he overestimated just how far right Australia had shifted. With every bum policy, with every gaffe, his polls sank and in February 2015 two small-time Western Australian MPs, Luke Simpkins and Don Randall, had had enough. Their electorates were mining communities and with the drop in ore prices their people were going through their own localised downturn. As they watched public opinion change, they sensed their considerable margins starting to slip away. The Queensland state election saw the sitting Liberal state government wiped out and everyone at a federal level knew they were in trouble. Something had to be done, so the backbench triggered a leadership challenge on 6 February and Prime Minister Abbott got busy counting votes.

South Australia was a problem. It had always been a problem for Tony Abbott. No more cars and no more ships meant no more jobs for its people and it was making for an unsettling feeling in Liberal electorates, which were already showing signs of rebellion on that weekend before the first leadership spill.

South Australia's role in the whole thing largely hinged on a mid-level South Australian Liberal Party senator, Sean Edwards. A moderate within the party, Edwards had branded himself a Liberal champion for the shipbuilding industry in October 2014 when he wrote to the prime minister to tell him he could no longer support the 'disengagement' with the industry. Once rebellion broke out in Abbott's camp, Sean Edwards saw an opportunity and reminded Abbott of his feelings on the matter. He didn't expect to hear from him, but that Saturday night, as he and his wife were getting dressed for a pirate-themed fancy dress party, the prime minister called.

There was no way Tony Abbott could have known whether Sean Edwards controlled one vote or seven. The actual number remains unclear. The senator won't talk about it, even though he implies he was one among many. Abbott couldn't take the risk, so he asked for a chance to speak to his Defence Minister about whether they could involve South Australian companies in any future submarine contract. Edwards didn't hear from him again until the next day as he was leaving for Canberra, when Tony Abbott called to say ASC would be involved, though the exact nature of that involvement remains unclear. Edwards asked whether there was going to be an announcement, or whether he could make it, and Abbott told him to 'go for your life', so Edwards did.

Tony Abbott won the spill 61 to 39 on the promise he would start to consult more with his backbench. There is a chance Senator Edwards's announcement helped give credibility to the idea that Abbott would actually follow through. Then, the Monday after the spill, Defence Minister Kevin Andrews publicly denied the essence of the deal made between the senator and the prime minister and it was back to business.

Over the next few days the media tried to nail down what Sean Edwards and the prime minister had spoken about that night in an attempt to work out exactly what had been said. The general narrative also made for a good story. A lesser-known, mid-level Liberal party senator from South Australia wedged a sitting prime minister during a moment of crisis to extract a significant concession about a multi-billion-dollar manufacturing industry on which thousands of people depended. It was a brave manoeuvre that instantly made Senator Edwards a pariah within his own party and a target of ridicule. Nor did he help matters when he gave a baffled interview with Sky News in which he struggled to remember the exact terms of his conversation with Tony Abbott.

As a state, South Australia tends to be fairly politically stable. There are precious few swing seats outside the former manufacturing district of Hindmarsh, where Matt Williams barely scraped a win for the Coalition at the 2013 election. Both major parties have locked down their strongholds and none really expected Tony Abbott's unpopularity to fester so deeply and then spread into Coalition safe seats occupied by key ministers such as Christopher Pyne.

But it did, and by 2015 Tony Abbott's people were getting nervous. The state Liberal Party had lost the election and was watching its numbers fall further. Christopher Pyne, a key cabinet minister, was facing a potential loss at the next election in his seat precisely because Tony Abbott, the prime minister for jobs, the infrastructure prime minister, had stood by as every major industry on which South Australia depended was closed down amidst talk of tough budgets.

So Tony Abbott went on the offensive. The prime minister started to spend increasing amounts of time in South Australia, but it didn't help and the polls kept sliding. Then, in August, the state's official unemployment rate hit 8 per cent and Middle Australia just stopped listening. On 4 August, Abbott even announced an $89 billion shipbuilding plan to offset the discontent that might be created in sending a $50 billion submarine contract offshore. No one cared.

A month later, on 14 September 2015, Tony Abbott lost his job. He had been given six months by his party to make it work and he got seven. The day before it all happened, Abbott had stopped over in Adelaide on his way back from Canning in Perth, where a by-election was running to fill the office of Don Randall, who had initiated the February leadership challenge. Among the finery of the Adelaide Club, an exclusive, men-only association frequented by the southern city's gentry, Abbott confronted Christopher Pyne about whether rumours of another rebellion were true. Pyne told him it was nonsense, that there was nothing to worry about, so Abbott was confident when he woke up the next morning and told reporters at a joint press conference alongside Premier Jay Weatherill that everything was fine. He flew back to Canberra, and just after noon, Julie Bishop told him he had lost the confidence of the party. At 3.15pm Malcolm Turnbull announced he would challenge. At 10.40pm, Abbott was made redundant.

A lot has since been written about Tony Abbott's last days by Canberra insiders and political reporters. Some of those on the factory line have their own insight. They call men like Abbott 'imagineers'. Imagineers are guys who come into a management job with an idea of how the place should run. They know the principles and the black and white of it, and in their mind they conjure up a perfect system, one in which everything should run a certain way. What they don't understand is how their actions translate on the shop floor. Out there, things go wrong. A machine has anomalies and the gauge wasn't built to spec. When it hits the part, it doesn't come out to the exact dimensions, it just doesn't get made right.

In fact, no part comes out to nominal specs, which is why the big companies all build in tolerances. Abbott had very low tolerances, and the fact is there are so many variables at play that the world as he imagined it could not exist. It still can't. In a perfect world, everything might work the way he intended, but as they say about the car industry, this is not a perfect world.

Chapter 22

OUR BOY IN CANBERRA

THE SAME RUST-BELT POLITICS THAT HELPED TAKE DOWN TONY Abbott have also helped forge Nick Xenophon, a man as uniquely South Australian as backyard zivania and frog cakes.

He is the politician who happened by accident. In 1997 the personal-injury lawyer ran a single-issue campaign as the No-Pokies MP for the South Australian Legislative Council and won on preferences. South Australia ended up liking him so much it asked him to stay on at the end of his eight-year term in 2006, but Xenophon had other things in mind when he ran for the federal senate a year later. South Australia didn't mind in the slightest and sent him on to be their man in Canberra with 24.9 per cent of the vote, more even than Labor, which finished up at 22.7 per cent.

Around that time, the general view of the local political establishment was that Nick Xenophon could not be trusted.

It was a feeling that went back to Xenophon's student days at Adelaide University when a group of overzealous Young Liberals got tricky with the vote for the editorship of the student magazine. While he wasn't involved in carrying it out, Xenophon benefited, and he would later confirm the election was rigged in a 1978 issue of the student magazine, after his editorship had finished. To this day, it is a story some use against him, but his willingness to talk about it publicly has also marked him as a person who does not hide from critics. Out in the real world of politics, senior political figures from both camps have always cursed the name Xenophon, and around the time the man left for the nation's capital, reports started to appear quoting anonymous sources talking about how he was an unknown quantity and meant trouble for Canberra.

Which served as a ringing endorsement for the people who voted for him. If those in power were saying Nick Xenophon was someone who wouldn't play ball, well, then he must be doing something right, as far as the street was concerned.

True to form, it didn't take Xenophon half a minute to start raising hell once he stepped off the plane. When Kevin Rudd wanted to spend $42 billion to stimulate the Australian economy and head off the devastation of the GFC, Nick Xenophon made him wait until he had agreed to bring forward $900 million in drought assistance for the Murray-Darling Basin. When Tony Abbott was elected in 2013, the scrappy Nick Xenophon united with the seven other crossbench senators to provide a counterweight to the prime minister's plans to remake the country. The ragtag group of senators, each with their own political agenda and level of experience, was a nightmare for the prime minister, who could barely contain his displeasure whenever he was forced to talk in public about the 'feral Senate' that bucked his authority.

It was the kind of attitude that drew comparisons to maverick Queensland MP Clive Palmer. Some say the charming, mild-mannered centrist Xenophon was just a South Australian export of the same stock. A kind of personality candidate who offered the allure of an alternative to the major parties but had no real staying power.

However, they were wrong. Clive Palmer was the product of mining-boom prosperity. A big-talking, blowhard businessman from the tropics whose credentials were based on the size of his bank account. Nick Xenophon was, by contrast, South Australia's favoured son, the quirky oddball who liked a joke but knew exactly where to apply pressure. The guy who put his career as a crusading personal-injury lawyer aside for a career as a crusading politician standing up for the everyday person. Clive Palmer's style was to yell and insult. Nick Xenophon's impulse was to care and mentor and co-opt. He was the guy Clive Palmer tried to be, but never could. Xeno, as he is affectionately called, was a gonzo politician. A thorn in the establishment's side whose success had been built on a basic formula of centrist politics, effectiveness, hard work, and his public image as someone who actually cared about other people.

As John Koutouzis, a grape grower in the Riverland, watched his business slowly die in the middle of a ten-year recession in the region's wine industry, no one cared. Even the local industry association representative had been telling growers to stay quiet out of fear the international press would catch onto their troubles and the price of their grapes would fall.

'Except Xenophon,' John Koutouzis said. 'He is the only one.'

When Nick Xenophon questioned the signing of free-trade agreements and in doing so announced that Australia was known internationally as the 'Free Trade Taliban', he caught people's attention. When autoworkers heard that Nick Xenophon had endorsed Guido Dumarey's plan to take over the Elizabeth car factory, they knew he was making an effort when up until that point, the Liberals had killed their livelihood and Labor seemed to roll over. Every time Xeno tried to nail the federal Liberal government over its attempt to offshore defence shipbuilding, those on the shipyards paid attention. When he wrote to Malcolm Turnbull the day after he took over from Tony Abbott to ask the new prime minister to move on bringing the projects forward, they cheered.

In fact, Nick Xenophon is likely the only politician who can get the same response from three separate grandmothers at the mere mention of his name. It begins with a slight pause, a narrowing of the eyes that suggests a deep and considered knowing, followed by the sentence: 'You know, I think Nick Xenophon has to be the hardest working polly out there.'

Every time Nick Xenophon sticks his foot in the prime minister's office door to extract his pound of flesh, South Australians beam.

'That's our boy.'

So when Nick Xenophon announced he was launching his own political party in December 2014, the Nick

Xenophon Team, or NXT, he was met with an eyebrow raise from those in the world of politics who knew him. It was an irony that the anti-politician politician was going to play the game. The humour in it only lasted until the polls started coming in predicting that NXT candidates had the potential to put some very important people out of a job. A CFMEU poll suggested that a no-name NXT candidate would win with 38 per cent of the vote in Christopher Pyne's seat. A Roy Morgan poll in February 2016 showed 20.5 per cent of South Australians were happy to vote NXT at the next election. A Galaxy poll suggested 24 per cent of the primary vote belonged to Xenophon. That was just South Australia, of course. The NXT was running candidates around the country. How they would fare in their home states was an unknown.

Around that time newspapers stared running stories of hushed plans by both major political parties to respond. Either they would attack Nick Xenophon's centrist public image or his anti-pokies stance and see what happened. Or they would wait and see. Xenophon's trademark formula worked as a lone independent, but trying to bind a team of separate people to a central platform across multiple states with competing political demands was another thing entirely.

So too was actually delivering. As an independent, it never mattered if Nick Xenophon won or lost a cause. Simply trying was enough because people knew he was going all-in for them, win or lose. With the new party, Nick Xenophon would face greater pressures to deliver. Just give it time, the thinking went, and the wheels would come off, just like Clive Palmer's.

Though no one will admit this on record, nor will they admit they are scared. Loose lips sink ships because no one trash talks Nick Xenophon in South Australia. He's the people's politician, the plucky senator who has the little guy's back, and so long as they feel that way, they have his.

Chapter 23

THIS IS WHAT A DOWNTURN LOOKS LIKE

THE NEIGHBOURS IN THIS SUBURB OF ELIZABETH DON'T KNOW when the house burned down; all they know is that it was there when they moved in five years ago and no one's touched it since. It's been left to rot, they say, and even if someone does demolish what's left, it'll be some property developer who will just stuff the block with units.

In the United States, they call this kind of thing gun rows: cheaply built houses with low ceilings, crammed onto a single block and rented back to the poor. They're going up all around this neighbourhood and back towards the shopping centre. Some see it as a sign the neighbourhood is being cleaned up and that the 'negative element' will slowly drift away. Most will believe that when they see it.

It's American living, the neighbours say. One is short, stocky with a thick neck and a name like Rick. The other is tall and thin with a name like Sam. They don't want their names on record, they say, they're too afraid of the thugs in the house across from Sam's who 'beat the shit' out of Rick one night after they had words.

Now the house is gutted. It's a new house too, built on the cheap. The ceilings are low and the rooms are tiny and everything feels hollow. The place looks as if a demolition crew just got started. A newspaper on the floor is dated Thursday, 26 March 2015. The wall in the living room has been ripped away and someone has pulled down the kitchen ceiling. Electrical wire hangs low and it's not clear whether it is live. The kitchen has been partially demolished, there are tags on the windows and some of the rooms look like someone has put their fist through the wall. Or maybe a sledgehammer. It's hard to tell.

Sam and Rick say to take a good look. It happened about six months ago, and for guys who don't want to talk on record, they're talking an awful lot. Rick says he's fed up with this kind of thing. He pays his rent and takes care of his house. Why shouldn't others? The guy who used to live in the house on the other corner was a meth dealer, Rick says. The junkies would park out the front of Rick's house, buy their gear, do their thing on the walk back to the car and leave the stems in his bins. Both say Holden leaving is only going to make things worse. Why? They don't really know. They just know that it is.

Mostly the neighbourhood is a nice place, they say, but there's nothing left for the kids. No work, no play. All

Rick's son wants to do is play video games. It makes Rick mad, but what can he do?

'American living,' Sam calls it, though he doesn't know how to fix it, he just knows it needs fixing.

Not many people in Adelaide would be surprised. The whole state has a way of laughing at Elizabeth and the region around it for its troubles. Heard a sad story about Elizabeth and its people? Why are you surprised? It's been that way as long as anyone can remember.

It hasn't, in fact. From the very moment Elizabeth, the city that bore the Queen's name, clawed its way out of a muddy field on 16 November 1955, it was a symbol for everything a post-war Australia wanted to be. Now people smirk at the basic Housing Trust constructions of the 50s and 60s, and there may be plans underway to eventually demolish them all, but what critics don't understand is that those cinderblock buildings offered their mostly working-class British residents things they never had, including indoor plumbing and gas ovens. Even for German, Italian and Greek outsiders in the 'Pommy ghetto', it was a lot better than the rubble pile that was central Europe at that time.

Few remember that for at least the first ten years of its existence, Elizabeth was one of the most photographed, talked-about and written-about cities in Australia. Before it became an outpost of the poor white Australian underclass, Elizabeth was the nation's first planned city and represented the triumph of reason and rationality over the chaotic, cutthroat market.

Orderly and neat and clean, Elizabeth was the place a post–World War II country first tried out the idea of importing a middle class from the Old Country on the promise of a house on a quarter-acre block, complete with indoor plumbing, gas and a backyard big enough for the kids and dog to run around in. It was going to be nothing like the dirty industrial towns of pre-war Britain, with poorly built housing clustered around huge factories that blackened the sky with smog. Every need of its projected 25,000 people would be met. There would be wide streets. Pleasant houses. There would be no heavy industry to dominate the horizon and pollute the baby-blue Australian sky. Growth would be controlled. People would be happy.

That's how Elizabeth started out, but the day General Motors signed on to build its second South Australian factory in the town along Philip Highway in 1958, everything changed. Everything was super-sized in the most American way. GM gave Elizabeth respectability and the promise of a strong manufacturing sector on which to build. Before then, there had been no real economic vision for Elizabeth. The town was planned, but how the local economy would function was really an afterthought. A car factory solved the problem.

Putting an operation like that in the middle of a field in 1950s Australia meant a neighbourhood would seed almost overnight. Towns and suburbs needed all the things factories needed. Electricity. Sewerage. Roads. Cheap housing. People. A supply chain. And once a supply chain was in place, smaller manufacturers making refrigerators, washing machines and sewing fabric could set up at reduced cost. Where there had once been cropland and empty plains, suddenly there was a functioning economy. For any state government looking to rapidly develop a piece of outlying real estate, car making was a godsend.

So with GM on board, Elizabeth was advertised across Europe and North America as a city going places, with strong local supply chains and a happy workforce free from radical union activity. Once the companies settled in, Elizabeth's fortunes were tied to the multinationals that built fridges and cars, meaning its future was always going to be decided around boardroom tables in faraway places such as Melbourne, London or Detroit. Ever since, Elizabeth has been at the mercy of the company bottom line.

It also meant Elizabeth became a city that made things. That is what Elizabeth did, that is all it ever did. It was the trade-off in bringing in the multinationals. Elizabeth's people gave up local control when they went to work in the factories, but the Holden factory and others to follow became a birthright that always promised good pay for hard work. Construction started in 1958 and four years later, the factory was hungry for labour as it started to churn out fuel-guzzling family sedans that quickly came to symbolise the Australian Way. Elizabeth built Holdens and Elizabeth drove Holdens. No one dared drive anything else.

In those days, a man in need of work could walk in off the street and into a job, so long as he could keep up. For Italian and Greek immigrants with barely passable English, it was a lifeline in a country that still thought itself porcelain white. Those were good times, for Elizabeth and for the rest of the country. But as Australia moved into the 70s, a cluster of global economic events cracked the economy. In 1973, oil prices skyrocketed when the world's petro-states announced an embargo; Britain gained entry into the European Economic Community, which foreshadowed the EU; and the first rumblings of globalisation meant Australian exports began to experience more competition in the world market. Coupled with protectionist economic policies, unemployment and inflation rose together for the first time since World War II in a phenomenon known as 'stagflation'. Soon enough, South Australia was haemorrhaging manufacturing jobs and Elizabeth was the exit wound.

Between 1972 and 1982, Adelaide alone had shed 10,000 manufacturing jobs. As of 1981, the manufacturing sector employed around 100,000 South Australians. During the recessions of the 80s and 90s, the number of retrenchments in South Australia grew from 23,000 in 1988 to 48,000 in 1992. One in three of those were in manufacturing and by 2011, the total number of manufacturing jobs in South Australia had fallen to 74,000.

In 1982, only 11 of the first 21 factories that had signed on to help pioneer Elizabeth remained. Smaller firms tended to flee or fold, while bigger firms like GM Holden pushed on with a reduced workforce. Four years later, only four of thirteen 'major factories' featured in a 1965 promotional booklet for Elizabeth remained. By the end of the first decade of the new millennium, GM Holden was the last standing.

But Elizabeth has been in a downturn since the 80s. Now what's left of the manufacturing base seems to be disappearing too, taking more jobs with it and leaving the state with what Premier Jay Weatherill has euphemistically called 'significant difficulties'.

The federal government's Small Area Labour Markets report for the September quarter 2015 had unemployment in Elizabeth at 33.3 per cent. Like a stone on the social fabric, Elizabeth was sinking and pulling down the areas around it. Davoren Park clocked 20.5 per cent. Smithfield and Elizabeth North: 23.9. Salisbury North: 12.2. Salisbury: 16.2 per cent. Parafield Gardens: 10.5. Across the state, the Australian Bureau of Statistics had the unemployment rates hitting 8.2 per cent in August 2015. Economists such as Dr John Spoehr expected the state-wide jobless rate to rise to 9 per cent by 2017 before going on to hit double digits. This was a jobs crisis, he told anyone who would listen, and it was one disproportionately affecting men.

Until recently the whole decline has been more or less contained; a slow rot occasionally worsened by the politics of state-government housing policies that concentrated single mothers, the long-term unemployed and Indigenous people into the one region. Now, as 2017 approaches, that process is speeding up, making what happens to Elizabeth, and the rest of Adelaide, anyone's guess.

And people always guess Detroit. It is the first word that leaves the lips of factory workers and politicians, bar-stool economists and street-corner intellectuals when talking about the state's troubles.

'We'll be just like Detroit,' they say.

Everyone knows the story of Detroit, the company town that rose with the Big Three car makers GM, Ford and Chrysler, and fell with them too. It's all in the name. Detroit, the place where Henry Ford set up the first production line to turn raw steel into a carriage affordable to the everyman. Detroit, the Arsenal of Democracy. Detroit, the city that called out to immigrants with the promise of a good wage when everyone else was paying the minimum. Detroit, the city that went boom and then bust during the 50s, right around the time the US started to globalise and companies started to experiment with decentralised production to maximise their profit margin. Around the time automation started and robots began to compete with people. Around the time the price of fuel started to rise. When a new network of highways delivered Detroit's mostly white middle class from the city into the suburbs that had sprawled out along the plains in those days when the city was the fourth largest in the country.

It was a time when free-market economics began its slow march to dominance and companies could no longer bank on the same level of protections to prop up domestic markets. That's when Detroit's rot started, slowly at first, as the smaller operations began to pull out. Later it went up the food chain to the very pillars of the city's success: Ford, GM and Chrysler. Once the Big Three started to sink, Detroit started to sink with them.

The decline picked up speed, and at its peak there was nothing anyone could do to stop it. It had taken on its own inertia. The glory days were over and the factories started to close, work started to dry up and so did the money. Higher unemployment exposed underlying social tensions, allowing race to re-emerge as a fault line in a city where people were being pushed to the brink.

In the Detroit of the 50s and 60s, race was a good indicator of class, and unemployment tended to hit the city's black residents hardest. This, coupled with racial segregation in housing and education, made 1967 Detroit the scene of the biggest race riot in US history and afterwards the white middle class thought nothing of leaving their black neighbours to their fate.

Throughout the 70s, 80s and 90s, the city continued to disintegrate as crime raged and people headed south as air conditioning opened up warmer climates with their non-unionised workforces. A shrinking population translated to a shrinking tax base in a city with high unemployment and heavy welfare participation. Whole factories were left to rust into 'brownfields', industrial ruins so thoroughly contaminated by decades of manufacturing processes running with virtually no environmental regulation that no sane, moneyed investor would touch them. Warehouses were boarded up and left to sit empty. The city didn't have enough money to demolish the decayed housing stock, so entire neighbourhoods became ghost towns.

At the 1950 census, Detroit counted 1.8 million people. Over half a century later in 2010, its population was just 700,000. Today, the plains on which Detroit was built have started to reclaim its neighbourhoods, with a third of Detroit having returned to prairie. Other neighbourhoods have been playgrounds for arsonists, and there was a time when every night a house went up in flames, making a funeral pyre out of another dead American Dream.

And all of this happened long before 2008, when the sub-prime mortgage crisis and the global financial crisis bore down upon world financial markets with all their fury. For Detroit, the falling car sales caused by the GFC pushed the Big Three over the edge and the day they officially filed for bankruptcy in 2009 was a particularly crappy day in a town where bad news is the norm. Today, even GM executives have their offices face Canada so they don't have to look out over their legacy that is downtown Detroit.

This is how Detroit, the mother of industrial blight, developed a global reputation for misery. How its name became international shorthand for failure. But it is not the whole story. Things may be bad, but Detroit is not dead yet. It still has Chrysler, GM and Ford, crippled though they may be. Detroit struggles on. All Elizabeth really had left was Holden.

Australia never had anything like Detroit, it just had a lot of little ones, like Elizabeth, like Norlane, like Broadmeadows. Some were in South Australia, more were in Victoria, which is why Melbourne is likely to be hit hardest when the industry goes. Dr John Spoehr's modelling from 2014 projected South Australia's job losses at 23,903 by the end of 2017, and Victoria's at 98,483. That work assumed the Australia dollar would fall back to US80 cents and investment in mining would drop off. It has since fallen to US72 cents at the time of writing and the Australian mining industry has been hurting as the prices of iron ore and thermal coal continue to floor.

Even then, Spoehr's figures were contentious. His modelling relied on multipliers to make a projection about the impact, and not every economist agreed. Those suspicious of multiplier projections tend to prefer the number cited in a Deloitte Access Economics report that optimistically put projected South Australian job losses at only 2000. This is a low-ball figure that only recognises the tip of the iceberg, the 1700 or so direct job losses from the closure of Holden itself. Those who cite it only see the Holden factory in isolation and never step back to look at the whole. Because of that they miss the web of little companies hanging off beneath.

And it is what lies under the surface that will make this worse than a couple of big-brand factories going under. The people hurt by this will be those living in the kind of places where local politicians positively spin the opening of the latest Hungry Jack's franchise as 'good for local jobs' because the official youth unemployment rate in the area is pushing 17 per cent or higher.

Which is why the death of the Australian car industry is a defining moment in Australian economic history. Those laid off from the factory line tomorrow will filter away and find work as security guards, or taxi drivers, or construction workers, but it is their kids who are fated to minimum wage and heart disease. Even those with an education have struggled to find work in South Australia and for years they've been rolling up their parchments, packing their bags and climbing aboard planes headed east or overseas for something better.

The South Australian state government, for its part, has been working hard to stay positive and trying to sell its vision for the 'New Economy'. Arts, tourism, food and wine is the future, they say. It's the 'food revolution'. But then these industries have never been known for their job security or the size of their pay cheque. Try raising a family on a bartender's wage. Or a federal arts grant.

Still, Elizabeth's leadership has been talking confidently about premium agriculture, food and wine for its future. What it sounds like is a lot of new industry based on low-pay, seasonal work with long periods of downtime, in a water-intensive business in a state with little water, at the very end of the Murray–Darling river system, in a drying climate. All it would take is one bad recession, or one long drought, for it all to be wiped away again.

So, want to know what's going to happen to places like Elizabeth when the factories go? You could look to Detroit.

You could look to Chicago or Cleveland or Flint or Lansing. You could even look to the Spanish city of Bilbao, where in the worst part of the 80s one in four people were put out of work as industry shrivelled up and which, with its one million people, is loosely comparable to the wider Adelaide metropolitan area. From these cities you can dig out the clues and hints at what a future without the factories looks like. But then Australia's Little Detroits have different stories, different histories and different people. There is no clear formula for what will unmake them and what will remake them. If there were, the people in charge wouldn't be running scared.

Chapter 24

THIS IS NOT A COMPLETE LIST

In April 2014, Arnott's biscuits cut 120 people from their Marleston site in Adelaide, South Australia. Aldinga Turkeys cut 79 jobs. ACI cut 60. Penrice, a soda ash company, closed, laying off 100 people. So too did The Cairn Hill Iron Ore, taking another 13 people with them. CARR Components was talking about laying off 70 people during its takeover by Precision. Pacific Brands moved 24 jobs to Queensland. SA Caroma Industries cut 76 people from their Norwood site. ABC Adelaide cut 37 people out of their operation.

In January 2015 Arrium cut 600 people from their operation in Coober Pedy and later in November another 305 people from its Whyalla steelworks. BHP cut another 90 jobs from Roxby Downs in January 2015, 140 more a few months later and another 380 after that. SANTOS cut 200 people from its Adelaide operation as part of a 565 person company reduction as well and another 1000 contract positions. The closure of Alinta's power stations cost 440 jobs. Federal funding cuts saw 400 social services workers out of a job. Fairfax cut 35 people from its regional papers after a round of restructuring. In July 2015, SA Pathology said it would cut 332 jobs over the next three years to make $42.2 million in savings. A plan to streamline the Department of Education was announced that would involve job cuts. Unibooks, a retailer of university text books and materials, closed down taking 100 people with it.

In January 2016, Oz Minerals sacked a reported 70 people from their operation, as they had at the start of 2015. In February 2016, Industrial Engineers and Springmakers cut 50 people because they couldn't compete with cheap imports. Dick Smith closed around the same time, putting at risk 2460 people nationwide. SMR Automotive cut 140 in March 2016 as a direct consequence of the end of the car industry.

In March Arrium's Whyalla Steelworkers went into administration ...

Chapter 25

GEETROIT

It's a Thursday afternoon in Grovedale Chicken and Fish in Geelong's south. The lunch rush has been and gone this day and it's just Mark Farnsworth behind the counter. For now the place is empty, making for a rare moment of quiet against the hum of the fridge, the white tiles and white walls of its interior.

Up on the wall is a framed aerial-view photo of Alcoa's Port Henry aluminium smelter. The smelter is dead now, just an empty metal shell that had operated for half a century until someone decided it wasn't needed anymore. The men and women who used to run it live all around this area, Mark says, and they come into his shop all the time.

Those who don't know Mark usually notice that photo, then they get talking about the state of things, ask him whether he worked at the smelter. He tells them he did.

They take a moment and tell him it was a gutsy move to spend his redundancy payout to buy the shop. Mark tells them it was fine; he bought himself a job with this place. Besides, he'd done the research. Food was a safe gamble.

Then Mark asks what they're doing with themselves.

It has been about 18 months since the closure, and the money from the payouts is starting to run out. Over the next six, around the time Ford is due to close for good, the 1000 people who used to work for Alcoa are going to show up in the official jobless numbers as they start to access the welfare system and other services. Right now, though, they show up in Mark's shop and that's when he gets the stories.

Some have got along just fine, he says, but others are struggling. From the people he talks to, he puts it at a 50–50 split. A lot of people who could get out have moved away, but others have found work locally, whether at Viva Energy, which used to be the Shell refinery and which by 2016 was making money again, or an hour away in Melbourne. Younger guys tend to go FIFO, a game older men and women with families try to stay away from because they've all heard the stories about divorce and suicide.

Then there are those who have stayed but are stuck in crappy jobs they hate. There's one regular who comes in, Mark says, who's selling Toyotas and Mitsubishis at a dealership in Geelong and hates every single minute. Other guys can only get part-time work or none at all. Some of them have sold their houses and have gone back to renting.

'It's scary, you know?' Mark says. 'Especially some of the Alcoa guys coming in now. They can't get work. They can't get anything. They've been trying and trying but there's nothing out there.'

As everyone likes to say around here, Geelong is a city making a change and change itself is not a bad thing. A long time ago it was the wool industry that made Geelong. Then one day that changed and it was cars and aluminium and steel that paid the bills. As of 2013, manufacturing accounted for 43 per cent of the region's economic output, with the rest being made up by services. That's when manufacturing started to slip faster than ever. Now room is being made for something else, the thinking goes.

Smart jobs, that's the future. So is agriculture and setting up the town to cater to the wealthy with its sun-drenched beaches and expensive gourmet restaurants. Clothing retailer Cotton On has been aggressively expanding its stores, adding jobs at its Geelong headquarters. Unemployment as of January 2016 had been the lowest in recent memory, falling below the regional average to 5.4 per cent, bouncing back from the slump when Alcoa closed its doors. From the city's centre, where Geelong looks and feels just like another Australian CBD, the future looks good.

Except the biggest cheerleaders for change are usually those with the most to gain and, at least in Geelong, things are still unfolding. Ford's engine works in Norlane is due to close down in October 2016 with the rest of the car industry to follow in 2017. About 18 months after those closures start, after the parts makers kick out the shoprats, the money will dry up and they'll be in exactly the same position as the guys from the smelter and the rolling mill.

In that way, Alcoa was just a dry run for the end of Ford. Alcoa's Geelong operations ran for 51 years across its sprawling industrial complex in Port Henry. The place kept 960 people employed and Mark says that for every person who worked there, there were at least three contractors. It was good money in a 24-hour operation.

Now the foundry is cold and the only thing left is the memory of what it once meant. Talking about the closure, everyone who worked at the place at the time says they had seen it coming for a while. Just like everyone else they had been watching the Australian dollar rise and the price of aluminium fall. There had been a review of company operations to work out if the place was economically viable and the agreement the company had struck 25 years ago for cheap power was due to expire. There had been bad news stories every other day and, for months, management at the company had been comparing the Port Henry smelter to other smelters Alcoa ran across the globe to get a feel for their odds.

Even so, the very idea that the smelter and its two rolling mills would actually close didn't seem possible. Even on the morning of 18 February 2014, there was a feeling it would go on, something would come along to save then. Then at 8am a meeting was held and Mark was among those who filed in, gathered around and together listened as the manager in charge told everyone they were done. The smelter was aging infrastructure, the company had decided, and it would be cheaper to go offshore and start fresh than it would be to try to save it.

Alcoa wasn't a place that ran on pretence and when the end came, management got right to the heart of it.

'We have shit days and we have not-so-shit days,' the manager said. 'Unfortunately, today is one of the first.'

As of July, 500 people lost their jobs when the final pot line was turned off at a cost to Alcoa of $49 million. In

December another 250 people went when the rolling mills closed, and just like that it was over.

Alcoa wasn't the only one downsizing at the time. The 300 people Qantas had doing maintenance at Avalon airport lost their jobs, and Shell was in the process of selling its refinery. Boral had cut 100 people in 2013 and Target let 260 go the same year. Geelong's mayor, Darryn Lyons, described it at the time as a 'tsunami' of job losses and called an emergency meeting to discuss the situation. Mark was just one of hundreds caught in the swell.

Before he signed on to do his 23 years with Alcoa, Mark was a musician. He used to play drums and sax, and he sang in a band. Teaching music helped him get by well enough until he had kids and needed a steady job, so he looked to Alcoa.

Just like the Holden factory, the Port Henry smelter had been a birthright. Mark's brother and father worked there – the latter for 27 years. Mark still remembers picking up his old man and driving him out to the refinery on the tip of the peninsula where the sheer scale of the place dwarfed even the bigger car factories and made him feel small. There were ten-tonne cranes and trucks, and machines 40, 50 feet high. They were fed by metal coils that stood to 1.8 metres in length and when unwound stretched 10 kilometres.

When Mark started out in the smelter in 1992 he was careful with his hands. The musician was scared of losing a finger in a place that was as hot as Hell and permanently smelled of sulphur. It was a genuine risk at Port Henry, an old smelter where they did things the old way. The pots ran at 950 degrees and the guys working them stood in between wearing heavy cotton shirts and pants, and thick gloves and masks to shield them from the heat. There was the occasional explosion and the odd injury. Every guy in the place knew they were taking a risk just stepping inside. Mostly, though, it was just hot, but for the money they were being paid they were all happy to be there.

Mark never had to worry about his hands. Seven years in, he spilled molten metal on his boot while he was crust-breaking at one of the pots. It was a process whereby a machine that works like a jackhammer is suspended by a crane over a pot of molten aluminium as it shoots down to break through the cooler surface. That day the pot had been overfilled and when Mark cracked the crust, a wave of liquid metal burst up, rippled out and spilled over the lip. The heat melted his boot and cooked his foot.

'There were worse than me,' he says, adding that Alcoa was good to him after the accident. Between skin grafts, he was off his feet for months and the company took care of him. They even did little things like regularly send someone around to mow his lawn. When he was up and getting around, they made him safety rep and put him through a university course studying occupational health and safety management. After that, he spent most of his time in the office.

The university qualification meant that when Mark lost his job at Alcoa, he wasn't overly worried. Towards the end, he says, there were guys crying in the lunchrooms. They were fighting with their wives, had no qualifications and no idea about what they were going to do. At least he had something to fall back on, he thought, until he started applying for jobs. It didn't take long, however, for him to work out he was wrong. He tried for 'everything OHS' from Inverleigh to Warrnambool and a couple of times he made it through to second-round interviews, but no further than that.

For a time, things looked bad enough that Mark thought about leaving, but he had two kids in their early 20s and a 14-year-old son still in school, so he wasn't really in a position to go anywhere. Packing up would have been an act of desperation. That's when he and his partner started looking at businesses. He did his research before finally settling on the chicken shop. Food was safe, he thought, and the former owner swore that when things were steady, he'd be working only about four days a week.

These days that promise seems like a joke. At Alcoa, Mark worked 12-hour shifts. Now he's 47 years old and working 13 hours a day, six days a week and on the seventh he is taking care of paperwork and seeing to the kids.

Mark's exhausted, he says, and the black under his eyes seems to confirm that.

His evenings are usually spent talking to his friends over the phone because it's the only time he gets to hear from them. Just the other day a friend told him he was 'getting on' and asked if he could keep it up. Mark shrugs. All he knows is that when he goes home, his hands are rough from constantly washing them in soap. The pedometer on his wrist says he's taken 14,000 steps just today. He's lost 16 kilos as well as his interest in food now that he spends every day watching chickens slowly rotate on a spit.

Asked whether the pay was better at Alcoa, Mark doesn't even hesitate. 'Shit yeah,' he says while working the grill. 'Better than what I'm making here. It was regular, too. You knew what you were getting. Here it's not like that at all.'

Mark doesn't pay himself a wage; the business pays for everything. It's a different scene from back when he and the others were on $100,000 a year with money to go out to restaurants or take a holiday to Sydney for a weekend. Those were good years. Losing the refinery meant losing something special.

'You used to walk into a place in an Alcoa jacket and people would know you, know you were making good money,' Mark says.

'You walk in now and they say, "Oh, you work in a chip shop?"'

Then there are the unexpected costs of doing business. Coke called earlier this week to ask how many bottles he wanted; that was $600 gone. The other day he found out there were nine keys to the shop in circulation and he only had two, so he brought in a locksmith. Then Mark was working so much his four-year relationship ended because there just wasn't enough time for her.

Which was tough. The couple had bought the business together. She was supposed to be the customer contact and he was supposed to work the grill so he didn't end up chewing people out when they behaved like jerks. When she left, it was all on him.

Mark's not bitter, though. It's not a bad job and at least he's working. He's made the transition. Every day he's meeting new people and he says he enjoys the 'challenges' the shop throws at him, though there's no denying things are pretty scary outside his front doors. Not even five minutes away, new developments are going up because housing prices in Melbourne are too high, but there isn't a decent paying job to be found within 45 minutes.

Which is why Mark's put up a notice on the front window of the shop advertising his 'Junior Employee Program', just like the one Alcoa used to run. He had the idea when he kept getting résumés from young people who couldn't find work because they lacked the experience. The program runs for four weeks at two shifts a week and at the end of it the successful applicant will get a certificate and reference to put on their résumé. They're paid according to the trainee award scheme and if they turn out to be a good employee, Mark says he may even keep them on.

It may not be much, in the scheme of things, but it's Mark's way of helping to fight back against something he had no part in making.

Chapter 26

THE WATERFALL EFFECT

IT'S NOT OFTEN THE ANGLESEA RIVER GETS TO TASTE THE SEA. The river runs from the Otway Ranges east of Winchelsea, and its water flows down, south by east towards Bass Strait. In its course it flows over buried coal seams, down past an open-cut coalmine and the power station that used to feed Alcoa's Port Henry smelter. From there it moves on slowly through wetlands before hitting the town at the end of the Great Ocean Road that shares its name.

When the weather is dry, the water makes its run for the coast, only it rarely makes it. Instead, sand from the beach crawls inside the river mouth and silts it up, making it possible to stand at the river's fingertip, at the very point where it reaches for the sea, only to be dragged back inland.

For years the river, and the power station up the way, had both been something of a flashpoint for the local community. The river is the main artery of the tourist town and some among its 2454 people have always looked to it with suspicion. Clean it up or close it down, they said, and in the end they got their wish, except they could not know just how much their river, as they knew it, depended on their power plant.

When a boardroom on one side of the world sneezes, the water level in a river on the other drops. Some might call this the butterfly effect applied to globalisation, but that lacks a certain feel for the chain of command. It's more like a waterfall. A boardroom in a tall tower somewhere in New York made the decision to close the Port Henry aluminium smelter. That decision dripped down and rippled out across the planet, where it trickled onto the heads of those running the multinational's Australian arm. From there the company put out a press release, and it started to rain on the workforce.

Once the news settled in, it didn't take long for that puddle to splash onto the power station along the river about 40 kilometres away. No more refinery meant there was no more need for the power station that had provided 40 per cent of Port Henry's power since 1969. The plant was old but well maintained, so Alcoa put it up for sale. The company didn't want to close it, but it had no plans to go into the power-generation business. The plant stayed on the market for about a year, and despite some interest a buyer could not be confirmed. In the end, Alcoa decided to turn off the power plant too.

What started as a trickle became a flood when that announcement was made and people realised that once the plant was turned off, the power station's pumps that kept water flowing into the river would be turned off too. This water helped balance the river's pH and kept the levels high when they naturally should have been low. It was a flow they depended on when every summer Anglesea's population surged with the tourists who made their way down the Great Ocean Road and stopped to sit by the river or enjoy their stretch of beach. And then there were the water pumps at the mine. No more power plant meant no one needed the coal from the mine next door. Because the mine was now redundant, there was no need to continue running the pumps keeping groundwater from slowly filling up the open-cut and turning it into an acidic swimming pool hostile to aquatic life.

That's how a drip from one side of the world can build into a tsunami. As far as closures go, the decision to close the power plant was relatively sudden. It all happened in the space of a year, more or less, and any plans that had been made about what to do should the plant one day close would have been based on a what-if hypothetical rather than a solid idea that it would actually happen in that person's working life.

Not that many in the town had been particularly sad to see the power station go. It had never been popular. It was an old, clunky plant that began operation four decades back and was supplied by the nearby coalmine at the bargain price of 29 cents a tonne. Alcoa kept the plant in good condition, but that didn't change the fact that the thing was built for an era when people did not know, or much care about, carbon-dioxide emissions, sulphur emissions and the health and environmental effects of burning 35 million tonnes of coal over a 36-year period. The plant was a big producer of sulphur-dioxide emissions, owing to the features of coal used in the process, and in the period from 2013 to 2014 it pumped out 43,000 tonnes of SO_2. The plant's size and output effectively made it one of the biggest emitters of the stuff in the country.

The locals first caught onto the idea that the plant might be dirty when the Anglesea Primary School was moved to a site beneath the power plant and some started asking urgent, probing questions. A group of parents succeeded in using Freedom of Information requests to get hold of documents, whereby they learned that the site was a serious emitter of sulphur dioxide. Concerns grew about what this meant for the health of the town's children attending the school and from those concerns the Surf Coast Air Action group was formed. This group began pushing for Alcoa to install $150 million 'scrubbers' in the plant's stacks, which would remove all the sulphur dioxide and any other heavy pollutants from the air, or to shut it down entirely.

Then there were the dead fish. Every now and then, the Anglesea River has a way of turning acid and killing the fish that live in its estuary. Since 2000, there have been several 'fish kills' in the river, and some in the community looked to the Alcoa operation as the root cause. And why not? The relationship between industry and the environment through history has been one of conqueror and conquered. Whenever industry drains a wetland or paves over pristine grassland, the rivers have run red and the soil is salted with arsenic.

Stories about industrial infrastructure polluting rivers are a dime a dozen. Flint, Michigan – another city that made and lost a good life on the back of General Motors – had a state of emergency declared in January 2016 when lead-contaminated water poisoned up to 12,000 of the city's children. The water it was drawing from the Flint River was so full of chlorides from road salts, it leached lead from the old pipes and became poisonous to drink in the time it took the water to run from the treatment plant to the tap.

The Cuyahoga River, which empties out into Lake Erie in Cleveland, another rust-belt city, was once called one of the most polluted rivers in America. It served as the intestinal tract for nearly every industrial process in the region. By the mid-60s no fish could survive in its water, and in 1952 the river burned, causing $1 million in damage. Then it burned again in 1969. The Cuyahoga has burned at least 13 times in its history.

Then there was the Dee River, a little closer to home. In 2013, the abandoned Mount Morgan gold mine in Queensland spilled acid and heavy metals into the Dee River after a flooding event. The chemicals turned the water a bright blue-green, killing fish and bird life downstream.

That's how Alcoa's plant up on the hill, with the white steam gently rising out of its stacks, made for a natural villain. The problem was, the people who thought that way were also probably wrong, according to Deakin University's Dr John Sherwood, who has studied the river and its geology. The real problem, he says, was a little more complex in that the river just happened to make it a particularly crappy place to be a fish. Nature is not always kind.

On its way to the coast, the river runs over buried, sulphur-rich coal seams and through marshland. When the water mixes with the coal underneath, it produces sulphuric acid. That's one source of acid. The other is the marshland. All it takes is a hot winter or a dry summer for the wetlands to grow thirsty and when they do, acid collects in the exposed earth at different points in the catchment. When the next rain comes, this acid is washed downstream, where it grows in concentration. At the bottom of the estuary right by the town is a layer of saltwater, which ordinarily gives fish a place to hide. When that water becomes stagnant because the river mouth has been closed for a long while, or heavy rain has washed that water out to sea, dead fish start floating to the surface.

The point is, the power plant was not a popular piece of infrastructure and on 10 August 2015 Anglesea's people marched in the hundreds calling for it to be shut down. Alcoa, for its part, did not want to bulldoze the plant. When the Port Henry closure was first announced in 2014, the company applied for a licence to sell electricity back into the grid from the Anglesea power station in the hope of making the operation more attractive to a buyer. It was a small plant in the scheme of things, but it was a piece of industrial infrastructure that had been well maintained and was connected to the grid. It made sense to put it to work and save 85 jobs. So with its newly acquired licence, the company put out a call for offers and it was rumoured that Exergen, a company specialising in clean coal, was front runner until it all fell through.

So on 22 August 2015 at 8.48pm, the plant powered down for the last time. That night those who had kept the place alive and running over four decades without a major incident gathered in the control room around the big red button that acted as an on–off switch for the boiler at its heart. The button was about 2 centimetres wide, and it used to be that if someone pushed it during daily operations, chaos would follow. So it was a sombre moment when the workforce watched plant supervisor Bryce Hutton push the button deliberately and with purpose that night to power down the station for the last time. The 85 people who relied on the place stayed on an extra week to help put the plant safely into mothballs ahead of its eventual demolition around 2020, and when they were done, they were out of a job.

Not everyone left, though. The company kept on three men at the lonely plant to help run the monitoring systems and keep the water pumps running temporarily. These were old hands who had been with the company for a very long time and knew every bolt in the operation. They were the kind of guys loyal to the company right to the bitter end, who kept coming to work in the shell of an old power plant as the wind whistled through it, and who refused to talk to a reporter even if they'd be out of a job in a few months' time anyway.

Their job was important. During its heyday, the plant drew groundwater from six separate bores. This water was used to cool the power station, and afterwards it was run through a treatment process to a standard set by the Environmental Protection Authority, so its pH could be carefully managed. Eventually, this was mixed with all the water piped from the bottom of the open-cut before being flushed back into the river.

Each day the power station pumped 4.5 mega litres into the Anglesea River. It was one of three water sources and the only one not dependent on rain. When the other tributaries, Salt Creek and Marshy Creek, stopped flowing through summer or a dry winter, the power station kept the Anglesea River alive.

About a month before the plant and its pumps were to be turned off for good, it dawned on the people of Anglesea that the water level in their river may fall without the power plant to help maintain it. It was a cutting issue in the small town at one end of the Great Ocean Road, which made its money off tourism dollars connected to the river and the nearby beach. As the concerns grew louder, the Victorian state government quickly stepped in, getting Alcoa to stick around and keep the pumps running until early 2016 so they had time to work out what exactly they were going to do.

But Alcoa wasn't going to stick around forever. Even if the company wanted to protect its reputation by taking care of its employees and rehabilitating the site, it was still a profit-driven multinational that wasn't going to be tied down just to maintain the water levels in the river of some no-name town at the end of the world in regional Australia. It also had a bigger problem to address in the work that needed to be done on the gaping hole in the ground it had spent the last 40 years digging just outside town.

For most of the locals, the fear was that the exposed coal seam in the open-cut might go up in flames the next time a bushfire raged, just like the open-cut at Morwell that fed the now-infamous Hazelwood power station. To head off the threat, and calm fears among the townspeople, the company promised to backfill the exposed coal at the mine site with a metre of soil. That might mitigate the fire hazard posed by an exposed coal seam, but it wouldn't do much for the possibility that the pit might be left to slowly fill with water until it became an acid lake.

Without the water pumps, groundwater would slowly seep into the pit, filling it until it reached the level of the water table. As this happened, the exposed coal would turn the water acidic, which in turn would mobilise heavy metals contained in the soil around it. Something similar happened to the Berkeley Pit in Butte, Montana, when the old open-cut copper mine closed in 1982 and was left to slowly fill at the rate of about 30 centimetres a year; in 1995 when a flock of 342 geese landed on the surface of the toxic lake, the pit swallowed them whole.

Not that the Anglesea pit would end up the same way. Different geology produces a different result but, even so, a slow-filling pool of acid creates its own problems. The closest homes to the mine are 500 metres away. Then there was the river. If heavy rain was to fill an acid lake in the mine, suddenly causing it to overflow, chances are the run-off would find its way into the river. From there it would wash downstream right into the estuary, and under the right conditions it would be lethal to anything caught in its way.

This, of course, is a problem that can be managed with enough time, forethought or money. It's possible to add chemicals such as lime into the lake as it fills. The United States does it, and so does Germany, though it usually means having to keep dumping chemicals into the lake over time. There are other approaches too, such as bioremediation, whereby organic matter is used to grow bacteria on the soon-to-be lakebed. This creates an aquatic community that will naturally balance the pH. For this to work, it means acting with speed from the moment the pit starts to fill and then trying to stay ahead of it.

At the time of writing, this has not happened at Anglesea. The government has opened up a tender process for solutions while the pumps are still flowing. Someone will eventually have to organise it all and then pay for it. Alcoa has set aside $55 million to cover the rehabilitation costs, but that money will only go so far and once the company is gone, it isn't coming back.

At least for now, it's still possible to walk the estuary bank and watch kids jump from bridges into the water. There are wives fishing with their husbands and fathers fishing with their young sons, who get bored and go play in the mangroves. The campground across the other side still fills up in summer and those people staying the night make tracks through the blocked river mouth over to the beach in the morning.

You can still see the power station up in the hills, even if the white plumes no longer rise from its stacks. It costs 30 bucks an hour to rent a canoe to see the sights. You can't paddle right up to the power station and the mine that used to feed it, but you can get pretty close. It takes an hour and a bit to make it up the estuary and back. The guys down at the boat sheds won't charge you any extra if it takes a little bit longer. They're pretty good like that. All they want is for you to experience their river.

Chapter 27

AUSTRALIAN RUST

A TIRED AUSTRALIAN FLAG HANGS FROM THE CORNER OF THE white, horizontal wood-slat house. Another building of the same breed has been painted purple-blue and its well-kept front yard is filled with garden kitsch. Down the way, a stained mattress lies out the front of a newer brick unit and the tall, gaunt occupant looks like he's fading as quickly as the black jumper he wears. A block over, there is a house with a boat parked out front. Another nearby lies vacant. Locals say it has been that way ever since they found its former owner dead on the floor.

This is Norlane in North Geelong, so named for Norman Lane, a World War II soldier who died working on the Thai–Burma railway after being taken prisoner-of-war the day Singapore fell to the Japanese. The neighbourhood that bears his name surrounds the point where the railway track from Melbourne runs into the factory where Ford Australia built its engines. The company has built cars, in one form or another, around these parts ever since it set up shop in 1925 as a distant, warm-climate outpost of Ford's Canadian arm.

In May 2013 the company announced it would close, after it lost $600 million over the previous half-decade. Now, the factory that began with prefabricated Model Ts will end with EcoLPi engines as of 7 October 2016, when Ford shuts it all down. Its Broadmeadows assembly line in North Melbourne will go too, effectively putting an end to almost 90 years of Australian production.

Where you find a doomed car factory, chances are it will be overlooking a sad children's playground. There are two bordering the old Tonsley Factory in South Australia and one that looks out over the Geelong Ford engine works that dominates the landscape out this way. The factory used to be even bigger back in the day, spread out over more land and, early on, the houses around it were built with wood from the packing crates in which the prefab cars were shipped. With time, and periodic downsizing, the plant has gradually withered and shrunk in size. Now with the rest of it packing up, Norlane gets a front-row seat as the production lines wind down and the foundries close and the machinery is ripped out to be taken away and auctioned off. Ford has a whole section of the company devoted to doing just that and, when they are done, nothing will be left but the rusting shell of an old factory as far as the eye can see. With no one to tend it, the weeds will grow, the roof will leak and the scrappers will work out a way in to strip whatever copper they can find from the walls. When they are done, it will be just another memory of what things used to be like and a good reminder of where they are headed.

Across the road from the main gate, there's an old man sitting on his front verandah. It's an image straight out of the American Midwest. The neat front yard, the white house with the wooden cladding that looks like all the others, the wooden fence and the white coffee cup resting on a wooden beam. The old man is dressed neatly, wearing a baseball cap and checked shirt with an old AM/FM radio sitting on his lap that he turns down when the stranger walks up his driveway. He doesn't say anything, at first. Just waits for the stranger to state their business.

He would have been a big man once. The kind who feared no one. These days his red walking frame stays within arm's reach and he won't give his name to a reporter. He's afraid it'll come back to haunt him in the form of a brick through the window. For the same reason he doesn't want his photo taken. Instead, he gives over his phone number and says if anyone doubts he exists, they can call him and he'll set them straight.

He and his wife have lived in this house for over 50 years, since 1962, back when it was an old Housing Commission home. All the houses around here were Housing Commission in those days. Still are, mostly. The couple were renting then, and they had nothing. Before the house they lived in a tiny garage somewhere near Melbourne with no money and two young children. The dole paid four pounds, ten shillings and rent was exactly four pounds.

So when they got this place, they stuck around. The old man was a boilermaker by trade and first found himself a job at the Ford engine plant, working in the foundry. He didn't last long, only about four months, because he hated every minute of it. It was the wrong kind of work for a man used to the outdoors, the kind of work that didn't change much going on up through to the 80s and into the new millennium. Smelters are strange places for that very reason. Outside it may be 42 degrees in the shade, but inside the forge it will be 52. The molten metal would be heated to 1400 degrees and there's something about the heat and the dust, the heavy lifting and the long hours that finds its way under a man's skin and into his bones. In no time at all, a soft 18-year-old who never held a job could be forged into a grizzled lump of muscle. The men who worked in these places were rough and they were brawlers, they spoke plainly and were not to be screwed with. If a guy wasn't crazy going in, he'd be crazy coming out.

The old man didn't mind the heavy lifting during his four months at the Ford plant, but he sure as hell wasn't going to spend his life in the heat with a roof over his head. Fresh air and open sky were what he wanted and he found just that at the old refinery, back when it was still owned by Shell.

Even then he couldn't escape the factory. Under a star-filled sky, he and his wife would lie in their bed and fall asleep to the constant, repetitive clang of machinery. Sometimes the factory would give off the smell of burning Bakelite, and the old man is still bitter about a time back in the 60s when he says Ford cheaped-out on capture bags in one of the stacks. Iron oxide drifted up with the hot steam and downwind to dust his home and car. He tells of a meeting with all the 'relevant authorities' from the EPA through to the mayor, and the way they treated him like maybe he was mistaken, like maybe he drove through a cloud of dust on the way home one night. That could explain the dust on the car, he told the doubters, but it didn't explain the red dust on the house.

Despite it all, he and his wife stayed. Their place was as good as any and the job at the Shell refinery paid well. They ended up taking a mortgage to buy the house, despite the noise, and there they raised three children.

Those were different days, the old man says. When he was 15, he and his family followed their father out from Holland. There was talk the Russians were going to march on Europe and his father had come to the end of the world first to pave the way. The old man says he landed on the Port Melbourne docks 'with a suitcase and fuck-all else'.

'There was work everywhere,' he says about his first decade in Australia. 'You finished at one place one day and started somewhere else the next. You could walk into Fords on a Monday and that was it.'

His father, he says, worked just down the road at International Harvester, which made farm equipment including tractors and trucks. It had set up in 1938 across 45 acres of land down the road from the Ford plant so it could be close to the supply chain and the Port of Geelong. When World War II kicked off, its factory built P-40E Kittyhawk fighters and British-designed Fairey Battle light bombers. Rumour has it one of the old planes lies buried somewhere beneath the old factory site. When the dust kicked up by the war settled, it was business as usual and the factory amped up its operation until drought and recession took root during the 60s and Australian farmers could not afford to buy the machines it was building. By 1982, they were shutting the place down.

'They bulldozed it and put in a woodchip factory,' the old man says. There is disgust in his voice. He hates the woodchip factory for the noise it makes, but also for what it represents.

For now the neighbourhood is a place where people still mow their lawns and garden gnomes watch the streets. There is a cluster of shops nearby where people sip flat whites on white plastic deck chairs under the sun. It's nothing fancy, but it's enough.

But these days things aren't looking so hot for the old man, or the neighbourhood, when the plant goes. He's had a couple of strokes and during the last one he fell, right there on the front step, and broke his hip. Now he has to move with a walker. His three kids have grown up and moved away, which he says is probably a good thing, because all the factories have gone the way of International Harvester. Once there was a company down the way that used to make windows for Ford, he says. Then, when they lost the contract, they went to 'Malaysia or China or Thailand'. Over the past few years, he has watched sections of the Ford plant be ripped down and another Bunnings rise in its place.

Union guys such as Tony Anderson of the AMWU say manufacturing more broadly contributes $10 billion to the local economy. Losing any chunk of it would be a big hit to neighbourhoods like Norlane, says Anderson, who started in 1983 in Ford's casting plant making engine blocks and crank shafts. Since the closures were announced, he has been the union's point man in Victoria, helping to manage the closure.

'The car industry, they're shitty jobs,' Tony says. 'But through the car industry, we've managed to get trained. These are skills that people would never get without the car industry and it assisted in reading and writing and gave them a decent life.

'We've got people in there that, when they finish at Ford, employers will look at them and not even give them a second chance.'

It's a point echoed by the old man. Even if the end of the plant means a good night's sleep, there isn't much left around here these days and unemployment is running high. The rest of Geelong may be getting along fine, but one set of figures as of November 2015 had the unemployment rate pushing 21.7 per cent in Norlane. The factory jobs seem to be going one by one and all that's left are angry young men with a lot of ideas about the way the world works and no clue how or why things got this way.

People tend to take out their frustration on the houses. The little wooden houses on their quarter-acre blocks that make up the neighbourhood here were never good buildings, but they were good homes. Good enough to raise a family. Good enough to get by in. These days if a property developer doesn't want to bulldoze the plot to put in two, three, maybe four brick units, the empty homes have a way of burning down.

'They take a match to them,' the old man says. He's talking about a time in 2006 when bored teenage girls burned down three empty houses for kicks and nearly killed a mother and her child the third time round. It's something that happens every so often and the last serious string of arson attacks happened in December 2015 when two churches in the area burned.

That's the way of things out here, he says, though it hasn't always been so. Once there was work enough for everybody.

'You know, money's not everything,' the old man says. 'But it helps.'

Chapter 28

DARRYN AND ME

THE MAYOR OF GEELONG DIDN'T HAVE TIME FOR AN INTERVIEW. It had been about two months since the first request. Christmas had come and gone, and just when the engine revved on a New Year and the mayor's people were finally answering their phones, they said the mother of Darryn Lyons's fiancée, ex-model Elissa Friday, had passed away from a brain tumour and he was absent without leave to be with 'the lady mayoress'.

'It's hit Mr Mayor hard,' his offsider said.

At the end of last year Mayor Darryn Lyons was giving interviews about how he had become a recluse in the seven months since his fiancée left to be with her mother. His party-boy lifestyle was a thing of the past, he said, and though he'd often talked about running for federal politics, he had not even made a decision about whether to run for mayor a second time. Until then, he'd always said it was a no-brainer, always hinted that stepping up to federal politics was guaranteed. Now the tone had changed. Before he made any decision, he'd have to weigh up the feelings of his fiancée, whom he made a point of saying had his deepest respect.

It was an unusual interview for Darryn Lyons, whose default setting is maximum volume. So far he has lived his life as the Tory Sid Vicious with his coloured mohawks and fake abs and his ability to make people mad just by existing. Only a month before he had posed for a photo with patrons at a beer festival in October in a T-shirt showing Madonna hitch-hiking naked accompanied by a Photoshopped caption that read: 'Gas, grass or ass, no one rides for free'.

The morning breakfast shows could never resist a little bit of Darryn at the best of times, so they ran the photos, asking their viewers whether the T-shirt was offensive. It made news around the country and Darryn Lyons did his best to apologise for it, calling it a slip-up and saying he regretted it. The incident even attracted a stinging editorial in *The Guardian*, the thrust of which was that the mayor of Geelong, the man who 221,500 people had chosen to run the city as its manufacturing base shut down should, to paraphrase the sentiment, focus on doing his goddamn job.

It had started with Alcoa. Then Boral. Then Target. Then Qantas. Eventually it would be Ford and whoever else. It totalled well over 1500 direct job losses, a short, sharp spike for early February 2014 that the newly minted mayor called a 'tsunami'. All had been announced within a few months of his election and prompted an emergency meeting of all local MPs to work out what they were going to do.

By the end of the month, the rising sense of alarm had given way to a steely-eyed resolve. Geelong was a city in transition, came the message from the mayor's office. Just a city undergoing a change from the old to the new. Geelong has done it before with the sheep industry, and it would do so again, though this time with smart jobs and health and tourism. In essence, it was the same message being spread by Glenn Docherty, the mayor of Elizabeth, though with somewhat less force of personality and none of the social-media presence. It was that same message the mayor of Geelong brought with him when he spoke to the *Financial Review* for a long feature on the city's transition that opened with Darryn Lyons telling the workers at Ford who wanted to be retrained on company time to 'get off their bloody arse':

> You've got to get off your bloody arse, and you've got to go out, and you've got to find it, and you've got to do it yourself. Stop the dependence on society, stop blaming governments and officials. There is work out there, it might be a bit grubby. I've been there and done it myself. I grew up doing it. You know, at the end of the day, stop this whingeing, whining and moaning for pay rises here and pay rises there. The fact of the matter is, sometimes you've got to go back to go forward.

It was not an unfamiliar feeling for Darryn Lyons, who forged a legend as a self-made blue-collar aristocrat. His ghosted autobiography tells the story of the tireless, sleepless, high-energy, workaholic, working-class kid from the colonies who made it in the Old Country, where he lived the high life.

The flesh-and-blood Darryn Lyons was the son of a mild-mannered architect who moved to Leopold, a nice middle-class suburb south of Geelong. Before he dropped out of school, he was dux. When he dropped out, it was because he landed a cadetship as a photographer at the local paper. The rest of the story unfolded when Darryn moved to London in his 20s with $500 in his pocket. A chance meeting with Rupert Murdoch in the lift on the way into his interview landed him his first job on day one. Darryn only slept four or five hours a night in those days, his autobiography claims, and the character presented is one of a simple lad who out of sheer dumb enthusiasm made a career for himself hanging out with celebrities and sports stars, covering the fall of Ceauşescu in Romania and the Bosnian civil war, and eventually building himself a business empire through the photo agency he established in 1993.

As a young photographer, he spotted the rise of the paparazzi early on and cashed in with Big Photos. His photo agency gave him a lifestyle that would eventually kill his first marriage, see him 'lost in a white cloud of my own creation' and build him a $58 million personal fortune, including a property portfolio with holdings in the United Kingdom, New York, Barbados, Dubai and Australia. It was also a lifestyle that eventually broke him and by the time the global financial crisis hit in 2008, he lost heart and watched his agency burn. Darryn Lyons told the *Sydney Morning Herald* that by the time the agency crashed into the ground in 2012, he had resigned and put a CEO in charge. When it went into liquidation in 2013, owing photographers $125,000, he promised he had nothing to do with it.

His agency gone, Darryn Lyons was getting older and his thoughts turned to matters of legacy. So Mr Paparazzi, the British reality TV star, Geelong's wayward son, came back home from the 26-year grand tour abroad. He moved into a big house looking over Corio Bay, decorated unapologetically in the style of new money with lion statues by the front gate, a bust of himself with a camera on the front step, Rod Stewart's Lamborghini in his garage and a private art collection. The Australian dream made flesh.

Which also goes some of the way to explaining why Darryn Lyons quickly became 'fed up' with talking about Alcoa and Ford, as he told his interviewer. It had been a month since the closures were announced, but those were the companies of the past, he said. The high-tech future was on its way in the form of advanced manufacturing of the kind embodied by the much-talked-about Carbon Revolution, a company that makes carbon-fibre wheels it sells to sports car manufacturers overseas. There were the CSIRO research facilities, and retail jobs coming in from Cotton On's head office, which paid just as well. Geelong, it was written, was making all the right moves in all the right places. Healthcare and social assistance were growth sectors; advanced manufacturing was employing people laid off from Ford and Alcoa who, 'once trained', the profile's author emphasised, made for 'great process workers'. Geelong was changing, the numbers showed – what was there to complain about?

By August 2014, Geelong seemed to be in a bad place. To end years of deadlock, the state government had taken control of large development projects under advisement from the Geelong Authority, a newly created advisory body made up of local business leaders. Geelong's unemployment rate was beginning to spike at just above 9 per cent, the bulk of the unemployed were women, and Darryn Lyons's role as mayor seemed to have been stripped back to a sales position with a $170,000 annual salary.

Which seemed to be fine by Darryn Lyons, the master communicator whose working life in the Fleet Street tabloids had trained him in the art of accessibility and volume. Make it clear, make it loud and people will listen was the recipe and it worked, every single time. All of it – the hair, the clothes and the bravado – made for an elaborate misdirection, a cunning bait-and-switch because while everyone else was busy weighing up the right or wrong of it, Darryn Lyons was going for the jugular.

Which, in a nutshell, was the playbook by which Darryn Lyons took office when he was sworn in on 26 November 2013 after final preferences were counted. He was a man who was never supposed to be mayor. He claimed to be running as a joke candidate. Whether he was serious from the start, or he grew serious along the way, doesn't matter, because the moment he put on those mayoral robes for the first time was an event that cast a hushed silence over the sombre old guard of the local Geelong business elite.

Their man, Keith Fagg, the 94th mayor of Geelong, started the whole mess when he announced his sudden retirement from office. It was an open secret that Geelong's town hall is a nest of vipers, one made official in a report handed down by Susan Halliday, former head of the Australian Human Rights Commission in October 2015. In that report, she identified an ongoing culture of bullying in the administration. Keith Fagg, a devout Christian who never touched the bottle, had been lowered into the pit by the business establishment and couldn't hack the stress.

With his resignation for 'health issues', Fagg triggered a mayoral race at a sensitive time. A state election was on its way and what then Premier Denis Napthine needed in Geelong was someone appropriate. A safe, quiet pair of hands. Someone he could depend on.

The catch was, the city council elections had been recently opened up to popular vote. This new model introduced a presidential-style election system for the mayor's office and had been billed as a democratising effort. Direct voting would bring a sense of dynamism to the race and guarantee that the winner was the best candidate for the job. Not only that, but with the backing of the people, the president–mayor could eventually become the focal point for all business and political life of the city, a unifying figure, a one-stop shop for business and politics whose decisions could be reviewed later on by the other councillors.

In effect, getting elected as mayor meant having to campaign across an area the size of two federal electorates, Corio and Corangamite. Anyone who wanted to make a serious run for the job had to be able to pay to make sure people knew who they were. A ballpark figure for that kind of effort is estimated at somewhere around $250,000, although those who ran a candidate in that first election have never gone on record to say exactly how much they spent and those who have talked about it like to play down the figure. Realistically, the only people who had that kind of money were the city's business community and their public face, Frank Costa, a local businessman and president of the Geelong Football Club whose own story began as a child of humble Sicilian immigrants selling papers until he eventually built a business empire out of fruits and vegetables.

Keith Fagg had let Costa down, so what Costa needed was someone else to take over on short notice. Frank Costa ended up finding what he was looking for in the recycled figure of Keith Jarvis, a former mayor from back in the 90s best known for a failed bid to bring a Guggenheim Museum to Geelong. Keith Jarvis was one of the old boys, it was understood. A team player. Someone who could be trusted to do the right thing at the right moment and never make too much noise.

There were sixteen candidates in the race but only two that mattered: Darryn Lyons and Keith Jarvis. To ensure the voting public of Geelong made the right decision, the business community took out full-page attack ads in the local paper, warning people not to vote for Darryn Lyons. Frank Costa even went so far as to suggest in an interview with *The Age* that should anyone other than a Liberal win, the state government might wipe the slate clean by sacking the council and appointing an administrator.

What they ended up with was the surreal form of Darryn Lyons, by 58,000 votes, delivered in part by a social-media presence consisting of 717,000 Twitter followers, T-shirts, trailers, nonstop public appearances and a few carefully timed self-deprecating jokes made to local reporters about his surgically enhanced abs. The man was a philistine, but he was Geelong's philistine, one who on some level cared deeply about the city. With a little push from Robert Doyle, the mayor of Melbourne and the former leader of the Victorian state Liberal Party who first met Darryn Lyons in 2002, the man who had once ruled Big Pictures from a red velvet throne with his initials carved on it now ruled Geelong. Old-money Geelong had no choice but to work with new-money Geelong if it wanted to stay relevant, and for a time it worked out. Even Frank Costa was pleased by the attention the city was getting.

It didn't last. During the election Darryn Lyons always said he couldn't be managed, and in office he kept his word. He had always traded on being just a little too far beyond anyone's control but just endearing enough to make it excusable. True to character, that's how he operated as mayor.

It started with the commercial depicting the rest of Geelong as zombies wedded to their manufacturing past and he, Darryn Lyons, as a Gandalf on horseback, washing the city clean with light. There was the billboard he put up on the highway into town showing his face and personal slogan, which he said was good advertising but others thought of as the birth of an imitation North Korean personality cult.

Then there was the new mayor's vision to upgrade the Yarra Street Pier in order to open up Geelong to international cruise ships. At first it was welcomed as a good idea, almost visionary, until Frank Costa started talking publicly about how his family owned the wooden Cunningham Pier and how it would be great if the council took it off his hands. From then on, The Mayor and the Big End of Town were opposed and no one wanted to get in the middle.

The Pier deadlocked and other projects ground to a halt for lack of investment, such as the Sustainable Farms Project, a massive greenhouse vegetable garden supposed to have been built over six years at Avalon Airport. At Christmas

2014 the council spent over $1 million on a floating steel and LED Christmas tree. The particulars of the tree were confidential, said the council, and they weren't at liberty to discuss something so sensitive, but they insisted it had attracted 250,000 visitors to the city.

In the meantime, Geelong was spinning its wheels. The city was in debt, councillors had been talking about tough budgets, and the local Meals on Wheels had its funding cut. The only relief came when unemployment figures across the city of Geelong dropped back to 3.6 per cent as 2015 closed. The optimistic put the August 2014 spike down as a one-off, but the realistic were saying it was an early tremor of what was to come when all those who lost their jobs at Alcoa started turning up in the official numbers.

As a final blow, a Commission of Inquiry had been established following Susan Halliday's report, which was about to go over Geelong Town Hall in detail. Just when Geelong's populist mayor needed friends, it seemed he was running out.

As long as Tony Abbott and Denis Napthine had been around, Darryn Lyons had marked himself as their man in Geelong by freezing out anyone seen as too friendly to Labor. Which wasn't a problem while the Coalition was ascendant across the country, but once a backlash against Liberal Government policy claimed both leaders and Labor once again began to assert itself, Labor neither forgave nor forgot. When the state Liberal Party lost the election, its central figures had little love for the colourful, upstart mayor in the east judging by Denis Napthine's tone, and Darryn Lyons, the man who described himself as Tory to his core, let his Liberal Party membership lapse.

At the same time the mayor's key staff, executive officer and former Liberal MP Alister Paterson and administrative officer Wendy Hatton, quietly moved to the second floor of the building. They had only just settled into their new ground-floor offices outside the mayor's door, which had been freshly refurbished at a cost of $150,000. When a copy of the Independent Commission's report was later leaked, it branded Darryn a bully who had tried to run the Geelong City Council as if it were a Fleet Street newsroom and in doing so created a 'climate of fear and anxiety' that had both key staffers not wanting to be physically near their mayor.

To top it off, the mayor was giving interviews saying he had become a recluse. Right when the city needed leadership, its mayor was AWOL and alone. By April 2016, Local Government Services Minister Natalie Hutchins had introduced a bill to sack Mayor Darryn Lyons along with the rest of the council, and replace them with an unelected administrator until 2020.

'I'm the first to admit that my razzamatazz and in-your-face style has not been to everyone's liking and I've stepped on a few toes, and even grumbled and yelled quite a bit in getting things done for my city,' Lyons said when he appeared on the television show *Today* the morning after, when he was torn apart by host Karl Stefanovic.

'But I've suffered the frustrations of any leader who wants to change the world overnight ... who gets impatient with those who haven't been able to keep up with the pace.'

A young man who once met the mayor at a Lyons family function told how Darryn Lyons took a shine to him. How when the young man mentioned in passing that he'd once imagined a career in the film industry, the mayor spent the next 30 intense minutes talking about how he was going to leverage his connections to help him out. He was serious, he said, but the young man never really believed him, and Darryn Lyons never followed through, though he certainly left an impression. It's the same thing everyone else says about Darryn Lyons: he cared when others didn't. That meant something, but caring alone was never going to be enough.

Chapter 29

RISEN

UNION TROUBLE KILLED THE HUYCK.WANGNER FACTORY IN Breakwater just south of Geelong. The year was 2008, around August when things start getting cold. The GFC was just heating up, and it was that time of year when the company had to negotiate a new Enterprise Bargaining Agreement with its workforce. The union representing the workers in the negotiations thought it could hold out for more money, but when company management asked their American bosses, they said hell no.

So the union called a strike, complete with a picket line and fire in a barrel around which men gathered to warm themselves. The Americans didn't budge and the dispute dragged on as the bosses a continent away grew furious. The Geelong Huyck.Wangner factory made huge sheets of felt used in the paper-making process, and orders coming in from Asia meant serious money. The company couldn't afford the downtime and if their lazy, good-for-nothing Australian workforce didn't get back to work soon, they said, they'd close the whole goddamn place down.

The union didn't believe them for a minute and, in doing so, completely overplayed its hand. In November 2008, the Americans told everyone the factory would stay open until 9 March and no further.

Scott Anderson, 39, was on holiday when he and his wife found out they no longer had a job. Both worked in the factory and it was where they'd met. That weekend they were in Port Fairy for the wedding of a friend, and Scott was in a pub when he received a text from a guy back at the plant saying something was up.

Then the news came on and Scott had the bartender turn up the volume. Scott listened as the reporter announced the factory would close next year. The bartender poured Scott another one on the house.

Not long after, an American executive arrived to tell the factory's management how it would all go. He put up a Gantt chart outlining what should happen as the company wound down to its inevitable close. A week later he flew away, leaving the details up to the locals like Richard Koris, the project manager at the factory. In those days it employed 210 people, 30 of whom were office staff. Once the line workers were laid off and the doors locked, the office became nothing more than an inbound call centre taking orders for the Asian market.

After that it was Richard's job to work out how they were going to gut the factory. The machines that wove the felts had to be dismantled and sold to whomever would take them. Anything else not nailed down could be flogged off as soon as possible. In no time at all, they sold the trolleys and the supporting infrastructure and all the other secondary equipment. Then they had some Chinese buyers swing by to look at the machines, but what they didn't realise is that the Chinese don't like to buy second hand. They might have had deep pockets, but they weren't just going to throw money away. They wanted new, right out of the box. It was almost a non-negotiable requirement. And even if they were willing to compromise on that point, they wanted to see the machines in action so they knew exactly what they were getting for their money. Except, all the machines had been turned off when the last of the line workers walked out the gate. Then the quote came in outlining how much it would cost to take apart the machines, box them up and ship everything to China. Richard puts the figure at somewhere in the region of $7 million.

Richard tried to talk the American bosses out of closing the factory. The accountant had crunched the numbers and put together a business plan for how, with a little money and elbow grease, they could reopen the factory and make it globally competitive. He made a presentation to those American bosses where he outlined the plan, but they didn't care. The factory was dead and it was staying dead. Nothing anyone could say would change their minds.

It took two months before the Americans realised they had made a terrible mistake. The decision to close down the factory was taken on the assumption that South America and Europe could pick up the demand from Asia. But a good run on a single felt only lasts up to 50 days and orders were coming in from everywhere. South America and

Europe had enough orders to soak up their capacity and anything going to Asia was being supplied from the tail end of their run. By May, lead times on orders had blown out to 46 weeks and the company couldn't keep up.

Out of nowhere Richard had a call telling him to reboot the factory. The company needed another six months, they said, then that was it. Get it done. So Richard started putting in calls to the old hands to see if they would come back. To sweeten the pot, he offered them a Christmas bonus if the plant did end up closing again at the end of the six months, and he ended up finding 52 out of 210 people willing to return to work. Almost half of those who did had not worked since the closure.

* * *

When the Andersons were laid off from the factory, they used their payouts to pay down their debt. The lay-offs didn't bother Scott's wife much. They had just started a family and she had been on maternity leave when it happened. Odds were she wasn't going back to work anyway and though she found something low key for a while after the kids were born, juggling work and family ended up being just too hard.

So it was up to Scott to keep the money coming in and the payout didn't last long. It never does. To an outsider, the money a factory worker gets when it all winds down seems like a lot, but the time between finishing up at a dead plant and finding a new way to keep the lights on goes by quicker than they know.

To keep things going, Scott found a job in a factory making emergency flares. Essentially, he was mixing

15 kilos' worth of explosives for $16 an hour. It was crappy pay and he never stopped looking for the next thing. Before long he saw that the prisons were hiring and he secured himself a new gig working as a guard in the high-security section of Barwon Prison just outside Lara, keeping men like Victorian gangland personality Carl Williams in check. The job was '99 per cent boredom and 1 per cent chaos' and it came with seven weeks of training and the constant threat of physical violence. Prison work was 24 hours a day, seven days a week, but for 18 months it paid the bills. The most exciting thing that happened in Scott's time there was the day Carl Williams was beaten to death by a fellow inmate.

Around that time, Huycks was on the hunt for people to come back in. Scott had a call from the company but all they could offer was six months and a maybe, so he turned them down. Not long after, he saw the job for Alcoa in the paper. He knew the company paid well and it was good work where they made things, so Scott put in an application, but was knocked back when the company decided not to put people on. It was the GFC, so he couldn't blame them. Then Alcoa changed its mind and asked him to come in. So Scott quit the prison and went to work in the finishing area of Alcoa's rolling mills. It smelled, it was dirty and it was hot, but it paid.

Huycks started back up around June 2010. When Richard Koris reopened the place, he surveyed the 52 returned employees to find out where they had been since they lost their jobs the year before. Of those first 52, he says 49 per cent had not worked since they had been let go, 29 per cent had part-time work they were unhappy with, and only 10 per cent had found full-time work again.

Five months later, the Americans decided they liked what they were seeing from the factory. Both management and the workforce held a grudge against the union, and while some workers kept up their membership, the unions hadn't moved back into the shop. Quality was high, production was up and all of Asia was lining up to buy felts from the factory. So the suits gave it another 18 months. That deadline came and went and by 2013, exports had hit $60 million. Things were going so well, the company set aside $5 million to upgrade the machinery and hire 20 new staff. The local paper reported it as a rare good-news story for a manufacturing town where everyone was saying, even then, industry was on its way out.

What they didn't mention was the shiny new factory the company was building somewhere in China after a previous effort to build a plant in Vietnam had fallen flat.

* * *

Around the time Huyck.Wangner was getting back on its feet, Alcoa started to look wobbly, but Scott had no intention of leaving. The money was good, so were the people, and there was zero chance of getting attacked by anyone like at the prison. Then 2014 came around and the night before the fateful day when Alcoa said it would close its doors, the Andersons were driving home from another holiday. Scott's supervisor called to let him know it was over; he didn't want Scott to first read about it in the newspaper tomorrow. Scott and his wife looked at each other.

So he had about ten months to find something else when he remembered Huyck.Wangner had been looking for people. He got in touch with a friend working there, and before long he had an offer to work nightshift, keeping the two departments running smoothly because of his experience with Alcoa. Scott said yes but asked if they would wait until January so he could get his redundancy payout. Management weren't happy about it and some of the higher-ups asked whether it was really worth it.

In the end they waited, which is how Scott sidestepped the collapse of Alcoa. Like the others, he came home to the factory where things were looking good. Orders were steady and the work was stable. The people from Huycks were back together.

Then in early 2016, work on the Chinese factory finished and its brand-new machinery started to weave felt and rumours in Geelong. People started doing the maths on the new factory and it didn't take long to recognise the threat and start asking questions.

'Shit,' the conversations went, 'this new factory is bad news.'

'I just tell the guys to keep turning up every day until we get told different,' Scott says. 'All we can do is keep making felt, and if they decide to shut us, they decide to shut us. Nothing we can say is going to stop that.

'Once things start happening, we'll be the last to know.'

That might be truth, but it doesn't stop the questions. Right now, it's six guys to a machine in China; Geelong operates at a ratio of two to one. How long till China catches up? The Geelong factory is 50 years old next year. Some of its machines still have muscle, but others are coming to the end of their run. One of two departments has already been dealing with a slump. So, how long have they got? Can the plant stay open?

'My mind says yes,' Richard breathes down the phone when asked the question. 'But my gut, being an accountant, says no. I can't see it happening. We have infrastructure problems. We're old. I mean, it's raining right now. We've got roofing problems. We can't replace the roof because it's asbestos. We can't get on it because no one will touch it. If the rain comes through ...'

In the background there is a crack. A freak storm at the end of another warm January is hitting Geelong. It came out of nowhere, and its thunder is loud enough to be heard a world away. It has taken the office staff by surprise too. In the background there is a deep, guttural sound of awe.

'When we left, we had $2 million worth of parts, not materials, and costs just from running it that we were spending a year in Geelong alone,' Richard goes on. 'And we maintained that we did everything we could using Geelong labour. Suddenly it was $2 million that disappeared off the face of Geelong. All the little companies couldn't believe their luck when we restarted.'

The rain is coming down hard now. You can hear it.

'And you know, most of our people, we've trained them up. But, and not to be offensive, more of them are from a different socio-economic level, they need manufacturing to exist. A lot of the people didn't want to go to school. Or they dropped out of school. So you've still got that problem in Geelong.

'Health and aged care is supposed to be the future here. Maybe Geelong will become a retirement village or a place for health, but I can't see it working for every one of these people here. They want to work, they want to build, I can't see them saying, "I'll just go into the health industry and become a carer." It's not as if people go, "Oh, I'll go to uni to get a degree."

'Even now, people – we've got their sons coming up to try and get work here.'

Richard says goodbye, but the rain doesn't stop when he puts down the phone. In the space of a few hours, a month's worth of rain, 42.4 millimetres, falls on Geelong. It is a 'once-in-50-years event', the weather bureau calls it, and the rain keeps pouring down until it comes through the old asbestos roof above the office in the 50-year-old factory. The thing just gives way and by close of business two inches of water has pooled on the office floor. All anyone can do is cut the power to keep the server and the computers and the machines alive while they wait for tomorrow to work out the cost.

Chapter 30

BOATS FOR VOTES

Leon White started 2016 with two funerals and no job.

Sitting in his living room at his home in North Sunshine, Leon is watching a daytime news segment on bushfires as the air conditioner hums to keep back the heat. He is a boilermaker by trade, and he looks the picture of a man who has spent his life working with metal. The 43-year-old is a big guy, tattoo sleeves up both arms, who speaks tersely with a voice textured like gravel.

The living room and kitchen are filled with porcelain knick-knacks, the work of Leon's girlfriend Julie. The pair have been together 11 years. She's not here at the moment, she's at work organising the next Variety Bash for the children's charity. Every year she does it, spending months doing reconnaissance, carefully plotting the route the car run will take as it moves around the country. The couple don't have kids, but they have a dog, 'the fur baby', Leon jokes. Between Julie's work for the charity and Leon's job with BAE at the Williamstown shipyard, they have been able to buy the house they're living in and make a place for themselves in a world that is rapidly changing.

The night before New Year's Eve, Julie's sister's partner died. He'd been sick for a while, Leon says. The doctors had told them it was laryngitis and they were running tests. Then something went wrong, he didn't feel good and Julie's sister had to drive him to the hospital. On the way there, he started to bleed from his mouth and slumped over in his seat. At the hospital they gave him four blood transfusions and had him on the operating table to find out where he was bleeding, but couldn't find it in time. He was 63.

Two weeks later, Leon's father died. He was 68. He had been diagnosed with oesophageal cancer two months before. Leon says his passing was a small mercy because by the time the cancer took him, he had really started to go downhill.

It's not something men like Leon talk about much, but it is a hard thing getting to the age where a person starts to lose parents and friends. It gets harder when the job goes too.

On 3 December, BAE told Leon another round of cutbacks was due, and he was one of those who didn't make it. Before it happened, they had the supervisors do assessments on everyone and Leon had gone through his result with his boss. He scored high overall, but the boss said he was easily distracted. Leon said of course he was: he was the main union delegate on site and he had 340 distractions, only what they called distractions he called members. None of that mattered to the supervisor and on that Thursday morning in December he and 80 of those distractions got the sack.

That morning, Leon was on leave doing a job for the union, filling in for an organiser who was away. He was on a site talking to another group of workers when he received a text from the company asking him to come in. Right then he knew what was up, and when he arrived, they brought him into the office, sat him down and gave him the speech.

After that it was open season down at the pub. Those who had lost their jobs waited out the back in the beer garden of the Stags Head Hotel to see who would come in next. As the day wore on, the afternoon shift started and a few of those guys started to filter in too. They were met by a warm welcome.

It was probably better than having survived, Leon thinks now. Sitting around at smoko the day after a cutback is never nice. Working somewhere for a long time makes the people a person works with almost a second family. Over the past two years, about 800 people have been picked off, one by one, from the Williamstown shipyard.

'After it happens, the next day, you're sitting around thinking, wish it was me,' he says.

Another 50 will go by March 2016, bringing the total workforce on site to just 150 people. Management haven't been safe either. The colour of a person's collar means nothing when there just isn't any work to be done. The contract on the Air Warfare Destroyer is winding up as the ships near completion and there are no other projects confirmed within the foreseeable future. It's an issue the unions have been trying to get both sides of politics to move on for at least half a decade, but the left couldn't keep it together long enough to do much of anything and the right's ideological grudge against organised labour trumped the call of a new voting base.

It's a damn shame too, Leon thinks, because it was good work. It was a crappy job some days, sure. In summer it was hot, in winter it was miserable. There are tight spaces to fit into and if something needed to be altered, Spain had to be emailed for permission because they owned the design. None of that changed the fact they were helping to build a ship from scratch.

'It's rewarding work, to start with a bit of flat steel, form it and watch it float away,' Leon says. It was something they were also teaching the next generation. Leon reckons 30 apprentices came through their shipyard over the past five years. They're now boilermakers, so they can do other things, such as structural steel in construction, but they know how to build ships, which is precision work on huge, complex structures. And there would have been more like them too. There was a training centre on site and if everything had worked out, if new contracts had come in, Leon would have taught more kids the trade, just like he was taught when he did his apprenticeship at the railway.

Things didn't go that way. No government moved quickly enough to bring on new work and BAE ended up letting its people go. Instead, the job he was doing for the union finished up on Christmas Eve. Now he has to update his résumé and find something new, but then no one's hiring just after Christmas. He's picked up some casual work down the road putting in steel on a new casting plant, but it's only a few days a week and then it will end.

What comes next he doesn't know, but he's not too worried. He's in a better position than others. He and Julie own their home in Melbourne's west, and while things are tough out there, he's never been out of work longer than a fortnight. He has set up a Facebook page for the former Williamstown crew. There are a few hundred or so on there and if he hears about any jobs going, he shares them to the page.

Like them, chances are Leon will get work in construction. 'There's always work in construction for a tradesman,' he says. Construction pays better than the shipyard, but it's even less stable than shipbuilding and it seems to be the only work Australia has going on lately.

Leon is more worried about the older guys on the yards, the ones who have spent 25 years building the country's navy vessels. When Leon was in school, there were only three computers in the place and he says anyone who knew how to work them was a 'nerd'. But it's not like that anymore. The whole world has changed. They can't just go to a newspaper and look through the classifieds, or overhear someone talking at the pub. These days nothing gets done without a computer and those guys who grew up in an era before the Internet and email are going to struggle.

Eventually nothing will be left of the shipyard, Leon expects. To pacify South Australia during his final months, Tony Abbott had been talking about how the federal government would build a fleet of patrol boats in the state starting in 2018, and how it would bring forward a frigate program with the earliest work to start 2020. If they had brought the patrol boats forward by now, they'd be cutting steel, Leon says, and he would still have a job. Instead, the shipyard will be dead by 2018. By that time he thinks BAE will close it down and sell it off. Then they might buy an empty field next door to ASC where they'll set up new, build the hull blocks right there and drag them next door. He can see ASC in Adelaide hiring back everyone who was laid off over the past 18 months and the government claiming a triumph in job creation, but then there won't be any calling people back to work in Victoria.

It's a vision of the future that might not be too far off.

In April 2016, about two months before the expected election in July, Malcolm Turnbull set his feet firmly on Adelaide soil and told the country a decision had finally been made about the subs. French company DCNS had won the contract to design and build a modified version of its nuclear submarine, the Shortfin Barracuda, in South Australia. The twelve subs would be built in Adelaide after all, Turnbull said, and they would be made from Australian steel, in a rolling build.

Hearing those words felt like victory. It was a win, a rare one for the state, and that is exactly what South Australian Premier Jay Weatherill called it. Opposition Leader Stephen Marshall agreed wholeheartedly and called it 'fantastic' news. Both said it put Adelaide on the French map.

This was certainly true long term, but the short term still felt like a bummer. The cynical saw this as a well-timed political manoeuvre to salvage support in South Australia: boats for votes. It was just two months out from an election and no one had seen a signed contract yet. Wait till then, they said, because if the last three years had taught anyone anything, it was that promises from politicians going into an election were not worth the paper they were on.

The cautiously optimistic were also holding back. They couldn't help but run out the best-case scenario. Work was projected to start sometime in the early 2020s, with the design work coming first and the actual physical work involved in cutting steel starting a few years after that, around 2025 or beyond. In the meantime, the Air Warfare Destroyers would wrap in 2018 and 1200 people would drift away. The building of a fleet of twelve offshore patrol vessels would commence at that time but only 500 people would be needed to put them together, meaning ASC would shed most of its skilled workforce. When the government shipbuilder finally started on the subs sometime in the 2020s, they'd be doing so with a near-new workforce and all the expense that entailed.

That could be ten years from the date of the announcement. Who knew what could happen in that time? Anyone who might once have had an interest in seeing an answer to that question probably wouldn't be around to find out.

Chapter 31

ENGINE GREASE AND WHALE OIL

It's a warm morning in the Heidelberg West workshop. The radio is on, the floor is well swept and Keith Sutton has his head in the engine of a blue 1965 Ford Mustang. Without looking up, he tells the stranger at his garage door to come back later.

'It's not a good time,' he says before calling instructions back to Peter Aitchinson in the driver's seat, unseen behind the hood of the car. It is Peter's first day in the workshop. Not so for Zeiko Zalac, who is standing on a stepladder, sanding back a rusting car body.

Over in the corner is a 1942 Dodge. The owner brought it in from America only to find rust all through the floor. The next one over is an XA Falcon Coupe, Australian made. It's rare, Keith says when he gets a minute, because Ford didn't make many. Out in the car park is a 1956 FJ

Holden panel van without windows that belongs to Zeiko. Around the corner, in the courtyard of the other warehouse Keith owns, is an orange 1970 Valiant Charger waiting for its windscreen to be installed. Just the other day, the guys finished up work on an old Holden Monaro.

For the past 42 years Keith has made his living as a mechanic, but since 1999 he has been trading in memories, giving old cars new engines and a fresh coat of paint. It's all Keith ever wanted to do. Growing up in the 50s, he never had a chance: car culture defined his generation. At school, he still remembers how he and the other guys would line up at the gate during lunchtime to listen to the muscle cars come over the hill. They couldn't see them, but they could hear them and that was all they needed to tell each apart by the distinct call of their engine. Ever since, Keith's blood has roared to the sound of a V8.

'That's all changed now,' he says. 'Since the 80s, it changed. It's all fuel injectors and electronic ignitions. You plug them into a computer or a scanner. That's fine for some, but not for me.'

These days, Keith is one of a dying breed. As a 15-year-old in 1953, Keith traded the classroom for the mechanic's workshop. During the day, he'd work on his clients' vehicles and then he'd go home to work on his own car. He still remembers trying to lift out an engine block by himself at five in the morning. Mechanics in those days knew every part of the vehicle, he says. If a starter motor broke down, they would rebuild it. Put it on the bench, pull it apart, remake it and put it back on the car. No one does that anymore. Now they just buy a new one.

It's the same story for panel beating. Old cars rust, it's a fact of life. It usually starts at the bottom where the water pools and slowly eats its way up through the steel. That said, each car rusts differently. The back window of that Ford Coupe in his workshop was never sealed properly in the factory, so water tends to seep in and the rust eats at the edges. Mending it takes work, but those who knew how to form a panel like they did on the factory line around 1955 are retired, bored by it or dead. All they do now is unpick a few spot welds and put on a whole new sheet of steel.

'We've lost the skills base,' Keith says.

Just another sign of the times, according to Keith Sutton. Every institution he grew up with is slowly being closed down or sold off. Australia used to make cars that growled and hummed and snarled. It used to make a lot of other things too and it used to send them overseas. Not anymore, it seems. Those who still remember hold classic-car rallies, the medieval fairs of the industrial era where the chrome still shines and the engines still growl. There's one that meets regularly at Hanging Rock, the very same Hanging Rock where the fictional teenage girls disappeared.

When Australia decided it wasn't going to make cars anymore, Keith wasn't surprised. He had been seeing it everywhere for the past decade and by then he had just stopped paying attention, which is why he can't remember where he was the day Holden announced it had no future and in doing so took Toyota down with it. Ask him where he was the day Elvis died – well, that's a whole other story.

Around the corner, Zeiko Zalac and Peter Aitchinson are sitting on the front step of the workshop having lunch.

'Welcome to the executive tearoom,' Zeiko says, arms open wide and a smile between each ear. During the 80s, he worked on the trim line at the Ford factory in Broadmeadows for three months. He was a Broady Boy, from a Polish family, but the factory wasn't going to be his life. He was going to get out. The job was only there to help him get by while he studied to be an illustrator.

Later he launched himself into a career as a courtroom sketch artist drawing Australian villains and outlaws and making graphics for commercial television. He hated every single minute. If he had known any better, Zeiko might have stayed at the factory. It might not have had the prestige, but the factory paid well and at least there he knew what he had to do.

'Better than working for arseholes who don't know what they want,' he says.

Not that Zeiko has any love for the car companies or their executives.

'You know they bailed them out, right?' he says, talking about the $50 billion the US government paid to pull the American car industry back from the edge in 2009. The year before, Rick Wagoner, Alan Mulally and Robert Nardelli, the men in charge of GM, Ford and Chrysler respectively, crawled out of Detroit and flew into Washington in their private jets to ask for $25 billion to save their companies. Congress told them to get back on their planes, fly home and come back two weeks later with a better plan to save their industry. And if they were serious, it was heavily implied, they should do so by car.

The executives took the hint and made the trip back to Washington in the cars their factories made. There they asked for $34 billion and were sent back a second time with nothing. George W Bush ended up giving GM and Chrysler $17 billion on 15 December 2008 to keep them going a little longer. Barack Obama later completed the transaction when he bailed them out on the condition the company file for Chapter 11 bankruptcy. From there the bad assets were separated out from the good, with 'old GM' selling those good assets to 'new GM' to give the company a chance at life.

Charlie Wilson, former CEO of GM and US Secretary of Defence from 1953 through 1957, once said what's good for GM is good for the country. Charlie LeDuff, a reporter from Detroit, said that if Wilson was right, that must also be true in the reverse. It is a thought President Obama must have had when he agreed to hand over the money.

Zeiko Zalac says they should have been left to die.

'Fuck them,' he says. 'Do you think GM and Ford give a shit about their workers? They had a chance to invest in electric and renewables but they didn't. Obama shouldn't have done it. They never gave a shit about their employees, in the end what always matters is the bottom line.'

There's a crunch as he bites into his apple and looks out across the road, where an apple-red Barina is parked on the street. Once, he says, cars were beautiful. Even if they drank petrol and burped carbon monoxide, at least they had character. There was something more to them. He points to the Barina and says they now look like that. Plastic changed everything, in his thinking. Once the companies started using plastic to keep from having to press out so much steel, that was it.

'It was a compromise,' he says, and once it was made, everything they built, they built ugly.

Which is all you need to know about the way of the world right now, Zeiko says. As he sees it, the car companies had their shot to go electric and fuel efficient, just as Australia had its chance to build for the future. Instead, the car companies kept building thirsty V6s and V8s, even as the price of fuel was pushing $1.50 a litre, while Australia bet everything on the mining boom. It was going to keep ripping coal and iron ore out of the ground to feed power plants and factories across Asia forever, it thought. Then the GFC happened and people stopped buying cars. Five years later, China's record growth started to buckle and Asia put away its wallet.

'Might as well burn whale oil,' Zeiko says almost to himself as he takes another bite of the apple.

Postscript, of course, is that GM has been turning things around under the watchful eye of US government overseers. In the final three months of 2015, GM recorded a profit of $8.7 billion.

Australia saw no future in its factories. It closed the production lines to liberate workers from their well-paying jobs and all the while it kept digging, even as the price of thermal coal and iron ore fell through the floor.

Chapter 32

WHOLESOME BROADMEADOWS

Walking around Broadmeadows, Victoria, somewhere between Dallas shopping centre and the Ford assembly plant, under the warm summer air. It's after dark and there are crickets in the grass and people on the street. A guy in a robe is sitting on his front step, talking on his mobile as the soft glow of the TV fills the living room behind him. Down the way, a couple of kids are shovelling potting mix into their parents' garden while talking about soccer.

Broadmeadows is a metropolitan suburb with a population of 10,768 people, about a 30-minute train ride north of Melbourne on the Upfield line. Unlike Geelong, it is close to the city, and unlike pretty much everywhere else in the state of Victoria, real estate is cheap. It's also a migrant neighbourhood where one-third of its people were born in a country that doesn't speak English. Greeks,

Italians, Poles, Turks, Arabs, Vietnamese and Somalis have all made their homes on this strip of land for decades. They came here to build their lives and they stayed because there were others who understood their struggle. Together they started families and went to work in the factories building the Ford Falcons Australia's other half had been born to drive.

Aslan Sener, 56, was one of those guys. These days he owns a bakery in the Dallas plaza, which lies in the Dallas shops about halfway between the Ford factory and the Broadmeadows shopping centre. There isn't much light in the central plaza when Aslan steps outside the bakery's front door. A dim yellow from a nearby streetlight rains down and illuminates the man. He is short, in a baker's apron, with a moustache and knowing eyes. Before he says anything, he apologises and explains he can't talk right now: he has to work last minute in the bakery to get everything ready for tomorrow. Give him a call another time, any time, he says.

Days later Aslan is sitting on the front porch of his house with his mother when he tells how both he and his brother Gazi threw in with Australia and got their start at the Ford factory. They came out from Turkey, from somewhere near Ankara, as young men. Aslan came first, Gazi later. Aslan says when he first came out, he had a letter from the government with his name on it saying 'welcome'. Getting it was exciting and it made Aslan feel like he had made the right decision, that there was something here for him. It doesn't happen like that anymore, he admits.

'Now I don't think the government does give a letter,' he says.

Aslan and Gazi each spent about eight years in the factory, give or take. Aslan worked in the plastics factory from 1980 to 1988. Gazi started driving forklifts in 1987 and left in 1996. For both, it was their first serious job, an introduction to the daily grind on the floor of the Ford factory, the great leveller where Turks worked the same line with Greeks, where Italians and Vietnamese and Lebanese all worked the same hours and took home the same pay. The promise made to each was always the same: good money for hard work and an education in the way this new country operated.

Aslan worked mostly nightshift, operating a 50-metre-long machine he knew better than any other man on the shop floor. In the event of a breakdown it would take a mechanic four hours to shut it down and work through it piece by piece to fix the thing. Aslan knew it so well it would take him five minutes. It was a good job, he says, and one he only left to open his own business. He has done all right since, he says. He started out with a textiles business and then sold that when the industry went to China. After that he opened the bakery.

Guys like Aslan came out for a better life, but over the past ten years the factories that gave them that life have started heading back to Asia. It takes poverty to compete with poverty, not that Aslan is complaining. Ford set him up for life. It did the same for many others he knew. It meant everything out here and, now it has been taken away, he doesn't know what is going to replace it.

'New generation? I don't know,' Aslan says. 'Very difficult at the moment. For me? Forget it. For myself, it's end of the road. The next generation. Who knows? What's left for them? It's very hard right now.'

He's not wrong. As of October 2016, the last car will roll off the line in the Ford assembly plant down by the train station. It's a sprawling facility along the road to Sydney that, just like its sister plant in Norlane, is hard to ignore. When it goes, it will tear out the cogs and gears at the heart of Broadmeadows and mark the start, or end, of one of the biggest events in Australian economic history.

It was Ford Australia's president, Bob Graziano, who brought home the message that it was all over. The company had been doing the numbers on the operation and decided there was nothing for it. Nothing left. There was no way the factory could be saved. It would be cheaper to go somewhere else, such as Thailand, to make the cars then bring the things in on the back of a ship. So every one of the 1200 people who worked across the Geelong and Broadmeadows facilities had to go as of 2016 and with them the Falcon would die too.

And there was nothing anyone could do. This wasn't like that time in 1972 when the migrant men who put together Australia's American cars faced down the police and the multinational to teach it a lesson. In those days before 457 temporary migrant workers visas, Australia had been hungry for labour, and from 1947 to 1972, 2.3 million migrants heard the call. About three-quarters of the Australian workforce were migrants then and a good many couldn't speak or read English. So when they walked into the employment office at the Ford plant, someone who knew letters would fill out their forms for them, sign them up to the union and for overtime, no questions asked. The migrant men would end up with some of the worst jobs in the factory and if they ever complained about safety, or pay, or speed-ups, the company couldn't hear them. Their accents were too thick or their English too broken.

Even the union leadership couldn't hear them until the workforce went on strike on 18 May 1973. Australia's car factories were battlegrounds at this time with different unions and different workforces fighting all manner of causes and some just acting in solidarity. To strike was often a cathartic experience, a way for those who worked the factories to be heard above the machines. Those running the union at the Ford plant in 1973 didn't want to stop work at this time, though what they wanted didn't really matter because the 4000 or so bodies, the 8000 hands that kept the plant running, wanted something different. Like the English migrants who had been brought out to Elizabeth, many of the Spanish, Greek, Italian, Polish and Turkish migrants on the line at Broadmeadows grew up in or around the union movements that faced off in the streets against fascism in the lead-up to World War II. Just like their counterparts in Elizabeth, they didn't take no for an answer when the company and the union told them to go back to work, and they stopped clocking on until 11 June, when the company tried to bring an end to the dispute by offering them a wage increase.

The union leadership said yes to the wage increase but the workforce said no. What they wanted went further than that. They wanted the company to make things safer, to make repairs, to hire women and to stop giving the migrant men the worst jobs in the factory. So on the morning of 13 June, assembly workers met outside the gates of the Broadmeadows Ford factory. When the police tried to arrest a shop steward, the 1000 or so men present broke down a brick wall and invaded the plant. Police reinforcements arrived later but every step forward was met with bricks and bottles. The battle lasted six hours and caused $10,000 in damage, or $89,729.17 in today's money.

Ford ended up closing the factory for the next ten weeks before they gave in and promised to make a change. Management said the dispute had cost the company $27 million in lost production, a little over $240 million today, so they caved. It was a victory in the face of threats to lay off 4000 people and offshore the whole operation to Malaysia.

For that brief moment, the men of the Broadmeadows plant were in control of their fate. They had faced down one of the world's biggest multinationals and their threats to offshore everything, the police and, for a while, even their own union to make themselves heard.

But that was also a different time. One when the company and the unions were hard. They were direct, sometimes downright rude, and when that didn't work it came down to muscle. Things don't operate like that these days. As one former union organiser told it, the age of union militancy in the car factories ended in the 80s when 'everyone, the company and the union, grew up' and once the announcement was made in 2013 that the industry was dead, the feeling was that the unions were weaker than ever.

The workforce had no say when Ford shut the factory. It had nothing to do with labour or the unions. Stay or go, the rank and file had zero chance of influencing the outcome. The numbers had been crunched, the decision had been made and it was final. The business is dead, they were told, they just weren't making money and when it went, everyone would have to find something else to do. Those 1000 or so people who worked for the car factories had to go somewhere else.

* * *

Across the road from the factory are the Fordgate shops. At a quick count, there's a pizza joint, four kebab shops, an Afghani barbecue, an Iraqi barbecue, a greengrocer, post office, a clinic and a tax agent. Upstairs is an Arabic radio station. The factory across the road is the first thing the shopkeepers see in the morning when they open up and the last thing they see when they go home. Once it is empty and the lunch rush gone, the question everyone is asking is whether they can keep going. As long as that factory was there, Ford has always given them surety. It would never go, they thought. Now Ford is taking it away.

The rest of the suburb is nice, just like any other. Broadmeadows is the kind of place that doesn't really make headlines unless there are gunshots or terrorism raids or stories about refugees trying to kill themselves in the local detention centre. Sure, there are empty houses in some of its streets, but for now it's a place where people mow their lawns and nod to passers-by. A place where those living in one house may build a two-metre shrine to Mary, Mother of Christ in their front yard, while their neighbour wears a full-face veil as she drives her children to the Islamic school in a big, petrol-drinking four-wheel drive.

Ahmed Yussuf lives not far over from the railway line and if he had to put a word to it, he would describe the place as 'wholesome'.

'People have a fantasy of places like Broadmeadows and that idea or fantasy is built up by what we see on television,' Ahmed says. 'They have this perception of gangs. And I'm not going to lie to you, I had friends who were part of the Broady Boys. But these guys were, like, 14. Seriously, if your gangs are adolescent teens, walking around, you live in a quiet neighbourhood.'

Gangs and Ford Falcons have been chief exports of Broadmeadows ever since they used to come with names like the Oak Park Boot Boys, West Side Sharps, King Street Sharps, Lebanese Tigers, Black Dragons and Olsen Street Sharps. There are still groups using some of these names. Occasionally they make current-affairs programs, where they stand in front of television cameras and run their mouths while holding a machete, which makes for good viewing. Australians have always loved the thrill of a good outlaw, even adolescent ones who live with their parents. Even as far back as the 70s and 80s reporters were travelling north of Melbourne to find characters for their stories only to have to tell their subjects to 'look tougher' while shooting their photograph.

Ahmed is a 22-year-old journalism student at La Trobe and his Broadmeadows is very different to what people watch on the evening news. He is one of the new generation, whose family have had nothing to do with the factory. His parents moved to Australia in the 90s. His father was forced into becoming a child soldier in Somalia before he escaped that life to wander Africa. He drove trucks around the continent and applied for his first passport in Tanzania. In Australia, Ahmed's father became a mechanic and Ahmed's mother a housewife. When they were looking for houses, his father wanted to buy a suburb over in Coburg, but his mother said no. She wanted to live near the mosque, near the school, near shops and near a train line for when they wanted to make the half-hour trip into Melbourne, so that's what they did.

'It's the brown Australian dream,' Ahmed says. Unlike Elizabeth, which raises its best sons and daughters to leave, Ahmed says here they're raised to stay. Walking around his neighbourhood, he talks about how things are. The school across the road used to be 'a shithole' until it was rebuilt. Down the road from his house lived one of the few white families in the neighbourhood. From their garage hangs an Australian flag, and Ahmed still remembers the time when he was 12 and the eldest son, about 16, chased him down the street for no other reason than he was African.

Crossing the train tracks to the Fordgate shops, Ahmed talks up the 'world famous' Katiks, and how he has been coming here so long the family who owns it lets him eat for free. The kebabs are good and cheap, the way food should be. It's getting near lunchtime and there's a line out the door. Behind the counter is Ali, who greets Ahmed warmly and shakes his hand across the counter. Ahmed orders a mixed kebab and pulls a Coke from the fridge before the two chat about university. Ahmed's doing well, he says, he's going to graduate soon and then he'll be out in the real world. He has a few opportunities lined up, so he says he'll see how it goes.

Broadmeadows may have a reputation for danger, but to Ahmed it's an enclave. A nice enough place in the world, the kind that gave him a chance at a decent education in a nice enough school, which enabled him to go on to university. Most of all, it's a safe enough place for someone of the Muslim faith in an increasingly suspicious and frightened Australia.

And the more suspicious and scared Australia gets, the harder it is to be anything but a labourer, because employers read a résumé and respond better to white-sounding names. One study in the United States found that having an Anglicised name gave a person a 50 per cent better chance of getting into a professional job. A similar study in Australia from 2009 sent out more than 4000 job applications across Brisbane, Sydney and Melbourne and found those with Indigenous or migrant-sounding names fared worse, with those bearing Middle Eastern names having to send out 69 per cent more applications to get a call-back.

'It's also how you dress,' Ahmed says. 'If you're a Muslim woman who wears a hijab. You're going to a job interview, your name sounds "Arabic", you walk in and from the get-go you're at a disadvantage.'

That's also the very first thing Abdiwahab Mohamed, or 'Abs', says when he answers the door to Ahmed. 'Do you watch TV?' he deadpans when asked about the neighbourhood.

'You know, when you go for a job interview, if they ask where you're from and you say Broadmeadows, that's it. You have to say you're from Coburg. Or Dallas.

'Dallas, Texas?' Abs jokes, as if he's in the interview. 'No, Dallas, *Dallas*.'

It has been a while since the two young men have seen each other. Abs has been a little hard to get a hold of lately, but the two embrace as if no time has passed at all.

After high school, Ahmed went on to university, while Abs fell into working whatever job came along. Ahmed remembers how in Year 12 all Abs could talk about was how he was going to be a mechanic and work on cars. Abs loved cars, still does, though he drives a beat-up, if well-kept, Ford Laser, which he parks with precision about 2 centimetres away from the front wall of the sharehouse he's living in. If he had his way, he'd be driving a Nissan Skyline or something else compact and fast. He may love cars, but he loves Japanese cars most of all. And if he gave himself a moment to dream, he would want to be an architect or a draftsman, but he never made the grade.

Four years on, Abs is now 22 and life hasn't yet worked out the way it was supposed to. After Abs graduated, the guy across the road started talking about how Abs should go to work with him putting in pipe lagging. Abs said sure, why not? And for a while it was a good job, right up until the point that the work was absorbed into the standard plumber's contract, which put him and his friend out of business.

Since then, he's been working a series of odd jobs, looking for something that sticks. How many?

'A shitload.'

He repeats the phrase and trails off before he explains how over the past four years he has tried on nearly every trade except the work of an electrician. In that time, he's collected enough stories about shifty bosses to make a legal dossier heavy.

What Abs wanted in those four years was an apprenticeship. An apprenticeship meant money, it meant skills and it meant a future. What he got were broken promises. The people he ended up working for were always happy to dangle an apprenticeship in front of him for another week's work. Or maybe a few months. Eventually, he'd get wise to the idea it wasn't going to happen and he'd leave. Maybe he'd finally get that qualification to be a mechanic, he'd think, but then someone else would come along with a smile and a great idea if he needed a job.

Like that Greek plumber he used to work for. After a two-day trial, the plumber told him he was a hard worker and he'd bring him on as an apprentice next week. He'd get the officials down here, the plumber promised, and they'd sign the paperwork then and there, Monday morning, first thing.

So Monday morning, Abs climbed out of bed with confidence. 'I thought, this is it,' he says, clapping his hands together. He spent the day watching the clock as the hours fell away and nothing happened. In the end, he decided to just hang in there.

Two months later, the plumber told him he'd been working hard and deserved a week off. When Abs called back a week later to find out what was on, the plumber told him there was no work and to take another week. That didn't sit right, so Abs called the owner of the business, who also happened to be the plumber's father. He too said there was no work. So Abs called the plumber's girlfriend, who told him the plumber was working in a tattoo studio that day, which Abs said was funny because he'd been told there was no work.

And the stories keep coming. There was the Turkish guy with a flooring business who paid Abs $25 for a full day's work that started at seven in the morning and finished at eight at night. There was that time he was working on a construction site, cleaning away broken glass beneath a window when another shard fell and stabbed his forearm. The scar is visible as he leans cross-armed against the door frame. There was the other time he sliced off the top of his thumb on a sheet of plaster. The site had an empty first-aid box, so he wrapped his thumb in tissue paper before the boss told him to get back to work, even as the blood streamed and his arm slowly went numb. When he finally had a doctor look at it, she said if he'd left it any later, infection would have set in.

If the Ford factory were still hiring, he'd be there tomorrow, Abs says. He's not big on Fords but he loves cars and he'd heard the plant paid well. A job making cars would be better than what he's been doing the past few years and maybe he could have started an apprenticeship so he'd know a trade. It would have made for a better life than eking out an existence working cash-in-hand in the residential construction industry, wasting time with bosses who exchange broken promises for an honest day's labour. It would have been a path towards joining in the shared prosperity that has so far defined Australian life.

Instead, the factory is closing. In fact, Abs thinks it has already closed, so he's surprised to learn it hasn't. But then it's not hiring. Hasn't been for a long time. May as well be closed as far as he's concerned.

These days Abs isn't working. He's one among those who make up the 22.1 per cent unemployment rate for the area. But Abs has a plan. Now that he has some time, he might finally do that mechanics course he'd been talking about for so long. Afterward, he'd set up shop right there in his driveway. He wouldn't have to work for a boss and he'd get to work on cars. Maybe it would keep him going long enough to get qualified as a draftsman and then he can work on cars as a hobby. Maybe buy that Skyline he's always wanted. Maybe then, things will get better.

Chapter 33

100 YEARS OF SAMURAI PRIDE

The Toyota factory in Altona first opened in 1994 across 75 hectares of land in south Melbourne. It replaced the previous Port Melbourne site but in 2009 the factory was completely rebuilt from the outside in so it could produce 450 hybrid engines a day, marking the first production of hybrid cars in Australia.

It was a massive effort across the seven separate plants, which took 16 deliveries of steel a day and turned it all into 90,000 cars a year, 70 per cent of which were destined for export. The company even let the National Geographic Channel inside the plant in the lead-up to the 11 December launch of the new hybrid Camry to film it all for an episode of *Megafactories*, and ever since the episode has been permanently posted to the company's website, where it serves as one part factory tour and two parts press release.

To add a sense of tension, the climax of the episode was set around the imminent arrival of former Prime Minister Julia Gillard to open the factory alongside Toyota Australia President and CEO Max Yasuda. Prime ministers used to love car factories. If one ever opened they wanted to be seen cutting the ribbon. These places symbolised progress, growth, all the good things they should be doing – and this was no different for Julia Gillard, who was shown being driven to the stage in a blue Camry Hybrid. Rows of dignitaries, including then Industry Minister Greg Combet and the Japanese Ambassador, were present to listen to the forward-looking speeches from the leaders of the nation and the company about innovation and pride, while in the background the stoic, solemn workforce silently watched.

Two minutes later, the whole show closed to a white Camry Hybrid driving majestically down a highway against rising orchestral music while a narrator summed up the company's history and how it was moving lock-step into tomorrow.

The new factory, built in the shell of the old, only made it as far as 2014. It was supposed to run for decades, and to make it happen the company had sunk $330 million into the place, including $63 million the state and federal governments had put in to help get it off the ground. Toyota had spent $108 million on the new Camry, including $23.6 million of federal government assistance and, in its time, the car had led the market in Australia. The hybrid engine was meant to give the Altona factory legs, and it was a symbolic move. Australia was the first country in which Toyota built cars outside of Japan and it has been the company's proving ground ever since it started thinking about going global. Since then, Toyota has built over 3.2 million vehicles, making Australia the first step in its expansion into the American market, where it wrestled Detroit into submission.

Toyota was heavily invested in Australia and never wanted to close shop. It was a matter of pride, though that's not the way the government of the day saw it. During his tenure, federal Treasurer Joe Hockey said it was the unions who broke it. To prove it, he dug out an interview with Max Yasuda from 2012 during which he had talked about labour relations being a problem, and a press release from the company issued the day after Holden announced its closure. This was evidence, the treasurer said, that the Toyota workers did it to themselves.

Toyota responded by putting out a new press release. It had never blamed the unions or the workforce for the Australian factory's closure, it said, and it wanted that fact written into the permanent record. Sure, there had been problems with the unions. In 2012, the company sacked 350 workers who, it said, were performing poorly. That was more than one in ten of its then 3350-strong workforce. Senior union representatives like the AMWU's Fadi Hassan had walked the floor with management that morning to help pick out the people the company wanted gone. It was a hard job and after it was done, management turned around and told him he was going too.

From there he went back to his office, where he was met by a security guard who escorted him down to the hall and out to where the other workers were lining up. They were then directed to rooms where they were read their rights and given a dollar figure for their loyalty. Fadi was not the only senior union rep to be laid off that morning. Thirteen others were sacked that day, effectively wiping out the senior union leadership in the factory.

Afterwards, there had been talk about taking the incident to the courts, but that ended up going nowhere. Instead, everyone in the factory went home knowing how blunt Toyota could be when it came to the crunch. If anyone had forgotten that fact, they were reminded of it when Toyota gathered its workforce in early 2014 to announce the factory closure, flanked by heavy security.

That was a tough time for the company, but blaming the unions for the end of Toyota is to give them too much credit. What put Toyota in a situation of having to look for savings by cutting back on labour at its still-new factory was the high Australian dollar. What brought down the axe was the prospect of a supply-chain collapse if Toyota went on without Holden.

As of 2017, Toyota will bring its cars in by boat. It will need maybe 200 people to move 200,000 cars a year. The rest of its workforce will have to go, and the expertise they have built up over a lifetime of work in the factory will slowly fade. It's a story supported by the stats on Toyota's workforce. As of 2014, about 15 per cent of the Toyota workforce was aged over 55; 20 per cent was under 33; leaving about 65 per cent who were middle aged. The longest-serving employee as of 2015 was 83 years old. He had been with the company for 42 years. The average length of service at Toyota is 15 years.

How they will fare is anyone's guess, though clues may be found in the experience of some former Toyota workers laid off during 2012. One we will call Ali didn't want to be named. What happened in the time from then till now has made him ashamed.

It all started out fine. When Ali was let go, he got himself a professionally written résumé and started putting in applications. He was 50 when it happened and willing to work, but no one would take him. He was just too old, he says. He even thought about going to the Middle East on a contract, but it turns out they didn't want an old man either.

Three years on, Ali now works as a casual security guard and sometimes as a supervisor at a railway station. 'One day on, five days off,' he says. They have him working nights, and he'll sleep through the days. Some weeks he'll bring home a couple of hundred dollars. Sometimes he doesn't work at all.

'You have to live by the phone,' he says. 'They call, and you work. They don't, and you don't.'

So far he has kept at it this long, but the money from the package ran dry a long time ago and there's nothing left, he says. He did his best to keep up with the mortgage payments on his home in West Melbourne, but now the house is sold and their stuff is in boxes. They're about to move away to somewhere else.

'What am I going to give to my kids?' he asks. It's a question that matters to him. His wife overhears what he's saying and starts yelling something in another language from another room. He translates. She's telling him not to worry about the kids, he says. They're all young men in university now. She says he has to worry about himself. First he has to survive, then he can talk about the kids.

His wife has been angry ever since he lost his job. Not angry at him, just angry. It's been hard living cheque-to-cheque for both of them and Ali doesn't know where he is going next. Things are getting hard for everyone, if you ask him. Just the other day at work he was called out to a fruit-and-veg shop after a 71-year-old woman, a pensioner, had been caught shoplifting. She had taken one bag of tomatoes and one green pepper. Put them straight in her bag and tried to make a run for it. She didn't make it very far. It was Ali who convinced the shopkeepers not to call the police.

'You can't have the whole country as freelancers,' Ali says. 'You have to have people working for the company. A lot of people don't know how to be freelancers. I've been on my own, I've been surviving for three years, but as you can see I lost my house, though I'm still going. Not everyone knows how.'

As of 2015, things started winding down at the Toyota factory. The Camry had an update and the last model to be built at the factory started coming off the line on 28 April. Around that time, the company were talking up what it was doing for its long-serving workforce. It opened transition centres, just like Holden, and said it was working with each individual employee to develop a personalised, tailor-made plan for life after the factory. It was a service all bundled up in the $66 million the company spent during 2015 to manage the closure.

In 2017, when the gates are locked and security escorts what's left of the workforce from the premises, Toyota expects to pay out $200 million to keep the men and women who worked its production line going for a year, or maybe two.

After that, they're on their own. The company will have bigger things to worry about, like working out how they're going to shut down a near-new, state-of-the-art factory.

And as they're dismantling the machines, everyone will be thinking to themselves how it was all such a waste.

They used to make cars in there and they used to send them all over the world, you know?

Chapter 34

THEY SAY TOUGH TIMES NEVER LAST

THERE USED TO BE A HOLDEN PLANT OUT DANDENONG WAY too. They started building it in 1951 across 61 hectares of land, just south of the old market town. When it was completed in 1956, it made 168 a cars a day and came complete with its own dedicated train station where the only way in or out was through the Holden factory gate. Four million cars began life in that plant by 1981 and in 1986 it was taken over by a joint venture between General Motors and Toyota called United Australian Automobile Industries (UAAI).

At the dawn of the 80s, the tariffs started to fall and GM was bleeding money. The company decided that factories such as Acacia Ridge in Queensland, where the streets were named after the cars its people built, and Pagewood in New South Wales had no future and shut them down. Dandenong, it was hoped, might be different.

The plant just south of central Dandenong built Commodores, the thundering chariots of the Australian way, right up until 1988 when all the work was sent to Elizabeth in South Australia. The company then found itself with a stilled plant on its hands and an obligation under the Button Car Plan, which opened up the industry to the free market, to cooperate with other big companies. Nissan had dropped out of its initial partnership with Holden, but Toyota happened to be looking for space, so the factory's workforce went back to work building Apollos, Novas and Lexcens, which were all more or less rebadged Camrys, Corollas and Commodores.

People hated the cars, or at least that's what the sales numbers seemed to suggest, and the marriage between the giants only lasted until Toyota shifted all production to the Altona plant in 1994. In 1996 the two divorced, the UAAI died and there was no hope left for the Dandenong plant. The factory closed, just like all the others.

Instead of making cars, Holden kept a chunk of the former site, where it warehoused spare parts. Later, a developer bought up Estate 1 and sank $500 million into building a new industrial estate on top of it. The General Motors train station along the Pakenham Line managed to stay open until 2002, even though the footbridge led to an empty field. At 4.42pm, on 26 July 2002, the last train left the station. It was a Friday.

A few years later, KEEP OUT signs were put up on the footbridge and the door to the signal box was nailed shut. That didn't do much to stop the weeds and graffiti. As of

September 2015, the only person getting any use out of the Melbourne-bound platform looked to be a homeless person living beneath it.

Dandenong seemed to rise and fall with its GM plant, though it had been dealt a bad hand ever since they ran the Princes Highway through the centre of town, cutting it in half. In 1989 a new shopping centre was built adjoining an existing Myer department store, creating 76,383 square metres of brightly lit, windowless, industrial-air-conditioned consumer bliss across three separate floors, complete with high-gloss finish and two food courts. The hope was it would be good for the town, maybe make people some money, only they built it in the wrong half so all the people had no more reason to come into the CBD. That's when the shops started to empty out.

Then manufacturing began to slide. Legend has it that up through the 80s, unemployment in the region around Dandenong and Clayton was at 0 per cent. Old automotive workers tell the story of how when Nissan still made cars, they had to bus people into the area from Melbourne because there weren't enough bodies on the line. Then the 90s opened with the closure of the Holden plant and ended with the Heinz factory shutdown in 2000 after a boardroom somewhere in Pittsburgh decided it was cheaper to offshore everything to New Zealand. In between, Nissan stopped making cars in Australia, while all the little companies that provided the services and materials to keep the automakers and their workforce moving crumbled.

When the main drivers of a local economy shut down, economists say people need to have a little faith. The end of one industry creates space for a new, more competitive one to step into the void. In Dandenong, that new industry was drugs. The promise of oblivion and easy money made for a strong business opportunity and the dealers sold their product in the centre of town, right in the middle of the street. Newspapers called Springvale, a nearby suburb, 'Heroin City' and there a balloon of heroin smuggled in from Southeast Asia cost $50 in the 90s. Chances are nothing has really changed over the past ten years: heroin isn't exactly a commodity indexed to GDP.

Locals prefer not to talk about those dark days. The memory is an embarrassing stain on their history. Instead they prefer to talk about how the city is fighting back and how the Victorian state government is spending $290 million to drag Dandenong back to its feet. The council just spent $29 million rebuilding the local farmers market, and $1 billion is said to have been lined up for other projects over the next decade.

The street dealers are mostly gone now too. For a time, the trade got so heavy the locals were talking about an amnesty, but the state government vetoed the idea and went tough on crime. Police cracked down hard and drove the dealers back underground. That's something else the locals like to talk about. And then there's the diversity. Over 60 per cent of Dandenong's 25,000 people have come from somewhere else. Two-thirds of the city speak another language. After the shopkeepers left, it was the new migrants who had the energy and initiative to move into the empty shops. They started businesses when no one else would and now there's a Little India with spice markets and restaurants that feature whenever Dandenong tries to promote itself to the world.

That's because ten years after the Heinz factory closed down, Dandenong has been going through a transition, partly because it has become too expensive to live anywhere else. There are big plans for the little town that has been swallowed up by Melbourne as the city sprawls outward. Standing in Dandenong's new central plaza in front of the new library, it's possible to get a feel for the change going on. A giant flat-screen TV is tuned to an NITV documentary about Australia Day, and downstairs people sit in the shade of a cafe. Dandenong has been getting a facelift; its streets are being opened up to bring in more light and make them feel spacious. In the architectural world it's called 'place-making', a kind of plastic surgery for beat-up post-industrial towns that tries to remove some of the social scarring by physically reorganising public space. It's why Lonsdale Street, which used to tie together the two ends of the Princes Highway, has been widened into a boulevard and a bypass built to keep the heavy trucks from roaring through the centre of town. Walking through it all, and seeing the people shop or talk on the benches, it's a change that at least feels like it is working.

And Dandenong needs it to work. Its people have come far and worked hard to turn it around. Right now there is hope tomorrow will be better and the day after will be better again. With the end of the car industry, though, things are a little more complicated. The car factories may be gone, but Dandenong's people still make the bits and pieces that go into Commodores and Camrys. As it stands, there are 189 car-parts makers across southeast Melbourne, many clustered in the Greater Dandenong area. They make components for Holden and Toyota, and when those companies are gone, some will get by exporting parts to foreign automotive companies such as BMW in Germany. Others will pick up new work from companies such as Jayco Caravans in Dandenong South. Some won't, or it won't be enough, and they'll have to downsize anyway.

Some will say one thing and do another. Nissan Australia, which quit making cars in Australia in 1992, still runs a casting plant in the area making parts for export across the world. In April 2015, Nissan made grand statements about how Australian manufacturing was not dead, promising that its plant would stay beyond 2020. The 160 people it employed went home knowing they still had jobs, what the future meant.

Two months later Nissan closed the warehouse across the road when it decided to outsource its logistics operations, sacking the 42 people who thought they were safe. The company defended itself by saying those jobs were independent from its manufacturing operation.

What does the end of the car industry mean for Dandenong? SEMMA, the South East Melbourne Manufacturers Alliance, has been saying that though it may be a bad bigger picture, it doesn't think it will impact Dandenong in any significant way. This is just more churn in the economy, the thought runs, and there is opportunity in the ruins.

Just like everyone else lately, the organisation has been talking disruption and innovation, and it even brought in a futurist to better identify new opportunities for its members. For the past ten years SEMMA has been telling its members connected to the car industry of the need to diversify, and the region has seen a growth in manufacturing start-ups.

Walking through Dandenong, the change is clear, but it's hard to ignore the little details that suggest the city's sinners haven't gone far. Dandenong's transformation may be underway, but it is far from complete. Half the town still bears its 70s façade. Those untouched streets are narrow and the light commercial shopping complexes are a maze of poorly lit, tight corridors. The new boulevards feel empty and hot. When Melbourne's jobless rate was averaging 6.4 per cent for the quarter ending September 2015, Dandenong's was at 21.3 per cent. Police still bust drug dealers carrying up to $20,000 of product. Alcoholics Anonymous runs Thursday through Monday. Narcotics Anonymous runs nearly every night of the week too. Whispering the right words at the local strip club earns discount entry and a free drink. Outside the train station is an advertisement for a local lawyer whose smiling face looks into the eyes of everyone stepping out of the station and into Dandenong.

'Going to court?' it reads, in big, bold print. 'Tough times never last,' it promises. First call is free.

Can Dandenong be saved? The tall, white Christian evangelical in a T-shirt, shorts and dark glasses says anyone can be saved – so long as they believe. It's as hot as hell in Dandenong today and he's standing in the public square talking Jesus to an African woman in a niqab as the cloth of her robe ripples in the wind. She doesn't argue, she just stays silent. Her eyes carry a faint hint of frustration.

'This is for you,' the other preacher with him says. He hands over a flyer the size, colour and design of a $100 bill. On one side is a picture of the bushranger Ned Kelly and a $1 million valuation. On the other is a sermon they've been giving all over town.

'Ask yourself the million-dollar question,' it starts. 'Will you go to Heaven when you die?

'Here's a quick test. Have you ever told a lie, stolen anything or used God's name in vain? Have you looked with lust? Which is adultery of the heart in God's eyes. Will you be guilty on Judgement Day?

'If you have done these things, God sees you as a lying, thieving, blasphemous adulterer at heart. The Bible warns that if you are guilty, you will end up in Hell.

'You broke God's law. But Jesus took the punishment. That means He can legally forgive you and remove your death sentence.

'Please, repent today. Trust in Jesus Christ alone, and God will forgive you and grant you the gift of everlasting life.'

His solution?

'Get a Bible, read it daily and obey what you read.'

Chapter 35

REVOLUTIONS PER MINUTE

THE TICK-TOCK SOUND OF THE BALL HITTING INSPIRE9'S TABLE-tennis table can be heard from the street. Once you've taken the elevator up to the first floor, the doors slide open to the dim hum of activity and a reception desk manned by the tall, dapper figure of community manager Rahul Soans, wearing his trademark fedora and friendly smile.

The co-working space began life in 2005 but moved to its current Richmond warehouse space in 2011. Walking through, Rahul explains he is an engineer who used to work in the telecom industry before he decided it wasn't for him and left to discover the entrepreneurial world of start-ups. Eventually he found a job helping run this place and so far it's a pretty sweet gig. Most days are spent hanging out and talking to people and signing them up. There are about 100 people in the place right now, give or take, renting space.

A desk is $550 a month for a full subscription and there are drinks on Friday nights and a stage at the back of the house where they put on events and talks in the vein of TedX.

Over in the back corner of the building, Rahul points out the people from Rome2Rio. They're the heavies, he says. Everyone else in the place is whispering about how they just raised $1.6 million in investment capital on the back of an app they made. Theirs is a 'multi-modal' search program that, according to their pitch, tells a person how to get anywhere by listing every possible route, by any means of travel, right to the destination. All up, their company employs maybe 18 people, spread out over two rows of desks.

'Things are fairly lean here,' Rahul explains. He's talking about the idea of the lean start-up, the business philosophy of American entrepreneur Eric Ries, who built upon the ideas of his mentor Steve Blank. The basic thrust is to eliminate waste by keeping new start-ups responsive to their customers from the outset so they don't waste time building something no one wants.

It's a way of thinking about production adapted from the car industry in the mid-1950s when Taiicho Ohno, an engineer who spent his entire career with Toyota, first talked about the need to be constantly eliminating waste. He first articulated the idea that a production line must continually improve and that everything should come together just in time, just when it was needed to maximise productivity. It was an innovative way of thinking and it ended up saving Toyota from bankruptcy. Eventually his ideas would be exported to the English-speaking world under the name 'lean manufacturing' and in turn applied to other sectors, including start-ups. What's old is new again.

'I say to people when they ask about why I work with start-ups that the nature of work has been changing and we're at the forefront of the revolution,' Thomas Anbeek says. 'The industrial revolution was about getting people into the factories. The digital revolution is about getting them out of the factories [and] making them independent again.'

Thomas, 26, is from the Netherlands and ended up in Melbourne when he followed his Australian girlfriend home. In the Netherlands, he completed a master's degree in psychology with a focus on entrepreneurship and afterwards he became involved with organisations that supported Dutch entrepreneurs. In Australia, Startup Victoria was just getting off the ground and was advertising for a CEO, so Thomas applied. The chairman thought he was a little too inexperienced for the role, but took a shine to him and brought him on as events manager anyway.

Rohit Bhargava is 28 and from Canberra. For as long as he can remember, all he had wanted to do was play cricket professionally. It was something he was good at, good enough he ended up making it into the Academy of Cricket in India, where he was scouted by Middlesex County. But his professional cricket career ended before it began when he picked up an injury playing soccer. He can't, or won't, remember exactly how it happened; all he'll say is that accepting the dream was dead when for a moment it was so real was a hard time in his life. He has kept on with cricket since, he says, coaching the team at the university where he studied engineering and economics. The injury also gave him the idea for his first start-up in sports medicine.

It didn't last. Out of that first experience Rohit learned a lot, he says, primarily that what he was doing was not always right. After that he set up his second start-up, a crowd-funding platform for fashion designers, working with a development team based in Melbourne. Rohit had a job with an engineering firm then, and as the only team member not in Melbourne, he counted his savings, quit his job and headed south to be closer to the action. Soon enough, he fell in with Startup Victoria.

Together, Thomas and Rohit lay out the basics of start-ups. Someone setting up a new neighbourhood dog-wash service and someone else launching a new social-media company from their garage are both starting new businesses. Strictly speaking, both are entrepreneurs and both are start-ups. The first may be happy to get by in their local neighbourhood, while the second has ambition to become a giant, quickly. This is what separates those at the top from those somewhere in the middle, and Startup Victoria is about getting more people to the top.

This is because start-ups also fail. They can be high impact, but they're highly uncertain. Of all the businesses that started in Australia over the past decade, be they dog-washers or those with global ambitions, only 3.2 per cent achieved real growth over the first five years and in doing so accounted for 77 per cent of all job creation among new companies. Once they made it that far, their productivity dropped. Of the rest, 96.8 per cent did nothing or disappeared in the churn. For every Atlassian raising $60 million, there are many more trying to scrape together $100,000 to keep going.

For start-ups to get going, they need to fail, Thomas says. Out of this churn eventually comes a winner, though he's quick to qualify this. It's not failure for failure's sake that matters, but the lessons that come from failure.

'Ideas are worthless,' he says. That's the lesson of the start-up world. It's not about the specific idea but about execution, though even getting that part of a start-up right is more art than science. There is no recipe or formula for what makes a successful business, no one way to do things right. Learning that usually comes at the end of a grinding process of refinement, with all the personal and financial costs associated with failure.

It's a reality at odds with the legend of the teenage start-up founder building a multi-million-dollar company from their bedroom – the kind of story that has caught the country's attention, fuelled by the business press, which treats tech start-ups and their founders, almost always men, as rock stars. At first this image was helpful in generating support for start-ups and their founders, though both Thomas and Rohit say fame is something of a burden.

'Stories about a 19-year-old founder that built a business that's worth millions of dollars, that's very interesting to write about,' Thomas says. 'Very clickable content. If you actually look at the stats, the most successful start-ups are founded by people in their 30s and 40s and not people in their teens.'

Not that the general public sees that. As corporate organisations, universities and governments have learned about start-ups, they've started to mimic the language without understanding what is involved. They now talk about disruption and innovation, and hold hackathons. Every day people talk about developing apps as a way to make quick money with no appreciation for the long hours, the unpaid work and the level of obsession that goes into building up a baby company from nothing.

'It's a bit of a gold rush,' Rohit says.

Instead of panning for gold, however, people are deserting their day jobs to pan for the next Angry Birds.

* * *

How other people talk about start-ups is the issue in a nutshell. Those who constitute the start-up community cast themselves as free-thinking independents, the underdogs of the business world, T-shirt-wearing insurgents making fools out of bloated corporations when they steal their business with a clever revamp that undermines the old certainties in their way of doing things. They are agents for change, but change for the better and this self-styled image makes those on the inside resistant to the ideas that those on the outside want to imprint upon them. In doing so, its people have a way of thinking themselves free. Free from corporate Australia. Free from politics. Free from old ways of thinking.

But they're not. With an economy in need of growth, start-ups have caught the attention of politics. This creates a tension between the hard work needed to gradually grow new industry through start-ups and the impulse to try importing a ready-made tech industry. If they could bring some of that Silicon Valley magic here, the political thinking seems to run, Australia could trade up. Exchange some of that big manufacturing with its unionised workforce for a big new industry of clean-cut, smart, young entrepreneurial professionals who made it in Silicon Valley and will remake Silicon Valley here.

This is how tech start-ups have come to be seen as an opposing force to manufacturing industries, when they never had to be. Making apps and building cars were never rival activities. The people who do one, or the other, are not going anywhere. Ideas need to be applied and even driverless cars need to be built somewhere. So too do their parts. The idea that it was one or the other is a story told when politicians with an election to win start talking about the future.

American start-up founders may have moulded themselves the vanguard of a libertarian utopia, but most Australian entrepreneurs working on their start-ups are happy just making it to the next financial year. Those who survive and achieve the scale they're looking for eventually represent the best of the knowledge economy in an environment where most never make it. What the car makers represent are the best of the manufacturing sector in an industry where not every manufacturing business was capable of being innovative or efficient. Car makers have to be, because if they are not, cars would still come without air conditioners or computers in their engines and the factories would still be forming steel by hand. The best companies in the Australian supply chains had to be nimble to survive because of the small volumes they were making. Australia needed its car makers as well as a home-grown tech industry, just like Britain and just like the United States, which has its Detroit and its Silicon Valley.

Australia has neither. It closed down its Little Detroits and eventually it will learn, like everyone else, that Silicon Valleys are born of a special time and place, not made through government policy. It was an outcome that could have been avoided with a little nuance, but those who thought the factories still worked like they did in the early 80s peered in through the front window of the co-working spaces and saw in them a greater agenda.

Which is how in August 2015 economist Richard Blandy, a man who doesn't like economic multipliers, wrote for *InDaily* about 'How start-ups could solve SA's jobs crisis':

> The economic transformation that South Australia is facing is similar to that facing all the developed Western countries. They are transiting from the industrial era to the post-industrial era. The death of major secondary industries is a symptom of this transformation. Our emerging economic base of electronically networked small to medium businesses is in conflict with our inherited political and institutional superstructure of big firms, big unions and big government ...
>
> Adelaide presently has about 8 per cent of Australia's 1000 annual start-ups. Start-ups could contribute more than 40,000 jobs to the South Australia economy in 20 years' time, far more than the 2000 jobs being lost at Holden. According to Crossroads, Facebook employs about 1500 people in its Palo Alto HQ, but has created an estimated 53,000 jobs for Facebook app creators and 130,000 jobs in related business services. Apple employs 12,000 people in Cupertino, but has created over 60,000 jobs elsewhere.

A month later, Christopher Pyne wrote for the *Sydney Morning Herald* about how he and Malcolm Turnbull want to drive a 'cultural shift' to unlock the potential in start-ups:

> ... with a changing global economy and a decline in traditional manufacturing, our great challenge as a nation is to not just have the ideas, but have the ecosystem

> that allows Australians to pursue them … However, innovation has to be more than just a collection of buzzwords and good intentions. We need a whole of government approach that will drive a cultural shift.
>
> Our aim is a country with a growing entrepreneurial spirit, a citizenry who are prepared to pursue their ideas, prepared to take a risk and prepared to try again if they fail. The future of our economy and maintaining our standard of living as a first world country depends on it.

To get ahead of the curve, Opposition Leader Bill Shorten was photographed visiting Inspire9 in early December 2015 to announce Labor's innovation policy, a collection of tax incentives, a bigger focus on teaching kids to code and the promotion of regional 'innovation hubs'. Two days later Prime Minister Malcolm Turnbull went bigger when he announced his first major policy as PM, a $1.1 billion bundle that included tax incentives, changes to bankruptcy laws and changes to funding regulations, which seemed focussed on luring the 20,000 successful Australian tech entrepreneurs and their heavy wallets back from Silicon Valley. Australia would be a 'start-up nation', the prime minister declared. Australia would become 'agile'. Start-ups are the future. They're honest-to-god economic growth in a tin.

'Those people out there don't give a shit about any of that,' Aron Mercer says, waving a hand across the floor of Inspire9. They've got businesses to run, they're burning through money trying to get traction, and chances are a lot of them may not make it to the end of the next financial year.

Aron, 41, is married with a three-year-old child and his wife still works for corporate Australia. She's the one keeping the lights on right now while he's putting in the hours as a co-founder on the start-up Make Some Change.

Essentially, the app makes money from advertising. Advertisers pay for viewers, viewers watch ads and movie trailers, then donate the money the advertisers paid to a charity of the viewer's choice using a virtual currency created by the development team. This is because Make Some Change is a 'social enterprise', a new breed of start-up born of the idea that the start-up community has been 'solving the problems of rich white men' long enough. Building an app to let someone hire a personal chef for the evening only helps those who don't need help. The kind of thing Aron is working on has so far, in its first two months of operation, helped 49 women be trained as community leaders in India and provided 20 months' worth of scholarships in Cambodia.

'The idea that start-ups and tech will take up the slack from manufacturing is wrong,' Aron says when conversation swings that way. 'Guys popping rivets on cars and driving trucks aren't going to be working in start-ups. They don't even have the networks to get those jobs.'

For the next five minutes Aron talks the real world of start-ups: the long hours, the unpaid work because start-ups don't pay until they begin making money, and the level of financial and emotional risk involved. Aron says he asks himself every day whether what he's doing is worth it, whether it's going to fall apart. He loves the life, he loves what he's learning and he loves what he's doing now, but even he says it's not all roses.

Still, this is where he's meant to be. He spent 15 years in the corporate world working at companies like Australia Post and Experion where he was one tooth on a big cog on a bigger machine. That time with corporate Australia trained him and introduced him to the networks he needed to hear about this job, which offered him the chance to do something meaningful with his skill set. It was the right move for him, he says, but he's the first to say it's not for everyone.

'There's no school for this,' he says. 'You just go have 1000 cups of coffee.'

Since he joined up with the development team, his job has been to sell the start-up to anyone who might listen. Getting an angel investor on board to back the business means it just may be able to survive beyond its life expectancy and it is Aron's job to make that happen. Each investor weighs every business slightly differently, though if Aron had to boil it down, he would say it's some variation on how easily the idea can be scaled up, how unique the idea is, how easy it is for the investor to get out with their money, and the measure of whoever it is making the pitch.

'Lastly, they look at you,' he says, pointing centre mass, right across the table. 'And those guys are sharks.' He says it with emphasis.

And start-ups still face the same temptation to offshore. Australia ranks as the seventh easiest place in the world to start a business, but Australian investors aren't like American investors who, Aron says, place bets.

'They'll fund ten, knowing six will fail and one will take off,' Aron says. The rest simply get by.

Australian venture capitalists only back one.

'The question we're asking ourselves right now is do we bother with Australia,' he goes on. 'It's such a small market. It's less than 2 per cent of the global advertising market. But you could make it in California alone.

'When we started, we had a couple of American venture capitalists say don't bother about here and just go straight to America.'

And the feeling across the floor at Inspire9 is that Australia is very late to the game. It is an old frustration among young Australians in that what happens elsewhere in the world takes too long to filter Down Under.

If true, it is also a state of affairs that could be turned to an advantage. Being in the middle of the pack takes the pressure off, which affords a chance to look around and learn from others' mistakes.

Which is exactly what Scott Shane of Case Western Reserve University was trying to get governments to do in 2008, when he famously wrote a report for the World Economic Forum titled: 'Why encouraging more people to become entrepreneurs is bad public policy'.

In it, he argued that the idea that start-ups were major drivers of growth in an economy was a myth. Over the long term, new firms are not more productive than existing firms; the reverse is true. Start-ups may teach through failure, but established firms also learn through survival. Start-ups don't pay until money starts coming in, don't offer benefits and rarely employ many people. In the United States, start-ups never compensated for their lack of initial growth by making up for it later on, because most only made it three years in the churn. They never grew big enough, or fast enough. Instead they stayed small and as they grew older, these small firms experienced a high rate of job destruction. Australia is the same.

The personal and financial risk involved in starting a new business is also why wealthier countries tend to have lower numbers of new companies. The unemployed face no such risk from trying something new, so from out of their ranks step forward a greater number of entrepreneurs.

'If you want to find countries where there are a lot of entrepreneurs,' Shane wrote, 'go to Africa or South America.'

As an academic who studies entrepreneurship, Scott Shane's paper wasn't levelled at start-ups or the entrepreneurs who run them. What he wanted was clear thinking by those in government. The message was that it is about quality, not volume. Boosting economic growth is not as simple as a lot of new entrepreneurs all starting dog-wash businesses, or people with no managerial skills putting their life savings on the line to develop the next big smartphone app. Only 3.2 per cent of Australian start-ups actually had potential to deliver and as Shane wrote, it was a bad idea to spend public money to get more 'marginal' businesses that never grow, never make money and eventually die off, leaving their founders burned out and broken.

Which is not what Australia needs, but it does seem to be the dispiriting vision on offer: an economy of 23 million people driving around in 13.5 million imported cars all dreaming of making it rich on their own Uber app. Add it all up and what it looks like is a kind of *Downton Abbey* for the information age. A digital *Grapes of Wrath*, with a lot at the top, a lot at the bottom and not much going on in the middle.

In this future, the kids who don't make it to university will be pushed out to the margins, where they'll work a string of low-paid jobs knowing there's nothing else out there but never knowing why. Everyone else will spend years studying to become designers and architects and coders, and when they finish they'll get all the prestige of calling themselves professionals but none of the pay those titles used to guarantee. They will work out of government-subsidised co-working spaces and innovation hubs in the same warehouses and factories where their grandmothers and grandfathers were paid by the hour to make stuff. They'll drink from glass jars and play table tennis during the work day. A pool table is also a possibility.

They'll freelance or work for start-ups in the trenches of the digital revolution where they'll work at all hours of the day and won't see a dollar until the business starts turning a profit. They'll pay their rent driving for Uber, or whatever comes after Uber, or by pouring microbrews, or making lattes, or waiting tables at the barricades of the food revolution. A lucky few will make it. The start-up they signed onto will take off, achieve the high growth and the sustainability it always had the potential for. When it does, they will be treated like heroes of the market and asked their opinion on all matters of business life.

The other 96.8 per cent won't. But they'll do it all again and again, and they'll do it happily because they've grown up being taught they should not be afraid to give themselves over to the churn. They'll tell themselves it is all worth it. They'll tell anyone who listens how they freely chose this life.

What choice did they have?

Chapter 36

STILL SCREWED

WHEN JAMES TACEY SPOKE TO 2GB RADIO IN FEBRUARY 2014, he said he was screwed. He had no choice. If things kept going as they were, his company was going to offshore production at their Heidelberg West factory. The 97-year-old operation employed 43 people to make fasteners, the screws, nuts and bolts that stitch together Australia's Commodores and Falcons. The average length of service was 15 years in his factory, and with Holden soon to be out of the picture, the whole thing was coming apart. They were better off going to Thailand.

'If I draw a line in a sand today, our manufacturing facilities are finished as of 2017,' James told the radio host. 'I have to go to a low-cost country because I've lost the economy of scale.'

Two years on, things are looking very different. He and his manufacturing director, Ray Cervelli, have managed to hold it together long enough to turn the business around and these days James Tacey is a hard man to pin down. Climbing the stairs to the Staetite office, James is not around for the 9am sit-down. He's lost somewhere in the factory, one of the staff says. When she goes to look for him, the door to the factory opens and in floods the noise of metal and machines. It's a monstrous, constant whir that pounds its way inside the eardrums. It closes again, seals shut, and the room is silent except for the sound of tapping keys.

A fortnight from now, James and his marketing director will fly to San Francisco to meet with the people in charge at Tesla. Things are busy, he says, when he walks in ten minutes later. He's dressed casually, wearing a grey T-shirt, jeans and sandals. He shakes hands with a medium grip. Once settled, he starts to tell about how they had an idea the industry was on the way out five years ago, so they started trying to diversify their operation. Others haven't been so lucky.

At the start, only about 4 to 6 per cent of their business was exports and they had been eyeing Thailand as a place where they could bring in new business. After setting up a small 'base of operations', they started knocking on doors for customers. At first they couldn't find anyone and years went by without much luck. By the time the announcement came, they had two or three contracts in Thailand, which was something but not enough to keep them going. Eventually, they signed with GM and also with Futuris Thailand to make parts for the seats that went into the Ford Everest.

It was Tesla that changed everything, though. Through Futuris, Staetite ended up supplying Tesla for their Model S electric car. Tesla wasn't used to getting the kind of service Staetite provided. American and Chinese companies made their money through scale and never really had to worry about the service they provided to their customers; if someone needed something unique, or redesigned on short notice, that was tough. It was a different story when it came to Australian companies, which have always had to be responsive to their customer base to survive in a market with low population and low volumes.

'After six months of working with Tesla, they wanted us to look at other business and they've just hit us with that many quotes,' James says. Once Tesla moved all the work on the Model X in-house, it tapped Staetite to supply the parts. Tesla liked what they saw and James says they've started talking about his company designing and making the nuts and bolts on the upcoming Model 3. It would make them the only Australian supplier.

These days, they have enough work to say with confidence that their factory is staying. 'We've made it,' James says, flat out. They're back to running five days a week and in the first month of 2016, they had 2858 orders alone. They've just won another GM quality award for the fourth year running and their export share has risen to 60 per cent. The numbers are looking good. The company will make it to its 100th anniversary next year and when it does, it will survive the end of the Australian car industry.

Not everyone has, and not everyone will. Over the past two years, James says, they've watched as people have disappeared. 'A lot of people have just gone,' he says. They've packed down their operations and disappeared into the night. When Ford leaves in October 2016, what's left of the already anaemic supply chain is going to collapse. Some will make it, many won't and that makes things harder for everyone.

Just as the big car companies needed all the little companies in their supply chain to keep going, the little companies needed each other. Some provided essential services required to make a product or maintain its quality. The competition also acted as knowledge banks, safeguarding skills learned from over half a century of operations. If someone left all of a sudden, or was talking about retirement, it was possible to bring in someone from a competitor who knew what they were doing.

Staetite saved itself by going global, but before any of that happened, there was a time when company management had been talking about offshoring everything to Thailand. It seemed to make sense then. They had already set up a base from which they were trying to court new customers, so the company thought it wouldn't take much to shift their entire operation after Holden went. They'd be close to a new manufacturing base and a growing market, and labour would be cheaper. Staetite Fasteners was built as an Australian company set up to sell to the Australian market, but there was no more Australian market, so it made sense to go somewhere new.

But the maths didn't work. The cost of moving the entire factory to Thailand, setting up, making money and then having to bring that money back into Australia meant they would, essentially, be taxed twice. While Thailand had a growing manufacturing base, there wasn't enough of it there to allow them to make their product to the same standard. Sure, the Thai government offered them tax incentives and land subsidies, but, James says, he had to think about them as temporary. Eventually, they would run out and then the company had to stand on its own. It turned out that land and rent were just as expensive in Thailand as in Australia.

Then there was the cost of labour, which had been rising by the year as the automotive companies set up in Thailand and started to poach skilled workers from each other, subsequently driving up wages. Where a day's wage used to be 300 or 400 baht a day, it climbed to 700 baht and was likely to keep going. It might have meant better living conditions for the new Thai middle class, but for a company looking to make savings from exploiting cheap foreign labour, it was a downer.

'If your only reason to move to Thailand is the cost of labour, it's the wrong move,' James says. 'A lot of companies have moved over there and found that it ain't what it is. We know a lot of people who have gone and are no longer there. We know a lot of people who are there now, Australian companies, and it is killing them. A lot of them moved on promises they would get this business, or that business, but it hasn't worked out that way.

'There's three or four massive Australian companies there now, automotive ... there's not much going on in their factory. Some are doing really well, some are absolutely struggling.'

* * *

Out on the factory floor, Andrew Eadrie, 59, shows how to thread a screw. He's from New Zealand originally and over the noise of the machines he says he wanted to be an architect, except he grew up in a rough neighbourhood and left school early.

'Only a small handful ever make it to what they want in life,' Andrew says. 'And you know, some people make it and aren't very good at it.'

But this job Andrew is good at. You can tell by his hands and the way he talks with a careful, even-mannered thoroughness. He has been with the company for 11 years, he says, and has worked every job in the place. These days, he goes where he is needed and the skin on his hands is thick like leather from a working life so far spent keeping machines alive.

He is going through the settings on the threading machine now, holding the order form on this batch, explaining what each number means and why it is important. Once it's running, he takes a bucket of blank screws and pours them into the feeding tray. Then he starts the machine up and the tray starts to spin. The screws line up and feed down into the machine where they're covered in a lubricant and threaded through a die before being spat out at the bottom.

Steam rises from the newly threaded screws and Andrew picks up a couple in his hand like a farmer bending down to pick up a head of grain. 'They come out quite hot,' he says as he passes one over. 'It's the friction.' He's not wrong. As it rolls about a fresh pair of hands it burns with a sour kind of heat.

On the other side of the factory Andrew opens up a panel on one of the machines to show how it forces a blank screw through its teeth. He works it manually, to show the motion, then pushes it out rapidly and puts another thread on a blank screw. He says the machine is currently set to 110 parts per minute, or 6600 an hour. This machine alone is capable of pumping out tens of thousands a day, and when the entire factory is running full tilt the numbers are staggering.

Every last part starts life over in one corner of the factory before it works its way around. Every screw, every bolt made in this plant begins with steel wire being fed into the forge. Afterwards, the blank screws need the head put on them before being threaded. Once that's done, they'll be put through fire to harden them. The furnace runs at 930 degrees, he says, but sometimes they'll come out too brittle for what was ordered. To make them right, they need to be tempered with thermo gas and air heated to 300 degrees to bring them down to spec. From there, they go off to quality control just inside the attached warehouse, before they're packaged and shipped away.

'You won't find these in Bunnings,' Andrew says. 'Those are cheap Chinese imports. Every so often, the head comes right off.'

It's something Andrew feels that people don't really understand, what goes into making something like a screw from scratch. They help hold the world together, and the ones Andrew helps make in this factory are stronger than anything on the retail market. Most people don't know that. They don't know the two main ingredients are carbon and manganese or that they can make them with a radius on the tip so some robot on a production line somewhere will never miss its target. People only ever see the whole and never stop to think about the individual pieces.

'It's the same for our manufacturing and the same for our farmers,' Andrew says when asked about the world outside the factory walls. 'Just go to the shop and buy it. Just go to Bunnings. Just go to the grocery store. They don't realise someone had to make it or grow it.

'That wire,' he says, pointing over to the metre-high coils of wire lined up in rows against the front wall of the factory. 'We dig it out of the ground and send it overseas. Then we buy it back.

'Manufacturing is dead,' he goes on. 'They're trying to make it go technical, but how many people can work with computers? Some people want to work with their hands.'

* * *

That's something Ray Cervelli wants to talk about, sitting at his desk in his dark office, the horizontal blinds closed behind him, his attention complete. Ray is a short man with sharp eyes and an equally sharp intelligence. He's the last of the old-school managers, a dying breed. When he speaks, he does so slowly and with weight.

Officially he works three days a week, but really he does five because the 70-year-old still has passion. Ask him what he thinks, on any subject, and he'll tell it like it is.

'You know, someone once wrote a technical paper and called it a marriage between art and science,' he says of the factory floor. He pauses to let the thought sink in.

It was Greek and Italian migrants like Ray who started all the business in this industry. He says his family first came over in the early 1960s. The family had been running a business in Egypt during the 50s but they had to quit the country quickly. He doesn't explain why. His father then brought them back to Italy for a time before he moved them out to Australia in 1963. It was no easier here, he says, but his mother had relatives. Asked what it was like, he talks about how the weekends were quiet, the shops closed at six, and the toilets were in the back of the garden.

'Egypt was a third-world country but had all the amenities,' Ray says. 'Australia, the lucky country, the toilets were outside.'

Still, they made the trip and, when he was 15, Ray got himself an apprenticeship as a toolmaker. After he finished, he quit that as soon as he could. He then put himself through 15 years of night school studying engineering and management, where he learned to solve problems, how to step back and look at the whole to find a solution that worked. It taught him that the theory always comes after the practice. The world worked the way it wanted to, not the way you thought it should.

When Ray joined the fastener business, designing screws and bolts to application, it was vibrant. There were 121 different companies doing something similar to what Staetite does now. They even set up their own institute in the 70s, but over the next 50 years, Ray watched the companies fall away. He knows of one or two still going in Adelaide and Sydney, but in Melbourne there are only really two making any money.

Ray doesn't call himself an engineer these days. He stepped out of engineering and into a management role after he put himself through an MBA in business during his 40s. He wasn't the only one. Many of those found there just wasn't a place for them anymore and, just like Ray, they went to other companies, many of them in automotive. Then that industry closed down too.

Ray was standing outside with James, having a cigarette, when he heard the news that Holden was folding. Ray smoked back then, and the pair's eyes met. Neither had to say a word. Both knew what kind of threat it posed to everything they had put into the business over the years. They had worked together long enough to get a good sense of what the other was thinking. Both implicitly understood what it all meant and what kind of work had to be done if they were going to make it. Both shared a rising sense of anxiety and Ray lit another cigarette.

The pair never lied to their people about the odds. The Productivity Commission heard evidence that 80 per cent of suppliers in the automotive chain might close down when the car makers go, and Staetite could have been among them. The company makes a product range of 4000 parts to order, and if they don't have what a customer needs, they'll design it from scratch. All up, automotive accounted for about 70 per cent of their business then. They supplied General Motors direct and made the nuts and bolts for Tier 1 and Tier 2 suppliers, which in turn made parts for GM, Toyota and Ford. As the months rolled by after the end of the industry was made official, the infrastructure that held up the big factories began to crumble. Everyone they relied on to put in orders and keep the machines running stopped calling and, soon enough, James and Ray were cutting back shifts. It went from five days a week to four, then to three and a half. Everyone could see which way they were headed.

It was a hard time for Ray. He has never closed a factory. Once, at a company he worked for in Sydney, he had to lay off 70 people in one afternoon. Tell them their job was done.

'Unless you're a robot, it really takes the shit out of you, psychologically,' he says. 'And I was not closing the factory. If I had to close the factory, I would go into a corner and pass by. The psychological impact would be that big.'

It's also why Ray can't understand how or why it all happened. Australia is full of talent, he says. 'That man,' Ray says about Andrew Eadrie, 'has a unique ability to solve problems.' He says Andrew will take a moment, step back and see the whole. Without this place, without the factories, people like him will have one less place to use that talent.

'Where are the next generation of engineers coming from?' he asks, before he starts to list the companies that drew their engineers from the ranks of Holden. Holden will keep an Australian design team around, but it's been shedding engineers over the past few years because with no new models, and no more upgrades, there's no work. Even those who stay on will be a shadow of what they could have been with the plants where they learned how everything worked. The 38-hectare Fishermans Bend plant, first built on swampland in 1936, will become a block of high-rise apartments, Ray thinks, and he's likely right. At the end of December, six buyers made the shortlist to carve up the $130 million site where Holden used to make its engines. Those six included some of the biggest property developers in the country. It's something we will never regain, Ray says.

'I honestly don't believe the government, in making the decision they made, knew what they were doing,' Ray says. 'Joe Hockey's a total fuckwit. I'm sorry about the language, but it's the truth. He didn't know what he was talking about. Between him, this Minister for Industry and the prime minister, to do this, I don't believe they know what they've done.'

Ray tells the story about a meeting he once attended. A session had been organised by a government body for manufacturers in the automotive supply chain to help them diversify into something else before it was all over. There, the government man stood and told his audience of manufacturers their best bet was to move into making parts for the mining industry. Australia was the world's largest supplier of iron ore, he said, and that wasn't going to change any time soon.

As is his way, Ray listened quietly before he asked a question with razor-sharp precision. Mining is cyclical, he said, and mining needs parts ten times larger than what his factory was currently able to make. It would cost tens of millions of dollars to diversify into the mining industry, to retool, to remake the machines and build parts big enough and strong enough to haul coal and iron ore over distances. Where is that money coming from, he asked? And by the time it was done, will it have been worth it if the price of iron ore and coal falls through the floor? Did the government really expect them to go through with it?

They did. The government man told him that Australia was the world's largest supplier of iron ore. Ray repeats the phrase. *Australia was the largest supplier of iron ore.* That was it. That's all the man would say.

Then there was that email a couple of weeks back. As it stands, Staetite has plans to expand, and for that their operation needs more muscle. It would cost them $300,000 to go to the next stage of development, to bring in the new machines and with that, he says, they could move to dominate market share in their industry. To make it happen, they wanted to apply to the government for $130,000 in assistance under a scheme, but they never received an invitation to apply. Instead, they received another email from the government not long after, offering to pay an expert to come in and advise them on what to do with their business.

'We've won the GM quality award four years in a row,' Ray says slowly and with force. 'For the last seven years, we've been audited, they couldn't find a fault.

'I don't want someone coming in here, borrowing our watch and telling us what time it is.'

Times like these make Ray think about writing a letter. This is not how a rich, modern, developed country should behave, he thinks. It is not meant to throw away the people who make things. A nation of shopkeepers and baristas and investment advisors isn't enough. It needs to make stuff. To solve problems. Add value. When something goes wrong it needs to step back, look at the whole and find something that works. Australia can, but most days it doesn't seem like it wants to.

Ray should be retired by now, but he keeps coming into work because he loves what he does, even if Australia does not. He's a proud old lion, the last of a dying breed, one the country has decided it doesn't need anymore.

Though Ray's not worried. Why would he be?

There's nothing left to worry about.

Epilogue

A EULOGY

THERE IS AN OLD BENCH RIGHT ACROSS THE ROAD FROM THE Holden plant. The green paint is coming off and the wood of its seat is slanted. The lawn along that side of the highway is well kept, but the grass around the legs has grown long and wild. Once it might have been a bus stop, but these days it serves no real purpose other than to let a person look out over a car factory, and no one would want to do that anyway.

Sitting on that bench beneath a cloudy sky the colour of midnight ink, a few hours after the last shift knocked off, helps to get a feeling for what's about to happen. For now the Holden logo still glows red in the night sky, but it is on borrowed time. Once it is switched off and the factory is stilled, things will move quickly. The car park nearby is empty and the streets around these parts are poorly lit and deserted. This time of year the wind grows cold, which makes the hairs on your forearms stand on end. As the leaves of the gum trees rustle gently in the breeze, the only people moving through here are those whose cars prowl the highway.

By the time this book hits the printers, the car industry will have entered its final stage. The plant will have ended the production of the Cruze model and will have started to chip away at the workforce. After that, it will keep going for another six months more, maybe.

When it happens, when the gates are locked on the factories of Ford, Holden and Toyota, and their machines shipped to China or Thailand or wherever, it will mark the start of a grand new social experiment. What will be left? Who will stay? It's impossible to know for sure. There is no real precedent for something like this. Nothing we can look to as an oracle of what to expect. Every city has a different history and follows a different path. Those who can find something else to do will get by. Those who have the resources to move away probably will. Maybe they'll move out west if the price of iron ore rebounds, or maybe they'll join the flow of people migrating east to the capital cities from where the country is run. Those who can't will start turning up in the official numbers about 18 months after each factory has been put into mothballs. That's when this experiment being carried out on six million lab rats across two states will kick into next gear.

I have sat through funerals before but nothing like this. Australia has never seen what can happen when an entire industry packs up so completely in such a short space of time. The closest we have ever come is watching the steel industry rust up in Wollongong over two decades.

So should we have saved the factory? Should the Australian taxpayer have propped up the car companies until they finally turned it around?

Does it matter now?

The reality is, the factories are gone. The same political figures who talked about jobs and growth decided the factories were unnecessary and deleted them from the Australian social fabric. In doing so they talked as if they were cutting out a cancer, only it was never as simple as that. A lot of people are connected to the factories and shipyards and smelters in some way. If they didn't work them, or make their living off those who worked them, their ancestors probably did to give them a shot at something better. Cutting out the car jobs also meant cutting out the muscle.

Symbolically, what killing the car industry did was take down the whole idea that there was some level of nobility to work. Your granddad might not have got rich spending a quarter-century with the company, but he got by. It was an honest way of living which guaranteed a person their slice of the shared economic prosperity that has so far defined Australian life. Closing Holden brought an end to all that and marked the moment when Australia ditched the ethic of hard work for the hustle, when it became a nation of freelancers loyal to none but themselves.

Now those who gave the company 15 or more years have been turned out onto a job market that is alien to them. There they will be joined by everyone in the supply chain and everyone else caught up in the growing list of lay-offs and closures that have quietly racked up over the past three years, the latest at the time of writing being Arrium's

Whyalla steelworks going into administration, putting at risk another 1000 people and the stability of the local economy.

Which is why it is hard to shake the feeling that for all the good work that has been done, that for all the retraining programs, for all the Transition Centres, things are about to get a whole lot worse for a whole lot of good people. And not just autoworkers. The mining boom that would never end has ended and the makers have been put out of business. Australia seems to be pinning its hopes right now on a service economy augmented by a tech industry it doesn't have and is too impatient to grow. At the very same time the federal government has been playing a shell game with funding for scientific research and talking about how it wants to reform education and healthcare in ways that will make it more expensive, or of lower quality, for the very people who need it most.

It is a crappy set of circumstances, straight up. There is no other way around it. The conditions are there to make what comes next ugly, and from where I sit all it would take is ten long years and a bad case of corporate indifference or civic mismanagement to make a crappy situation desperate.

Though I hope it doesn't get to that. I'd like to believe it's possible for us to sidestep the worst of it, that we will find some way to fight back, that the promises of new jobs in advanced manufacturing and 'smart industries' might actually be more than hollow words.

However, people have been talking about these new jobs for a while now and outside a few notable examples, they're not here. When those same promises were made over a decade ago to the people of the American rust belt, those jobs never eventuated there either. It's why, these days, when I hear conversation turn this way, it sounds less visionary and more like the desperate talk people get into wherever the local industry shuts down.

And when the last of the factories go, it will happen among those regions whose people were among the first to be liberated from the factories in this great new experiment. While the rest of Australia got rich quick from ripping ore out of the dirt, these people were liberated from their good jobs, liberated from their good, dependable pay, liberated from their unions, liberated to build better, freer lives. All they need is to stay positive and have a little self-confidence, the thinking seems to go. Take another job, any job. This is the lucky country, after all. What does it matter if the pay isn't as good? Or the conditions are a little less friendly? No one gets rich in a day.

These are the people whose kids might need to lie about where they live to get that start in a low-paid, dead-end job that numbs the brain and offers no future. The people who try for an education only to graduate just as the funding has been pulled. The people who might lose their house because they can't keep up the payments as a disposable worker in the freelance economy. The people who might live in a neighbourhood where a house gets burned down and doesn't get rebuilt. Where they are afraid to give out their names because they fear a brick through the window or the thugs around the corner who may come back one night to teach a lesson.

Ask them what they think, and they will tell you how it is American living. Australia's very own American Dream.

Postscript

JULY-ISH, 2016

RAYLENE MULLINS, SIXTY-FOUR, IS LEAVING.

It is a Tuesday afternoon and things are scattered throughout the house she and her husband and partner of fifty years, Alan, rent in the town. Ever since Alan lost his job at Arrium, there has been no reason for them to stay.

The Mullins aren't the first to leave, and they won't be the last. Arrium ran the steelworks out this way, and since the company went into voluntary administration, the whole town has been wondering what will come next.

A future without the steelworks was once unthinkable in the 23,000-person town. So was a Whyalla without Raylene Mullins, ever since that day in March 2016 when she walked right up to the prime minister, Malcolm Turnbull, during a press conference and, without fear, gave him a lesson on the way of things.

Turnbull had planted his feet in the town to announce that a rail upgrade would be brought forward to assist the struggling steelworks. Arrium was in financial trouble, had been for a while, and though it hadn't yet entered administration, it was the closest thing the company was going to get to a bailout under a federal Coalition government.

Raylene already had the words formed in her head, she tells me while we sit in her backyard one afternoon. For a long time she has been watching the factories close down and go offshore. It is this thing happening to the country; something big and potentially bad. Things have changed a lot since Malcolm Fraser, the last prime minister that Raylene remembers with any warmth. He might have been an Oxford-educated career politician, but he was raised in rural Victoria and went back to the farm after he retired. Fraser was the reason Raylene has voted Liberal almost all her life.

'[Fraser] worked with his hands,' she says. 'He knew what he had to do for the country.'

As far as she's concerned, everyone who has come after has just been in it for him- or herself. It has been that way for so long that Raylene's faith has begun to waver. That's why she defected to Nick Xenophon at the recent federal election.

Her feeling is that the major parties have stopped talking to ordinary people, and when they try to do so, it is with a degree of condescension. During her exchange with Malcolm Turnbull, he listened politely and didn't interrupt. Manufacturing was dead in Australia, Raylene told him in front of the nation's media. Australia had killed it through the relentless pursuit of free trade agreements.

She told him a country needed to make stuff to keep people employed – and in case there was ever another war.

'You can't just have health jobs and office jobs,' she said.

'I understand your concern, I really do,' Turnbull responded. 'But our future is bound up with open markets.'

* * *

Truth is, the rust had set into Whyalla long before anyone knew it was there.

Steel had always been Whyalla's business. Steel built the roads out there. Steel built the houses. Steel brought in the people. Steel made the factories and drove the trucks. On bad days, steel seemed to hold up the sky.

The town's infant steelworks opened in 1941, alongside a shipyard, and Whyalla's people went to work building the warships the country needed to drive fascism out of the Pacific.

After the war they built merchant ships for BHP, and when the plant was upgraded in 1958 it became one of the largest steel production sites in Australia.

Nineteen-seventy-six was Whyalla's golden age, when its population swelled to 33,000. Two years later the shipyards closed, putting 1800 people out of work. The town plunged into a local recession, and South Australia's third largest city began its slow downward slide until that fateful day on 7 April 2016 when Arrium, the entity that owned the steelworks, went into administration.

That was the day of the crash. A Thursday. The Whyalla steelworks employed about 20 per cent of the town.

Everyone knew the prognosis was bad, but none had a real sense of it until Dr John Spoehr of Flinders University released an impact study in May which found that the end of the steelworks would hit harder than the decline of the auto industry in Detroit.

'In some ways Whyalla captures all our worst fears because it is so concentrated and so intense,' he told me. 'I've used the "Detroit" word, but in some ways Whyalla is in a much more precarious situation than Detroit because it's much more isolated. It doesn't have the advantages Detroit has in size, even though Detroit was dependent on the auto-making industries.'

So how did it happen?

In a word: hubris.

During the height of the mining boom, when the price of iron ore was over $100 a tonne, company management didn't just want to make steel, it wanted to mine the ore too. Arrium had invested heavily in high-stakes mining operations across South Australia's iron triangle while it worked the machines at the steelworks into the ground. According to the oral history of the workforce, no one in management seemed to want to shut the place down to make any upgrades. They were making too much money.

When the mining boom ended with a whimper and the price of iron ore fell, the company had to keep those old machines pumping just to cover costs. Steel was in oversupply around the world, the threadbare machines were no longer globally competitive and all the bad decisions made during the time of plenty started to be felt across the entire operation.

This is evident in the deal Arrium struck when it took over Southern Iron in October 2011. The company had bought the ore mine from WPG Resources and had to renegotiate a contract with US firm Genesee & Wyoming, which ran the rail link from the mine to the town.

Under the arrangement Arrium agreed to take what the mine sent down, or pay a penalty. In negotiation, Arrium fiddled with the volumes, but not the length of the contract, which it was agreed would run until 2017.

When the ore price fell again and Arrium had to mothball the mine in January 2015, it was still expected to pay $70 million under the contract for a service it was not using. Rumour has it the guys paid to run the rail line were turning up to work just to sit in the lunchroom and do nothing.

A little over a year later and a month before the company would go into administration under $2.3 billion in debt, Arrium asked its workforce to take a 10 per cent pay cut.

* * *

Acting mayor of Whyalla Tom Antonio never had a choice. Since Arrium went into administration it has been his job to guide the town through the crisis. Whyalla's local leadership had been in a 'unique situation' after Jim Pollock resigned as mayor in May 2016 for health reasons and sadly passed away a few months later, leaving Tom working alongside an acting CEO and an acting NBN supervisor.

As acting mayor Tom has been putting in fourteen-hour days, while also trying to keep his electrical retail business afloat. He has three sons working at the steelworks, and for a time has been trying to get the word out that Whyalla mattered. When I ask whether he was scared when the news broke of Arrium's collapse, he doesn't quite know how to answer. He goes to say yes, but catches himself quickly.

'I don't want to say scared,' he says. 'I was certainly extremely concerned. Absolutely. But I've taken this as a challenge.'

It sounds like safe politician speak, and there's a damn good reason for it. For months Tom Antonio has been speaking to everyone who will listen about what it would mean if Australia's last producer of structural steel closed. He's also been talking to state and federal politicians who are working with the administrators, who in turn were talking to the people at the banks.

Once Tom had their attention, the next task was to make sure the townspeople knew Whyalla was not doomed or risk the town emptying out.

Two days before we spoke the company made it known that it expected to be out of administration by Christmas 2016 while the steelworks and accompanying port would be sold off. Once that happens, Tom explains, it would mean a better future for Whyalla, as a commercial port would open up other opportunities in the region, like exporting iron ore.

The message, he says, is that Whyalla is fighting back against circumstances not of its making.

'Things will get better,' he says, though he can't put a definite timeline on it. It could all happen next week, or it could happen in six months.

* * *

Talk in Whyalla has a way of turning back to the town's troubles. Whyalla's people are angry on good days and anxious on the bad. They feel betrayed by those who used up the town during the best years of the mining boom and walked away for the worst, leaving them to clean up the mess.

And people have looked around at their town's empty houses losing value as they sit unsold. They can count the 'for lease' signs going up in storefront windows. Then they start wondering whether they have a future in Whyalla.

Bruce Baulderstone and his wife, Lorraine, have been thinking about leaving. They own a fish-and-chip shop, the oldest in the town. It has been around for forty years, they tell me. Up on the shop's walls are black-and-white photos from Whyalla's golden age which were saved from the rubbish heap by a local historian when BHP pulled out of the town in 2000.

'If you were in Year Twelve right now, would you stay?' Bruce asks me. 'There's just nothing else here.'

When I ask what his plans are, Bruce says he doesn't know. Tax time is coming up, and soon he will ask his accountant how long they can keep on. They used to employ five people in the shop, not including themselves, but now they are down to three. If they hadn't laid people off, they would have already gone bankrupt.

'But I can't sell up because no one's buying,' Bruce says. 'You know, I've always put something away in the good times, knowing there was going to be hard times, but I never knew it was going to get this bad. Some people don't realise how hard it is when you actually live here.'

* * *

When she left school in 1969, Raylene Mullins started working life as a machinist on a sewing machine. She was sixteen years old.

'I can put a zip in without tacking and pinning it,' she says. It is a point of pride.

Throughout her working life, Raylene sold Avon and Hobbytex paint and Tupperware door to door. She worked night shifts at Coles from six to nine, three times a week, while her husband stayed home with the kids. For a while she did repairs on the clothes at a dry cleaners in Victor Harbor, and in 1987 she started driving.

At first everyone told Raylene a woman couldn't drive a school bus, but she did it anyway. Later, in 2003, she wanted to drive taxis, and the same people told her she couldn't do that either. Raylene is short and doesn't approve of swearing; there was no way she could deal with the drunks and deadbeats late at night.

Raylene didn't care. 'That's life,' she said. She drove taxis for ten years.

Driving taught her how to get the measure of people. She had only six runners during her career, and she knew it was about to happen every time. Driving also meant she talked to people, got to know them, and that's how she collected stories about engineers who couldn't engineer, teachers who couldn't teach, and lawyers who couldn't lawyer.

At the same time she watched the local factories close down, one by one, as Australia traded the tangible for the intangible. The everyday items people used – the paperclips, the rubber bands, the zips, the garden shovels, the dinner plates, the furniture, the bricks, the clothing, the hats, the buckles, stuff of every size and shape – all started to be brought in on the back of a ship.

What Raylene has witnessed is the Great Transition: the move from making things to the 'New Economy', which concentrates economic activity in east coast metropolises like Sydney or Melbourne where people work on laptops in innovation hubs or trade bonds. The jobs of the future in her part of the world are health and tourism and services, she hears. If this doesn't work out, people might try construction or flipping houses in real estate thanks to negative gearing, a feature of Australian economic life which has been described as a Ponzi scheme by economists such as Yanis Varoufakis.

Raylene Mullins just calls it a betrayal.

What if you can't afford an education in this new Australia, she wonders. What if you make a mistake? And what if you just don't work that way?

'Some people aren't good at school,' she says. 'They are good with their hands. They can make. My older two sons didn't do well in school, couldn't grasp it and it was help at home that pushed them through. Otherwise they would have been lost in the world. People like them, they get told they are dumb, but with manufacturing, they can prove they are not. They go to work happy that they can do something and prove to people that they are not dumb, and that they can do it.

'Now these people have no choice about where to work because there isn't a choice anymore.'

* * *

In that way, Whyalla is no different to anywhere else across the country where the compact between labour, industry and government has been abandoned or undermined. Whyalla could be Wollongong from the 1980s, or Elizabeth in South Australia, or Geelong, Broadmeadows or Dandenong in Victoria when the car industry closes for good.

The factory, the steelworks and the smelters helped create a more evenly shared prosperity than Lenin's Socialist Republic. Now they are dead or dying in communities where a new housing development might go up overnight but there isn't a well-paying job within a 45-minute drive. Left behind by technological change, abandoned by the ideology, those places where identity is defined by town, work and family are watching their kids leave. In 1920s America, the Okies went west to California. In 2016, South Australia's sons and daughters go east to Melbourne or Sydney.

This is an Australia increasingly divided between the winners and losers, and politics is the latest victim. At the July 2016 federal election, almost a third of all South Australians voted independent; the bulk of them cast their ballots for the insurgent Nick Xenophon Team. Rowan Ramsey, the incumbent Liberal candidate for the electorate of Grey, in which Whyalla sits, only narrowly survived. So, too, did the federal Coalition, forming government with the slimmest of majorities on promises that include corporate-tax cuts and a $2 billion welfare crackdown. It is an approach that will only deepen the antagonism between ordinary people and Canberra.

At the time of writing, the For Sale signs are still slung over Arrium with no federal bailout in sight, Ford has gone and Holden's closure has been confirmed for 20 October 2017. At Elizabeth, unemployment is averaging 34.5 per cent. Whyalla is currently at 8.6 per cent.

Among the people who live in these places are the Australians who might be working two jobs, or no job, or be going out of business. They may now be able to choose between 350 different new car models sold under 67 separate brands, or 747 types of beer if they buy online, but many feel like they no longer have a choice. As the prime minister told the steelworker's wife, Australia's future is 'bound up with open markets'.

Sources

The stories contained within have been produced through interviews, on-the-ground observations and secondary sources. Some stories have been supplemented with insight and observations of others who have been willing to share. Secondary sources have included books, feature articles, news clippings, official reports, statistical data, pamphlets and online videos, the most significant of which are listed below. The profiles of Nick Xenophon and Darryn Lyons primarily draw on secondary sources, as does the account of the leadership challenge and the political climate following the 2013 election.

BOOKS

Bageant, J., *Deer Hunting With Jesus*, Portobello Books, London, 2008.

Bramble, T., *Trade Unionism in Australia: A history from flood to ebb tide*, Cambridge University Press, 2008.

Haigh, G., *End of the Road*, Penguin, Melbourne, 2008.

Horne, D., *The Lucky Country*, Penguin, Melbourne, 2009.

LeDuff, C., *Detroit: An American Autopsy*, Penguin, New York, 2013.

Lyons, D., *Mr Paparazzi: My Life as the World's Most Outrageous Celebrity Photographer*, John Blake Publishing, London, 2010.

Marmo, M., De Lint, W. and Palmer, D., *Crime and Justice: A Guide to Criminology*, Thomson Reuters Lawbook Co., 4th edn, Sydney, 2012.

McClelland, E., *Nothing but Blue Skies*, Bloomsbury Press, New York, 2013.

Peel, M., *Good Times, Hard Times: The past and the future in Elizabeth*, Melbourne University Press, 1995.

Peel, M., *The Lowest Rung: Voices of Australian poverty*, Melbourne University Press, 2003.

Schultz, J., *Steel City Blues*, Penguin, Melbourne, 1985.

LEGAL CASES

Fair Work Ombudsman v China Sanan Engineering Construction Corp [2013] Federal Circuit Court of Australia 1177.

OFFICIAL REPORTS, DOCUMENTS, POLICY PAPERS AND OTHERS

Allen Consulting Group, 'The Strategic Role of the Australian Automotive Manufacturing Industry', *Report to the Federal Chamber of Automotive Industries*, 2013.

Australian Manufacturing Workers' Union, 'Final Submission', prepared for The Productivity Commission Review into the Australian Automobile Industry, 2014.

Barbaro, B. and Spoehr, J., 'Closing the Motor Vehicle Industry: The Impact on Australia', The Australian Workplace innovation and Social Research Centre and the National Institute of Economic and Industry Research, University of Adelaide, April 2014.

Barnes, T., 'Detroit: What Lessons for Victoria from a "Post-Industrial" city', Research Paper No 2, Institute for Religion, Politics and Society, Australian Catholic University, December 2015.

Bertrand, M. and Mullainathan, S., 'Are Emily and Greg More Employable Than Lakisha and Jamal? A Field Experiment On Labour Market Discrimination', Working Paper No 9873, National Bureau of Economic Research, July 2003.

Booth, A., Leigh, A. and Varganova, E., 'Does Racial Discrimination Vary Across Minority Groups? Evidence from a Field Experiment', Discussion Paper Series No 4947, Institute for the Study of Labor, May 2010.

Corangamite Catchment Management Authority, brief history of Anglesea River taken from 'Anglesea River Estuary Management Plan 2012–2020'.

Deloitte Access Economics, 'Business Outlook: Eyes on China', March 2014.

Department of Defence, 'Defence Issues Paper: A discussion paper to inform the 2015 Defence White Paper,' July 2014.

Edwards, S., Submission to South Australian Nuclear Fuel Cycle Royal Commission, 3 August 2015.

Halliday, S., 'Culture Review 2015–2016', City of Greater Geelong, October 2015.

Hausmann, R., et al., 2013, The Atlas of Economic Complexity: Mapping Paths to Prosperity Part 1, Massachusetts Institute of Technology and Center for International Development, Harvard University.

Hendrickson, L., Bucifal, S., Balaguer, A. and Hansell, D., 'The employment dynamics of Australian entrepreneurship,' Research Paper No 4, Department of Industry and Science and Australian Bureau of Statistics, September 2015.

Holden Historical Services, 'Who built what and when?', <www.holdenhistoricalservices.com.au/cars/who-built-what-and-when>.

Hugo, G. and Harris, K., 'Population Dynamics in Outer Suburbs 2006–2011', Australian Population and Migration Research Centre, Vol. 1, No 2, February 2013.

Kellard, K., Honey, N. and McNamara, T., 'Evaluation of Work for the Dole 2014–15', ANU Social Research Centre, November 2015.

Keneley, M., Dimovski, B. and Stevenson, S., 'An assessment of structural change in the Geelong labour market 2014–2016' School of Accounting, Economics and Finance, Deakin University, August 2014.

Kent, A. and Hurley, K., 'The Devil is in the Detail: What's behind manufacturing growth and decline in Melbourne, 2001–2011', paper presented at The State of Australian Cities conference, Sydney, 26–29 November 2013.

Maher, W., 'Anglesea River Water Quality Review', Independent Review, Victorian Department of Sustainability and Environment, October 2011.

Nuclear Fuel Cycle Royal Commission, South Australia, 'Tentative Findings', 2016.

Productivity Commission, *Australia's Automotive Manufacturing Industry*, 'Inquiry Report No. 70', March 2014, Canberra. Copyright © Commonwealth of Australia, Productivity Commission, reproduced by permission.

Productivity Commission, *Australia's Automotive Manufacturing Industry*, 'Position Paper', January 2014.

Productivity Commission, *Australia's Automotive Manufacturing Industry*, 'Preliminary Findings Report', December 2013.

Productivity Commission, Inquiry into Australia's Automotive Manufacturing Industry, proceedings, Melbourne, 10 December 2013, 8.28am (transcript, Mike Devereux).

Roskam, J., Paterson, J. and Berg, C., 'Be like Gough: 75 radical ideas to transform Australia', *IPA Review*, August 2012.

Shane, S., 'Why encouraging more people to become entrepreneurs is bad public policy', *Small Business Economics*, Vol. 33(2), 2009.

Spoehr, J., 'Industrial Rejuvenation: Lessons from National and International Experience', WISeR working paper prepared for Department of Manufacturing, Innovation, Trade, Resources and Energy at the Stretton Centre, 2014.

StartupAus, 'Crossroads 2015: An action plan to develop a vibrant tech startup ecosystem in Australia', 2015.

NEWS MEDIA

Allard, T. and Patty, A., 'Tony Abbott's work for the dole scheme doesn't add up', *Sydney Morning Herald* (online), 2 August 2014.

Badham, V., 'Giddy up, Darryn Lyons. Geelong needs more than a Mayor on a bender', *The Guardian* (online), 13 October 2015.

Bennett, J., 'GM to shift production to Asia', *Wall Street Journal* (online), 8 December 2013.

Blandy, R., 'How start-ups could solve SA's job crisis', *InDaily* (indaily.com.au – Adelaide independent news website), 20 August 2015.

Blandy, R., 'Richard Blandy: Our Post-Industrial future is a rejection of bigness, centralisation and bureaucracy', *The Advertiser* (online), 12 March 2014.

Bowe, W., 'Poll Bludger: why the Coalition can afford to throw SA under the submarine', *Crikey* (online), 11 September 2014.

Burrow, V., 'Mother, daughter flee arson attack', *The Age* (online), 24 May 2006.

Chenery, S., 'The Emperor of Geelong,' *Good Weekend* (online), 22 February 2014.

Dowling, J., 'Who killed the car industry?', *Sydney Morning Herald* (online), 13 November 2015.

Dundas, G., 'Geelong Mayor Darryn Lyons no longer a Liberal Party member', *Geelong Advertiser* (online) 4 December 2015.

Garcia, S., 'A timeline of recent South Australian job losses', *ABC News* (online), 16 November 2015.

Harkinson, J., 'Death wears bunny slippers', *Mother Jones* (online), November/December 2014 issue.

Harkinson, J., 'That time we almost nuked North Carolina: And other terrifying near-misses, mishaps, and scandals from our atomic arsenal', *Mother Jones* (online), 10 November 2014.

Hunt N., 'Chinese paid $1.90 an hour to dismantle Mitsubishi factory', *The Advertiser* (online), 18 July 2010.

Jean, P., 'Prime Minister Tony Abbott says Future Submarines project will involve a "massive amount of work" in Adelaide', *The Advertiser*, 22 August 2014.

Kendzior, S., 'The peril of Hipster Economics: when urban decay becomes a set piece to be remodelled or romanticised', *Al Jazeera English* (online), 28 May 2014.

Kerwin, K., 'Mitsubishi's Marketing Makeover: lacking new models, new North American chief Finbarr O'Neill is working on the carmaker's image. It's a big job.', *Bloomberg* (online), 14 October 2004.

LeDuff, C., 'Hard times in Paul Ryan's home town', *Mother Jones* (online), September/October 2009 issue.

Linley, M., 'Norlane church communities left reeling after two arson attacks', *Geelong Advertiser* (online), 6 December 2015.

Lyons, J., 'Nick Xenophon is going national, but will voters go with him?' *The Australian* (online), 28 November 2015.

Madden, D., 'Gentrification doesn't trickle down to help everyone', *The Guardian* (online), 10 October 2014.

Manne, A., 'Joker in the Pack: On the road with the irrepressible Nick Xenophon', *The Monthly* (online), November 2015.

Masanauskas, F., 'Mohawk Mayor of Geelong admits he abused drugs but vows to revitalise the town', *Herald Sun* (online), 26 November 2013.

McGowan, S., 'Dusting off our past – Australian air conditioning', *HVACOR Nation*, July 2008.

Millar, R., 'Old school ties and six packs', *The Age* (online), 13 November 2013.

Mitchell, N. and Kerr, P., 'Ford plant closes after strike riot', *The Age*, 14 June 1973.

Opray, M., 'Tony Abbott's South Australia problem: on the front line of the Coalition's war to win back votes', *The Guardian* (online), 4 August 2015.

Porter, I., 'Here's who to blame for the coming recession', *The Age* (online), 7 September 2015.

Porter, I., 'The Government's car crash of an automotive policy', *The Age* (online), 13 January 2016.

Potter, B., 'The Fall and Rise of Geelong', *Australian Financial Review* (online), 28 February 2014.

Pyne, C., 'Australia can be the start-up and innovation nation under new Prime Minister Malcolm', *Sydney Morning*

Herald (online), 22 October 2015.

Redrup Y., 'Follow the rules and still get fined: Why this Chinese company was fined by Fair Work even after doing the right thing', *Smart Company* (online), 2 September 2013.

Robertson, J. and Johnston, C., 'Car parts makers gear up for a diversified future', *The Age* (online), 14 December 2013.

Rule, A., 'Inside Geelong Mayor Darryn Lyons' den', *Herald Sun* (online), 23 May 2015.

Solnit, R., 'Detroit Arcadia: Exploring the post-American Landscape', *Harpers' Magazine* (online), July 2007.

Squires, M., 'Geelong Mayor Darryn Lyons says he is lost and sad without the love of his life Elissa Friday', *Geelong Advertiser* (online), 24 November 2015.

Starick, P., 'Inside story of Malcolm Turnbull's coup to become Prime Minister and Tony Abbott's leadership downfall', *The Advertiser* (online), 18 September 2015.

Walker, J., 'From brash Young Liberal to Senate linchpin for Nick Xenophon', *The Australian* (online), 28 June 2008.

Whinnit, E., 'Dandenong is just fine and dandy', *News.com.au* (online), 26 June 2010.

Williamson, B., 'A sleepless night in a contaminated home at Clovelly Park', *ABC Adelaide* (online), 3 July 2014.

'AMWU angry over Nissan decision to close parts warehouses across Australia, 58 jobs lost', *ABC News* (online), 7 July 2015.

'GM has record sales in China in 2013', *Automotive News* via Reuters (online), 7 January 2014.

'"Not enough skilled workers" to fill automotive industry job vacancies', *BT news* (online), 9 February 2016.

MODELLING, DATA AND STATISTICS

Australian Bureau of Statistics, 2011, 'Regional Profiles':
- City of Playford
- Norwood
- Salisbury
- Unley
- Prospect

Australian Bureau of Statistics, Labour Force:
- National
- Victoria
- South Australia

Australian Bureau of Statistics, 'Prisoners in Australia 2015'.

Australian Production and Sales Statistics, Federal Chamber of Automotive Industries.

Brotherhood of Saint Laurence, 'Youth Unemployment Snapshot', February 2014.

Department of Employment, 'Small Area Labour Markets Research Australia', September Quarter, 2015.

International Labour Organisation, 'Global Employment Trends For Youth 2013: A generation at risk', 2013.

International Production and Sales Statistics, 'International Organization of Motor Vehicle Manufacturers'.

Investment in the Australian Mining and Manufacturing Industries since 1960, data sourced from Australian Bureau of Statistics 5204.0, Australian System of National Accounts, Table 64, Gross Fixed Private Capital Formation (Chain Volume Measures).

Melbourne Institute of Applied Economic and Social Research, 'Poverty Lines Australia: June Quarter', University of Melbourne, 2015.

National Institute of Economic and Industry Research, 'Full Motor Vehicle Closure: The impact on Australia and its regions', report for the Australian Workplace Innovation and Social Research Centre, 2014.

Office of Crime Statistics and Research, 'Australian Bureau of Statistics Recorded Crime – Victims, Australia 2014: The South Australian Perspective', Attorney General's Department of South Australia, 2015.

Office of Crime Statistics and Research, 'Offence Profile: South Australia 2014', Attorney General's Department of South Australia, 2015.

Rose, N. and Sced, M., 'Recorded Crime in South Australia, Metropolitan South Australia and Regional South Australia', Crime Mapper 2007–2011, 2013.

United States Census Bureau, 'Profile of General Population and Housing Characteristics: 2010, Detroit city, Michigan'.

Vinson, T., Rawsthorne, M., Beavis, A. and Ericson, M., 'Dropping off the Edge 2015', Mapping Disadvantage:
– Victoria profile
– South Australia profile

VIDEO AND AUDIO

Agenda, Sky News, 'Senator's confusion over submarine tender', 9 February 2015, viewed 12 December 2015 <https://www.youtube.com/watch?v=VWwqSavHbZ0>.

LMCSXUrbex, 'Abandoned: General Motors railway station', 11 September 2015, viewed 3 February 2015 <https://www.youtube.com/watch?v=fI73kIkjO4I>.

2GB Radio, 'Richard Riley and James Tacey', *Money News*, 11 February 2014.

Acknowledgements

IT TAKES ABOUT 30,000 COMPONENTS TO MAKE A CAR, RIGHT down to the smallest screw. Turns out books aren't much different.

My deepest thanks and gratitude goes to everyone who spoke to me for this book, those named and unnamed who showed me their cities, invited me into their homes and trusted me with their stories. You, the people of Elizabeth, of Geelong, of Broadmeadows and of Dandenong are proud people, good times or bad. You have my deepest respect.

Thank you to my mother, Marina, who taught me justice, taught me the alphabet and taught me how to write my name.

Thank you to Jennifer, who was there through it all.

Some of this work has appeared in other forms in *Kill Your Darlings*, *Al Jazeera English*, *Vice* and *The Guardian* Australia. My deepest thanks goes to editors Hop Dac, Julian and Rob for saving me from myself.

Thank you to Amy Maynard, Gideon and to Sophie for helping to make it happen and my deepest gratitude to Claire, Tom and everyone else at Hachette for taking it those next few steps.

Thank you to my lawyer Russell and my friends Alanna, Shane, Laura W, Laura Pi, Issy, Annie, EP, Matthew, Peter and especially Tanya for listening.

Thank you to those who lent me their couch or a spare bed on short notice, especially Anna, 30 Eveline, Pam and Russ and their kids, Elizabeth and Mary. All we have is our word.

Thank you to Greg Combet and Sean Edwards, to Jon Gee, John Camillo and Paul Difeliche and Tom Skladzien.

Thank you to Dr John Sheerwood for your insight. Glen Dalimore for the names and Amy Noonan for the hook-up. Thank you to Bill for being a sounding board and to Adam Reynolds for holding it together.

Thank you to the reporters from *The Age*, the *Sydney Morning Herald*, the *Saturday Paper*, *The Guardian*, the ABC, *The Advertiser*, *The Australian* and the *Geelong Advertiser* whose work I have relied upon to reconstruct events and timelines. Also thank you to my fellow stray Max Opray for pointing out 'Abbott's South Australia problem'.

During the production of this story, my beat-up old car fell in the line of duty. It was a Japanese import from the 90s with as many owners, and enough backyard repair jobs to make it 100 per cent local. May it rest in peace. It was a good workhorse.

Preface

The modern Australian politician should be of the people, but not one of them. They should enjoy beer, but never fall drunk in public. They should swear in private with their friends and allies, but not in public and never at their enemies. They should talk plainly. They should be charismatic. They should know how to give a speech to a room full of people who love them, and how to give a speech to a room full of people who hate them. No matter what, they should never react angrily to scrutiny, or heckling, or personal attacks. They should know poetry and literature, but only talk about these things in private, otherwise they will be seen to be weak.

An Australian politician should be tough. They should respect sportspeople and follow a team. On Grand Final day, they should watch with the nation and know the result. They should not back down to bullies. They should always say what they feel, but show restraint in what they say. They must have a considered opinion on all things, or be willing to bluff convincingly. They should answer direct questions, no matter how painful. A politician should never lie, unless it is in the national interest, or a time of national emergency, and then they should lie well, so people can respect them for it.

A politician should be intelligent, but not superior. They should be educated, but not arrogant. They should be of the land, of the factory, and of a trade. They should know how to work with their hands and this knowledge should inform their political work. They should work hard and live frugally. They should respect the public purse. They should be successful, but not rich, and if they are they should never advertise it.

A politician should have a family and cherish it, but never deploy it as a political weapon. They should cherish their children and govern with their future in mind. They should cherish their god and live by their beliefs, but never judge those who do not. Australians hate a preacher.

They should respect their leader, respect the process and respect their office. They should read the polls, and respond to them, but know when to hold through the flak. They should be comfortable with power, and know how to wield it like a scalpel, or a sledgehammer, but should never covet it. They should have vision and show leadership. They should include everyone, but know when to make a decision. They should bend, but never break, no matter how much pressure they are under. They should work to improve the lot of all.

This is the ideal of Australian political leadership; a person who cannot exist, has never existed and probably will never exist. Politicians may be afforded the dignity and authority that comes with public office, but politics is full of well-meaning, respectable people, as prone to dumb mistakes, petty vengeance and arrogant self-delusion as anyone else. Some are stone-cold stupid, with no imagination or passion for anything outside their own limited experience. Some may chafe at the party platform but never break ranks. With nothing to say, some may fall back on campaign slogans or talk in folksy clichés. Under threat, some may lie. They may talk big, but never act. They may love to win, at any cost, or have discovered a twisted interpretation of the world and their place within it. Others have simply had their naked ambition confused with talent.

With enough time, many politicians can make peace with their flaws and may even overcome them, putting them to work as something personal and unique. Sometimes they may have an opportunity do so some good in a city like Canberra where party lines are being erased and it feels like everyone has become a free agent. Sometimes they may even make something out of that opportunity.

Everyone, eventually, falls short. Every single one. And when powerful people start to look ordinary, those who vote for them start thinking that ordinary people might do a better job. Break the illusion enough times, and people start casting around for alternatives.

This is a book about those alternatives. It is not a political polemic or a sociological treatise, though it has something to say on both those accounts. This book is a snapshot of a time when the rules of the game seemed to be changing, when Pauline Hanson had returned despite the odds and people were grappling with what it meant.

For five months in 2016, I went to work for Senator Nick Xenophon as his media advisor. I left after being given an opportunity to write a book about what happened after the mining boom. Around that time, I started getting asked to write about US President Donald Trump and whether what happened to the USA could happen in Australia. People wanted to know about Hanson. People wanted to know about populism. People wanted to know about the lives of poor and working-class people, and whatever it was they were thinking.

I didn't end up writing those stories. Instead I was offered the chance to put together this book as a field report on the health of our democracy, asking why politicians seemed to be unable to see the barbarians coming until they were storming the gate. In doing so I had to revisit my brief time in politics – a hazy montage of memories – and work out what I had learned in that time. Then I had to build on it.

The more I thought about that time, the more I came to understand I had gone in cynical and I had come out the other side still cynical, but in a different way. Politics, I learned, is a place where the full range of human potential is on display, every day. There are good, decent people in there doing their best, and there are ruthless, calculating psychopaths who don't care at all.

All, I learned, are prisoners of their circumstances and the certainties of their worldview.

Nothing encapsulated this message more than the unexpected return of One Nation. In a lot of ways, Hanson was the political story of the decade, though as far as I was concerned, Pauline Hanson was the least interesting thing about Pauline Hanson. She was someone who preyed on the hopes and frustrations of working class and country people. Too much ink has been spilled on taking her apart.

I was more interested in the environment around her. I wanted to know *why*: Why now? Who voted for Pauline? And what had happened to us, and to the rest of the world, when fear-mongers and conspiracy nuts were suddenly put in charge of nuclear codes and the national budget?

To answer these questions I set out with my pen and pad to outline the lives and careers of some of those political leaders Australians had chosen from outside the major political parties to represent them and, where possible, to sketch the people who had voted for them, or those who hadn't. In doing so, I wanted to piece together what had happened in order to understand this 'populist moment', although I did not want to write it from the perspective of the major parties, be they blue, or red or green. Instead, my book would be told from the perspective of the rogues and the strays who are now sitting in parliament.

This is also book I never intended to write. I kept no notebook during my time in politics, though sometimes I would threaten Nick Xenophon with the idea that someday I would write his biography. The stories and observations I share from this time are memories fleshed out as best I can with the aid of documents, records, news articles, press releases and conversations with the people I worked alongside, and those who I met along the way. A few chapters have been the product of previous journalism, while the rest has been put together by working the phones and heading out on the road, because politics, I still believe somewhat earnestly, is more than the process of passing a bill. It is something that happens *out there*, on the street corners, in the coffee shops and fields, even in your living room. Power is a cooperative relationship. Parliament may give, and parliament may take, but it's the people living on the other side of those decisions – the powerless – who define what is acceptable.

So, I figured, if I wanted to understand something like Pauline Hanson with any real clarity, if I wanted to know what the hell happened *out there,* I had to be out there with the rest of them.

Chapter 1

Canberra's Religion Has Angry Gods

It was about three in the afternoon when we decided we needed a drink.

We had made our way down to the staff cafeteria through the winding corridors of Parliament House in Canberra, the seat of Australian democracy. An eerie silence had settled over the building and the whole place fell still.

'It's a little bit like the apocalypse,' Jono said.

We were seated in the couch section, over towards the back, and a chef in the staff cafeteria offered to get us some beer from a fridge in another room. While we waited, we tried to make sense of what just happened.

Jono and I had been working up in senate suite S1.56 while the votes were being counted. We had turned up to work at 7 am that morning, maybe a little earlier, and turned on the television, along with the whole world, to watch the final crescendo in a thundering presidential campaign, to find out what the American people would decide.

For months a sense of denial had knocked about the world of politics. Trump had no chance, the thinking had gone. He was crazy, crooked and vile. Hillary wasn't perfect, but she was safe, she was experienced and she knew what she was doing. It was only when the results started to roll in that the collective delusion lifted and the realisation dawned that Hillary had no chance. It was Trump for President 2017.

Rome burned, and all its allies could do was watch. Donald J Trump might not have been an Australian President, but the very fact he had climbed his way out of Trump Tower to take control of the biggest economy, military and nuclear arsenal in the world suddenly marked a dramatic shift in what was possible. Every rule of the game seemed to have been redefined. Trump defied every tenet of basic human decency and yet had somehow triumphed.

Jono belonged to that group who had never really believed Trump had a chance. He was Nick Xenophon's legislative advisor, a lawyer and a canny tactician with a sunny smile from a working class family in small town Burnie, Tasmania. As a kid he had visited Parliament House and rolled down its green hills. Something in that grass must have gotten under his skin, because from that moment on, all he had wanted was a chance to work in the Big House.

He got his chance with former Senator Ricky Muir, an average guy pulled off the street and elevated to Parliament by sheer dumb luck. In his job interview Jono told Muir that he had never really worked in politics, but he would work hard if given the chance. Muir liked his honesty and had agreed to give him his shot. Together, they got about two years out of it before the major parties ended their streak by rewriting the rules so an unknown quantity like Muir would never be allowed to take office again.

Once the result on the eve of the federal election in 2016 was known, Jono had wandered through Parliament House, thinking those were going to be his last hours, until Nick Xenophon floated the idea that Jono might want to come work for him.

The other camp – those who saw Trump coming a mile off – was represented by Philip Dorling, a bespectacled, jaded ex-Fairfax journalist who had been around Canberra longer than anyone could remember. He had a $100 bottle of wine riding on the outcome of the election with a staffer from another office, and from the moment the count started he closely monitored the result.

'Just look at that map,' Philip said from across the office as the votes piled up. On his computer screen splashed a map showing counties in the US. California and New York had gone to the Democrats and turned blue. Everything else in between had gone firetruck red, bricking up the centre of the country and dividing the world's last remaining super-power right down the middle.

At that point, the count was only halfway, so I asked whether he thought Hillary still had a chance.

'It's over,' he said. 'Just take a look. There's no coming back from that.'

'You just don't want to believe it.'

He had known Trump was coming, he said, ever since he went on a Defence Force study tour during which he ate crabs along a riverbank in some hick part of the US near where he was working. The Americans he dined with that day were obese, loud, deeply in debt, with no education and no real future for their kids, he told me. These were the people who voted for Trump. They were good, god-fearing people who didn't care about bad manners and heard Trump talk about how he was going bring back the good jobs, drain the swamp and make America great again, and liked it.

It was a line of thinking that made a lot of sense to me. I was a skinny kid from Adelaide's north who had graduated from an under-resourced public school where I once got stomped on the oval by a guy with 'newboys' tattooed across his forearms. The further north you went, the higher the unemployment figure ticked, well above the national average, even as the rest of the country went about its business without a care in the world.

Politics took no real interest in us while I was growing up, and when it did, it talked about the whole region as a problem to be solved, or forgotten, instead of consulted about its future. In the national scheme of things, we were losers. Politics was something the rest of the country did, something we watched briefly on the evening news before they cut to the sport. Not once do I remember a candidate knocking on our front door to ask my family about their views and talk about their problems, and if they had, we'd probably have pretended we weren't home anyway.

A few months before I started working for Nick Xenophon, I had published a book about my people, who were watching on as the car industry, the backbone of the local economy, shutdown. It was a strange book, for both me and for the local community. People with my roots don't often become writers or work in media, because it doesn't occur to them that they might, and the people I wrote about don't normally get their stories told in any depth unless some dumb kid leads police on a chase through the outer suburbs.

It was a book that had to be written, however. Politics might not have taken much of an interest in where I grew up, but in that moment politics took away the last good thing the community had left on the basis that the rest of the country was no longer willing to subsidise it. During that time, I saw the confusion, frustration and grief in people's eyes. I listened to them as they wondered aloud about their future, about how they were working two jobs, or no job, and how they worried for the future of their children. And then I wrote it all down in the name of journalism.

It was Australia's American Dream, I had written, and we were about to wake up to the nightmare.

I might not have known Donald Trump was coming to the US, but I knew something was happening Down Under. I had seen enough to know that when people start worrying about their future, they start looking for alternatives.

Before I had signed on for a couple of months with Nick Xenophon, or Nick – as he prefers to be called – I was working as a freelance journalist, a stray grinding out copy for any news outlet that would have me. I had covered Reclaim Australia rallies in two states and watched the return of One Nation with a sense of foreboding. Donald Trump was just a local American chapter of a global story, but whatever happened, however it played out, I knew it would come here eventually.

So when Nick made me an offer to come work in his press shop about a month after my book came out, I took it. I had spent the last four years living cheque-to-cheque, and had become exhausted by the hustle. To top it off, one crisis after another had taken over the lives of my parents. When that happens, and someone offers to help pay your rent for the foreseeable future, you don't say no.

Then there was the sense of adventure: it was an opportunity. Agreeing would mean embedding with the 'feral senate', that loose band of political rebels who resisted Tony Abbott's hard-wired authoritarian impulse to rewrite the way of Australian social and political life.

These senators, those who existed beyond the ranks of the major parties, were outsiders. A defiant group of contrarians – and occasionally – straight-out freaks, who had gradually come to represent those Australians who had been left behind. In turn, they became kingmakers. This group of people was simultaneously riding the same global forces which had delivered Trump to the White House while still largely keeping to the rules of the game.

In amongst it was One Nation. They were something new-ish, a kind of expeditionary force for the Trump campaign, who had clawed their way back from obscurity at the 2016 federal election, securing four senate seats. In the months afterwards, we watched the situation develop through our daily routines, and, sitting in our office, we came to the understanding that those with the most to lose from the return of One Nation were the independents. Once Trump had gone global, all it would take was one heart-felt lie in a post-fact universe for One Nation to sweep through those areas of the country which were so cynical, so withdrawn, they'd turn the whole system on its head for a laugh.

And on US Election Day, One Nation were the only ones celebrating as we walked down to the cafeteria. In their suite, they had popped the cork on a Champagne bottle and had extended an invitation for everyone to join. We had politely declined.

So while Philip Dorling ducked out early to collect on his bet, Jono and I went to the cafeteria to take stock.

'This is one of those days we will remember,' Jono said. 'Where were you when Trump was elected? Sitting in the seat of Australian democracy. Some day we would tell our grandchildren about this moment.'

We clinked our bottles.

'You think it could happen here?' Jono asked after a moment's pause.

'No doubt,' I said. 'It already is. There's a whole horde of angry people out there in search of a leader. If Canberra's religion is politics, we are sinners in the hands of angry gods.

'It's only a question of who, and how long.'